The Actor's Right to Act

The Actor's Right to Act

JOSEPH MACLEOD

published for the friends of Equity by

LAWRENCE and WISHART LTD
LONDON

published for the friends of Equity by
Lawrence and Wishart Ltd
39 Museum Street,
London WC1A 1LQ

First published 1981
© Joseph Macleod

Printed and bound in Great Britain at
The Camelot Press Ltd, Southampton

Contents

List of Illustrations   7

Preface by Alex McCrindle   11

Author's Foreword   13

1 Stock Companies and Actor-Managers   15

2 Speculators and Syndicates   26

3 Charity, Hope and Faith   45

4 The First Attempt   56

5 Actors Associated   66

6 Actors Limited   75

7 Breakaways   86

8 'The Struggling Mass'   100

9 How the A.A. became a Trade Union   113

10 Exercise Develops the Muscles   125

11 The Managers Dig Themselves In   137

12 The Stage Guild   152

13 The Making of Equity   169

Postscript   189

Appendices

   I Letter from Charles Landstone, January 1951   190

   II Letter from Felix Aylmer, March 1951   194

   III Letter from Gordon Sandison, May 1951   196

   IV Letter from Godfrey Tearle, June 1951   197

Index   199

Play Index   206

List of Illustrations

Between pages 64 and 65
Granville Barker
Charles Carson
Lewis Casson
Norman McKinnell

Between pages 96 and 97
Cecil Raleigh
Ben Webster
J. Fisher White
Sidney Valentine

To Alex McCrindle

Dear Alex,

Books are fulfilled only when they are read: and without your energy, determination, and devotion to the cause of the actor this one would have had an existence very limited indeed. I dedicate it to you in admiration and gratitude; as I had hoped to be able to do before I knew that you would be writing a Preface. May all theatre folk be grateful to you for the gift, and indeed the gifts, you provide for them!

Joseph

Preface

by ALEX McCRINDLE

Joseph Macleod has written what the General Secretary of Equity has described as the definitive history of the Actors' Association, which was the first attempt of members of the profession to improve conditions of work in London and outside.

But the story he tells is no mere record for the activist. He is not only a fine historian, but, as a man of the theatre, he cares passionately about the long and confused struggle of actors and actresses for professional justice and dignity; he reveals the conditions in detail, before the formation of the Actors' Association in 1892.

The decline and disappearance of the provincial 'stock' companies had resulted in an influx of experienced artists into London, where theatres were multiplying and booming. This in its turn had resulted in a general lowering of wages, while the completion of the country's railway network made touring companies additionally profitable.

The London managements were the first to see the advantages of forming a combine, including that of keeping salaries depressed. The touring managers were not far behind. Then came the 'bricks-and-mortar men' who bought theatres as investments for mere rents: and finally the business men, accountants, and others, who invested in and largely controlled with their near monopolies *what was to be offered on the stage.*

Meanwhile the profession itself suffered penury and hardship, and its members had no voice in their own lives.

It was this that led Robert Courtneidge to call together fellow pantomime artists at Manchester, which was the spark igniting what would become the Actors' Association. But another forty years had to go by for reforms.

One of the chief confusions was that many actors were actor-managers. Some of these left the Association and founded one of their own, the Stage Guild, which proved a rival to the A.A. and nearly killed it.

The amalgamation of the two made Equity; and Joseph Macleod, with personal experience as artist and manager (even, I believe, of the problems that can exasperate both sides in provincial touring), is a proper person to tell the tale.

London 1980

Author's Foreword

This book owes its existence to a request from Gordon Sandison, the General Secretary, and Charles Farrell, the Honorary Treasurer, of Equity, that I should write a short pamphlet about our Union's past history for 1951, the twenty-first year of its life. This I planned to complete within three or four months to be ready for the Jubilee. But on examining the material, I felt that Equity's past would not be fully understood without some account of the associations which led up to it; and none of this material had been collected.

No scholar, I think, ever had a more fascinating task than the breaking of this virgin soil. And no scholar I am sure, can ever have compiled with more heartfelt gratitude a list of acknowledgements to those who have provided him, and indeed trusted him, with irreplaceable 'sources'. For months my study floor has been covered with packages containing what may one day be library treasures.

To the following I would express my special thanks:

Mr Gordon Sandison and the Council of Equity for Minute Books of the old A.A. and other organisations, for press extracts, notes, and various documents.

Mr Felix Aylmer, OBE, for much help and information and for permission to print one of his letters.

Mr Godfrey Tearle, for information and for a series of letters explaining many points.

Mr H. Russell Sedgwick, for a whole suitcaseful of unique holograph letters, notes, MSS, press cuttings, and historic scribbles, mostly relating to the fusion of the A.A. and the Stage Guild, and for a personal account of that incident specially compiled.

Mr G. Carlton Wallace, for a quantity of documents about the Stage Guild.

Messrs Mander and Mitchenson, for the loan of papers and literature from their collection (an act of rare grace among collectors!).

Mr Alfred Lugg for information and press cuttings.

Mr Nat. Day of the Association of Touring and Producing Managers, for information and some Minutes of the Stage Guild.

Mr W. G. Gray, of the Actors' Benevolent Fund, for a gift of material, printed and verbal; Sir Kenneth Barnes for information about various schemes for Training Schools which I would have welcomed more space to use; and Dr C. Knight McDonald, for time patiently spent in medical research on the matter of theatre sanitation and industrial disease. Also Miss Eve Saville and the Home Research Department of the Fabian Society, for information. Nor can I omit the initial work done by Mr Alex. McCrindle, which greatly helped in the starting of my own.

Mr T. O'Brien of N.A.T.K.E., Mr J. Isaacs, Mr John Parker, Mr Stewart Cruikshank, and Mr Horace Collins, have given me prompt and courteous replies to questions with which I have bothered them.

The Editor and Staff of *The Stage* gave me much information and put bound volumes (with a place to study them) at my disposal. To these I am very grateful.

Besides these, there have been many who have helped to fill in details or track down other sources by their unstinted goodwill and reminiscence. Among the many, I would name the special: Mrs Anna Fisher White, Sir Lewis Casson, Mr Miles Malleson, Mr Harold Scott, Mr Charles Laidstone, Mr Charles Farrell, Mr Gerald Lawrence, and other colleagues of the Green Room Club. This book would have been better if I could have drawn more memories from them and from others; but time was lacking.

I have tried to make the book as objective as possible; naturally in my explorations I have come upon old sores forgotten but not healed. The exposing of such things, where no need appears, seemed to be fruitless; and where, for health, some such operation proved inevitable, I have kept the salt jar out of reach.

Joseph Macleod
Edinburgh, 1951

CHAPTER ONE

Stock Companies and Actor-Managers

*In a word we are so needful for the common
good that in some respect it were almost a sin
to put us down.*
The Stage-Players Complaint, 1641

What ever may be thought of the drama of the nineteenth century, which is more interesting than it is sometimes made out to be; and whatever may be thought of its styles of acting and staging, which despite our sometimes irreverent laughter did drive steadily through the generations a road to truthfulness and sincerity; certainly it cannot be denied that the ways in which our theatrical forebears kept themselves alive were of the utmost importance and interest . . . and are so still: for what happened to them then affects us all today.

In the 1800s the whole nature and composition of stage life altered; vividly and profoundly. In the first half of the century England, Scotland, and to some extent Wales and Ireland also, were covered with small, permanent theatrical units. Some were mobile, with no premises of their own, continually on the move, in more or less fixed and regional circuits of short seasons, or weeks, or two-night stands. Even little towns like Newport Pagnell, Alloa and Huntingdon had premises of some kind, occupied week after week by different companies, with eager audiences to receive them: small theatres, assembly rooms, halls, or, in the humblest case of Helensburgh, the large room of an inn, proudly if misleadingly entitled 'The Theatre', or even 'Theatre Royal'.[1] The standards of such constantly moving companies varied from crude vampings of strolling players to the careful and conscientious productions of William McCready, Senior.[2]

But others, some growing out of these, were static. Their managers took longer leases of premises, or even came to own them; and in time grew organically in the leisure life of city, small town, or locality, like McCready of Bristol and the West of England, Ryder of Perth and the North-East of Scotland, or Robertson who built his own theatres in the Lincolnshire circuit. Touring the neighbourhood in the offseason, they created a kind of aristocracy in local companies. Many were family concerns, the leads played by father and mother, till sons and daughters could graduate from juvenile parts to more powerful ones.

In the main, within their modest limits, they were prosperous, contented, sincere; and they did good service, took themselves seriously as creative artists. The work was hard, but one learned one's craft by endless diverse experience. Three or four or even six plays might be done in a week. If one play failed, there was no cause for dismay: another would succeed. At least somebody in the cast would have pleased somebody in the audience. And everybody would have learned something. Members of one company might leave and join another; but the company continued. Riches and fame were to be had, for the lucky ones, in London. But not everybody could get there and not everybody wished to get there. W. C. Macready debated a long while before leaving the 'country theatres', where he was popular and well-to-do, for London, where he might prove neither.[3] Harriot Murray was a well liked London actress when she chose to go to Scotland; and not the invitation of Edmund Kean to play opposite him in the English capital could persuade her to leave the Scottish one. Later in the century, more than one star-to-be, like Squire Bancroft, decided after two and a half years of Birmingham, Dublin, and other 'provincial' theatres, that they could still give him more tense and alert experience, and therefore more wide and accurate a technique, than London could.

In London, matters were not so pleasant. By a clever political and business move as long ago as 1737, a Licensing Act had been obtained, giving to the Patent Theatres (Covent Garden, Drury Lane, and in summer, later, the Haymarket) a virtual monopoly of drama, not only in London but throughout the four kingdoms. Any company, in any premises, performing a stage-play for profit, was henceforth to be treated, except within certain rigid and narrow limits, as if it consisted of rogues, vagabonds, sturdy beggars and vagrants; to be either whipped (men and women alike), or fined £50 in respect of each performance, their goods seized in default, or if they had none, to be thrown into a debtors' gaol from which they would have no possible method of extricating themselves for the rest of their lives.[4] This vicious ordinance was constantly evaded by legalistic tricks; but the 'minor' theatres in London were always suspect and circumscribed; and so were those in the country. Outside London, the centralising process made local drama difficult, but audiences were less subject to political pressure, and informers were infrequent. And in 1788 a slightly more lenient Act made it possible for travelling companies (still under stringent command to perform London-approved plays only) to legalise themselves in any district by applying to magistrates for permission to perform under certain drastic stipulations.[5] Grudging though it was, this later Act made the 'stock companies' possible; and the formal abolition of patent theatres in 1843 enabled them to grow.

However, by that time it had become too late for the local companies, which comprised the huge majority of the working profession, ever to establish first-class local theatres like those to be found in Germany, Russia, and other countries at that time. Already the stock companies were carrying within them the germs of their own dissolution: London had infected them.

'A stock company', wrote Ellen Terry,[6] referring to J. H. Chute's company at Bristol which she had joined in 1861 as a girl of fifteen, 'was a company of actors and actresses brought together by the manager of a provincial theatre to support a leading actor or actress – "a star" – from London. . . . Sometimes the "stars" would come for a whole season; if their magnitude were of the first order, only for one night. Sometimes they would rehearse with the stock company, sometimes they wouldn't.' And Chute's was among the best of the kind! His wife was Macready's half-sister; and actresses later to be Lady Bancroft and Dame Madge Kendal were at certain times members of it.

These stock companies gave beginners an excellent training.

Although for decades the stage had been understocked with actors, it was not easy to become one. Squire Bancroft relates that when he decided to go on the stage as a lad of nineteen, he addressed a 'shoal of letters' to the lessees of the leading country theatres, to most of which he received no answer, until Mercer Simpson of Birmingham granted an interview and took him on at one guinea a week. 'Upon this modest salary', Sir Squire continues, 'I feel some pride in saying that I lived.'[7]

That was in January 1861. By July he had played some thirty-six different parts. He then went to Cork, where in thirty-six nights he played forty different characters. And in the course of four years and four months he had no fewer than 346 parts behind him – within him, rather. The qualities developed by such a life were a photographic memory, since a new play was often put on at a day's notice; a retentive memory, too, since any new engagement might require the performance of quite a long part in a revival; observation of the same experienced players in a great variety of parts; alertness and initiative and loyalty to the show in all too frequent moments of artistic peril – 'Practice', says Sir Squire, writing in the late 1880s, 'which no young actor in this or any other country can now obtain'.[8]

So the stock companies provided the best theatres both in London and outside it with a constant flow of experienced newcomers.[9] But if this was their good side, they also had a bad side; and it was their bad side that drove them out of existence. Marie Wilton (Lady Bancroft) in her girlhood was in a Bristol company, which like most stock companies, grand or humble, went on tour of the neighbourhood during the summer 'vacation'. A star actor came from London to play in *The Lady of Lyons*. The company actress who was to have played his widowed mother was taken ill; and Marie Wilton was told to study the part in a few hours 'and do the best she could with it'. The performance was a fiasco. She knew nothing either of make-up or of impersonating old age. Apparently there was no rehearsal, certainly none in costume; and when she appeared on the stage looking half the age of her 'son', the audience was seized, audibly, with irrepressible mirth, and the star, visibly, with irrepressible wrath.[10]

Nor was this exceptional. With companies limited in number to what was economic, and with capital limited in resources by the necessary incidence of failures, and with both strained to their utmost by a continual demand for London novelties, it was natural that the standards of the stock companies should be rough-and-ready. But meanwhile, with the growing sophistication of local life, with the spread of illustrated magazines, and a greater ease of communications, local audiences wanted artistry closer and closer to London standards. And at the same time, the development of the London theatre was draining the best talent away from the stock companies. For the number of London theatres had increased enormously. With the abolition of the patents in 1843 some seventeen 'minor'[11] theatres became legitimately open to stage plays; and in the 1860s some nine more were built. The spectacular dramas then in vogue required large casts; and the best country talents found plenty of employment there. In consequence, it was the second-rate talents that stayed outside.

Moreover it was just these spectacular dramas which the 'country' audiences now wished to see. Each depended on a multitude of scenes, elaborately mounted; and indeed the appeal of each new show, because the plots were for the most part stereotyped, depended largely on the novelty of place, period or people to be seen in it. Old 'palace' or 'hall' sets no longer sufficed. Costumes must be more accurate than formerly. But few stock managers had the finance to commission three or four, still less a dozen, new scenes for each new play; nor would there have been time to build them if they had. And in any case, London gave ample employment to competent designers, and these too were leaving the country theatres. The only solution was for the 'stars' to bring their entire productions with them, cast, scenery, costumes, prompter and all: and this, so soon as the railway network provided adequate and cheap wherewithal, was what happened. London stars found new audiences at the end of their season, or, when long runs of single plays came in, new audiences and fresh wealth for themselves after the London public had been drained dry. Country audiences got better cast, better acted, better staged, and better disciplined performances, for which they were willing to pay a little more.

So the old stock company withered away. Mercer Simpson claimed that he was the very last manager to give it up, about 1880;[12] and very likely he was right, although the younger generation of that time did give 'stock' seasons, under such men as Wingold Lawrence at Birmingham in 1897, or at Bristol in the following two years.[13] Other and later seasons called 'stock' were in fact anticipations of local repertory theatres, though less permanent, and even harder-worked, some putting on two plays a week. No stars visited them.

Yet, if the old stock company withered away, its personnel, experienced, trained and wedded to the theatre, survived and planned to go on doing so. Some, it is true, had to abandon the stage and keep public-houses or tobacco-shops, or sell patent medicines. But many managers retained their leases and sub-let to the London tours, thus creating a new class, the provincial theatre manager, who, if he was clever, ended by owning, if not the company of his youthful dreams, at any rate a very profitable theatre property.

In London the case was very different. The stock company in a new form had transplanted itself under a London actor-manager.[14] This actor-manager was now faced with an influx of all the unemployed survivors of the country companies, trooping up to London in the hope of an engagement, no matter how low the salary offered. Their quality, perhaps, was not quite so good as that of those who had already arrived in London; but they were experienced and able and desperate for employment. Their presence tended, therefore, to reduce the salaries which managers would pay for 'supporting roles'. That comparatively few of the actor-managers, at least at first, did take advantage of the new raw materials, is greatly to their credit. But there was a danger that other kinds of managers would; and this, as will be seen, was what happened.

The theatre, unlike most other professions, is not a place where, once a man or a woman has attained a certain position of prominence and authority over others, the rest of their lives are spent in extending that authority over more and more employees. On the contrary, an actor might be a manager one year and employed by his own employee the next. This happens today; and so it did in the times we are describing: not only in London, but outside it too. T. C. King, for example, 'an excellent actor, but rarely seen in London', says Squire Bancroft, after being an employee in Birmingham would run his own season in Cork. Moreover, actor-managers had mostly been poor and struggling themselves: and although the Victorian attitude to personal success did not very often in commercial circles induce a self-made man to remember those he had outstripped, in artistic circles, especially in the theatre, it frequently did.

Also, it should be remembered, to have a good, though not too good, supporting company, was sound business. The shrewd, as well as the conscientious, actor-manager, once he had proved the worth of a newcomer, liked to keep him in the company, and the company together as much as possible. 'Those who were fortunate enough to join one of these companies,' Julia Neilson wrote about Irving, Tree, Alexander, Hare and Wyndham, 'were usually given a contract for a one to three year period'.[15] A. E. W. Mason, the novelist, who had been an actor himself, confirms this of Alexander; 'A continuous management meant very often continuity of employment; in play after play at the St James's Theatre, the same name occurred in the cast'.[16] A good player, even when engaged merely for the run of a single play, would usually be signed up for the next one.

It was sound policy too. Alexander followed the Bancrofts' habit of never allowing a play, however successful, to reach a point of saturation in public interest; so that he always had a popular play to revive at a few days' notice if a new one proved unpopular.[17] This meant keeping a fairly permanent company; and he knew very well that an able artist would be soon seduced into a rival house if he were not satisfied with the salary Alexander was giving him. To some extent, and in such cases, the good oncoming actor had some protection against the pool of mediocre ones. But the virtue of the actor-manager system lay in its being genuinely competitive and having high artistic standards.

It must not be thought that actor-managers were all rich, elderly people who bought themselves positions of tyrannical power, or had financial backers insisting on quick returns. The Bancrofts started a new era in British theatre management, when they were both very young, on £1,000 borrowed without security from Mrs Bancroft's brother-in-law. Without any experience of management, they took a low-class theatre in a slum district off the Tottenham Court Road, popularly known as the 'Dust-hole'; did it up in a new and elegant way; and by careful attention to detail and by a craftsmanship equalling only that of Madame Vestris at the old Olympic earlier in the century, but with the additional advantage of 'discovering' the leading dramatist of the century, T. W. Robertson, they created the leading successful theatre of the seventies and eighties. But by the opening night, their entire financial reserves stood at £150.[18]

After they retired from management, at the height of their powers and popularity, the rising star of Alexander shone all the brighter; but he had opened his first theatre at the age of thirty-one. Wilson Barrett, the elder, was thirty-three when he started his first company; Tree, thirty-four; Hare, thirty. Wyndham went into management at the Criterion in 1875 with £30, 'and never had a backer'.[19] Many others, though previously earning good salaries, had not been at their trade long enough to put by more than a quite modest capital; and although by prudence, judgement, courage and a certain amount of luck, they did amass considerable fortunes, many of them risked these in building or buying their own premises. Thus the Trafalgar Square Theatre (later called the Duke of York's) was built by the actor Frank Wyatt and his wife. Seymour Hicks built three: the Aldwych with a partner; the Hicks Theatre, later called the Globe; and the Queen's with a syndicate. Alexander reconstructed the St James's in 1899 for more than £7,000, the cost of a new theatre-building in those days, which made a very large hole in his savings.

Nor should it be thought that all actor-managers were more interested in themselves than in the play, a charge that is often brought against their memories. It is true that in 1897 when Irving had a fall and twisted his knee, *Richard III* could not be played in his absence, and the theatre closed.[20] But in that respect Irving was a survival from an earlier period. We have on the other hand an eye-witness account of the distress shown by George Alexander at rehearsal, when he noticed that he was playing an entire scene in the centre of the stage. 'You see', he explained to A. E. W. Mason, who was watching from the stalls, 'we play to sophisticated audiences here, and if I'm in the centre of the stage, they'll say "There of course is the actor-manager!" and the illusion of the play is gone.'[21]

Even before audiences not so sophisticated the tide was receding from that old practice. The importance of the solo star diminishes in proportion to the overall goodness and significance of the play itself; for a play with only one important character is not dramatic. Even in 'one-man' plays, though no other single character may outweigh the central figure, each that is in conflict with him must be given due importance in any scene, or there is no conflict. At this time plays, which had for more than half a century been of a very low standard, imitations of each other, or pirated versions of French successes, were improving fast. Of this improvement the Dramatic Copyright Act and the International Copyright Agreement were both cause and effect. Gone were the days of Buckstone and Boucicault. Dramatic authors now drew royalties and had an interest in the success of the play. They were to be taken seriously. T. W. Robertson, W. S. Gilbert, H. A. Jones, Oscar Wilde, Barrie, Shaw, were at work. The great names surrounding Granville Barker were beginning to learn their job. It is not without significance that many of the pioneers of real Victorian drama were men of the theatre, and produced their own works ably, not to say authoritatively.[22] Pinero, for example, at rehearsal was a well-informed and subtle martinet. Even a weak play could be sustained, not so much by a single performer, as by a unifying brain in the management of it. Charles Wyndham made the Criterion a centre of fine comedy, and could 'conjure into success play after play that in other hands would have gone off like a squib on a damp tennis-lawn'.[23]

It was T. W. Robertson's *Caste* which introduced the new era. All Britain wished to see it; and indeed it has the reputation of having sounded the death knell of the old stock company, because of its unprecedented success on tour with a company properly trained, produced, and equipped.[24] Other London companies followed this lead; and a gap was thus filled in the theatrical year. Hitherto it had been customary for theatres to close in London and the other principal cities after the end of the 'season'.[25] New stars formed a habit of regular autumn tours, complete with London company;[26] and swagger affairs they often were. 'When these great actors went on the road', Lena Ashwell recalls[27], 'the company travelled in a special train with the name of the manager and the names of the occupants of each carriage printed in large type and pasted on the windows.' Sir George Alexander expected his entire company to look as smart as possible, because there was always a concourse of distinguished society people at the station to see them off.

Very remunerative affairs too, they were. Alexander's autumn tours of twelve or fourteen weeks brought in, after all expenses were paid, net profits of over £4,000. Such sums were pure extras after a successful run; and could even balance out a failure.[28] Seymour Hicks and Ellaline Terriss travelled 130 people in *The Catch of the Season*, which cost £800 a week, but brought in sometimes £2,250 a week, and even, at Birmingham, £2,500.[29]

At first, in the eighties and nineties and while still in the control of actor-managers, such tours had considerable artistic merit. When Mary Anderson, the American actress whose 'natural' style created a sensation on this side of the Atlantic, went on tour in the

British Isles, she took with her a better company than she had had in London. In judgement of a play, the cities outside London, even though Shakespeare was not always a great draw, often proved keen and selective. The play *Claudian*, for example, was supposed to be 'above the heads of the provinces', but in fact faults were noticed in the conception of that piece which had escaped notice in London.[30] For less successful managers the country theatres offered livelihood while retrenching after a London failure. Edward Compton in 1892, having failed at the Opera Comique, sensibly decided that as he had made a success in the 'provinces' before he went to London, he could do so again till he had saved enough for another try there; which duly came to pass.[31]

We have spent all this space on the actor-managers, because there was a wholesome aspect of their activities, and they played an important function in theatre history. That they grew rich in an expanding theatre industry did not necessarily mean that less distinguished masses of artists had to grow poor or had to remain so. But the considerable fortunes which the successful ones did amass drew toward the theatre the speculative gaze of greedy and unscrupulous men, who were responsible for the deplorable conditions that now began to obtain. These greedy and unscrupulous men, copying and perverting the actor-managers' methods, in the end drove the actor-managers out of existence. Most of them came from outside the profession; but unhappily many, and these not the least notorious, came from inside it.

To complete our picture of the conditions under which our theatrical forebears worked, we must now examine the rise and development of the theatrical speculator and the commercial syndicate.

Notes and References

1. There is a mass of material concerning the little local theatres, embedded in the memoirs of many players. An account of the Helensburgh 'theatre royal' is given by John Coleman, *Fifty Years of an Actor's Life* (London, 1904, Vol. I, pp. 216, 229).
2. For the standards of William McCready, see an account of his promptbooks at Bristol by Kathleen Barker and the present author in *Theatre Notebook*, Vol. IV, No. 4, (July–September 1950).
3. Macready's *Reminiscences and Selections from his Diaries and Letters*. Ed. Sir F. Pollock, London, 1875, Vol. I, p. 124.
4. *10 Geo. II, c. 28.*

5. *20 Geo. III, c. xxx.*
6. *Ellen Terry's Memoirs*, London 1933, p. 35.
7. *Mr. and Mrs. Bancroft On and Off the Stage.* (8th edition. London, p. 65).
8. Ibid., pp. 66–7, 80.
9. W. Davenport Adams, '*Stock v. Star Companies*', *The Theatre*, Vol. I, pp. 277–81. 1 November 1878.
10. *Mr. and Mrs. Bancroft*, etc., p. 34.
11. They were anything but minor in size, some of them. The old Olympic seated 1,500; the Lyceum, 1,835; Sadler's Wells, 1,800; and the Adelphi, 2,135. *(Appendix No. 2 B (1) of Report of Select Committee on Theatres and Places of Entertainment, 1892: Theatres in existence before the the Passing of the Act of 1878.)*
12. Ibid., 2623.
13. *Green Room Book.* London, 1906, p. 204; and p. 215 under Stuart Lomath. John Hollingshead got a company together in Manchester, but his actors were not up even to the old standard, and his company came to grief. W. Davenport Adams; '*Thespis en Route*', *The Theatre*, N.S. Vol. III, pp. 295–302. 2 June 1884.
14. 'In London every theatre has its own stock company.' Mercer Simpson in evidence before the Select Committee, 2625.
15. Julia Neilson, *This for Remembrance*, London, 1940, p. 44.
16. A. E. W. Mason, *Sir George Alexander and the St. James's Theatre*, London, 1935. Lady Alexander's Appendix to this, p. 231.
17. A. E. W. Mason, op. cit., p. 212.
18. *The Bancrofts*, Marie Wilton's narrative, p. 86.
19. Florence Teignmouth Shore, *Sir Charles Wyndham*, London, 1908. (Stars of the Stage series), p. 50.
20. *The Theatre*, N.S. Vol. XXIX, p. 115, 1 February 1897.
21. A. E. W. Mason, op. cit., p. 4. But see also Clement Scott (quoted in *The Theatre*, 2nd MS. Vol. XXII. 1 August 1893: 'Except in extreme and exceptional cases the actor who becomes a manager is inimical to the encouragement of talent and any progress in art.'
22. *Dame Madge Kendal*, by herself, London, 1933, p. 42.
23. *Seymour Hicks, 24 Years of An Actor's Life*, by himself.
24. Percy Allen, *The Stage Life of Mrs. Stirling.* London, 1922, p. 190.
25. *Ellen Terry's Memoirs*, p. 28. Actors, like the rest of the world, were still entitled to their annual summer holidays. Ellen Terry says this custom of closing the theatres ended about 1906, when swifter means of transport brought more visitors to London in the 'dead' months. (p. 48, n. 1).
26. Julia Neilson, op. cit., pp. 44–5. The author gives 1914 as about the end of this custom.
27. Lena Ashwell, *Myself a Player.* London, 1936, p. 60.
28. A. E. W. Mason, op. cit., pp. 213 and 215.
29. Seymour Hicks, op. cit., p. 275.
30. W. Davenport Adams, *Thespis en Route.* loc. cit., pp. 295–302. Mercer Simpson, giving evidence before the Select Committee already cited, ascribed the lack of success of Shakespeare to the fact that the companies playing that dramatist's works frequently contained too many amateurs. See below, pp. 36–8.
31. *The Players*, Vol. I, p. 126. 26 January 1892.

CHAPTER TWO

Speculators and Syndicates

*The economic organisation of the theatre is
based on the asssumption that actors and
actresses are normally unemployed.*
Anonymous article in
The Saturday Review, 18 January 1919

We have mentioned already the rise towards the end of the
nineteenth century in the cities and big towns outside London of a
new type of employer: the provincial theatre manager. As time
went by, many of these began to think that if it was profitable to
own or to control the lease of a provincial theatre catering for
London tours, it would be more than doubly profitable to own or
to control two such theatres; and a chain of them might make a
fortune. Quite a number put this thought into practice.

There was, for example, a certain Andrew Melville in the West of
England. When he was little more than a schoolboy, his father,
who had been a gay, handsome, irresponsible actor and manager,
left him in possession of a theatre which he soon found to be
bankrupt.[1] The lad had great ability, and after a while made the
premises run at a profit. He was himself a passable actor, and
played Rip Van Winkle later in life for his own farewell benefit at
Derby in 1893.[2] He was also something of an author. That adapta-
tion of Washington Irving's story was his own; and it was said that
once in Birmingham he had re-written an entire melodrama, in

order to make it fit a stock of posters he happened to have on hand.[3] Not a man of very great artistic integrity, therefore; but before he retired he had control of the Grand, Derby, which he built; the Grand, Birmingham, the Grand, Glasgow, the Theatre Royal, Bristol, the New Theatre and Star Opera House, Swansea; a theatre in Walsall, and a big house at Shoreditch, where opera was performed.[4] According to H. G. Hibbert, he always reserved to himself the profits from the bars, from sales of refreshments, sweets and programmes, and from the management of the cloak rooms; a source of additional revenue by no means to be despised.[5]

A smart fellow, in fact. One who had grown up in the theatre, but not a theatre artist. A man of box office experience; one who had eaten the fruits of the tree of the knowledge of loss and profit; one who used his knowledge of the theatre to make money. And he made it; he died worth £90,000.[6] Not a very generous man, either, though he could make generous gestures. Twice within two months we find him taken to court by his own employees. A scene-shifter sued for personal injuries received in his service two years previously because of a slippery floor; he got £100 damages.

A scene-painter said he had not been paid wages due to him. But in the eyes of the magistrate, when Andrew Melville defended his right not to pay, scene-painting was not manual labour but 'high art'; and so there was no protection for the plaintiff within the Masters and Servants Act. As the contract was made, not in London, where the case was being heard, but in Birmingham, it should have been taken to the County Court; and that was the end of that matter. Melville waived his costs, including his own first-class fare to London.[7]

J. B. Howard was an actor good enough to play Iago when Salvini visited Edinburgh in April 1884. He had then lost his tenancy of the Theatre Royal there, despite his offer of a £2,000 rent with security for half that sum from Irving himself.[8] He joined Fred Wyndham, son of a former lessee of that house, and together they built the Lyceum Theatre, Edinburgh, which Irving opened in September 1883.[9] Within eight years these two men were proprietors of the Theatre Royal, Glasgow; lessees of the Royalty and lessees and managers of the Theatre Royal, Newcastle. Today the company they founded controls the seven principal theatres in Edinburgh, Glasgow, Manchester, Newcastle and Liverpool, and the booking of eleven other provincial theatres.[10]

By 1891 many other men were digging in the same gold rush.

William Bennett, at Leamington, Coventry, and Kidderminster; Robert Arthur at Dundee, Aberdeen and Wolverhampton; Edward Darby and Ellis Brammall, to name a few. Financial speculation was in full swing. Bigger and bigger theatres were built all over the country. There was a boom in what was becoming a theatre industry; and all manner of speculators, knowing little of theatre business and caring less for theatre art, were eager to be 'in on a good thing'. We can measure the size of it only by turning our wistful stage eyes upon the analogous cinema houses of our own day; for the figures are hard to believe. In Liverpool by 1892 there were no fewer than nine major legitimate theatres, three of them seating about 2,000, two of them just under 3,000 and one 3,000 fully. This was not to count Hengler's Circus, which seated 3,300 nor the preposterous figure of 397 music halls.[11] In Great Britain that year there were 313 legitimate theatres.[12]

In London it was the same. The abolition of the patent houses in 1843 had not resulted in a big rush to build new theatres: a score of them was then enough for a population of 286,067. It remained enough, or nearly enough, in 1881, though the population had increased nearly fourfold. But on the other hand by 1901, the population had increased only two-fold, while no fewer than twenty-five new theatres had been built. Nor was this in response to the growing suburban population; for suburbans did not at that time go regularly in any great numbers to the West End,[13] preferring the big local theatres that were built for them (outside the figures quoted above), where tours of stars ended or began, and they could see their favourites at half the price charged in 'town'.

The rush in the theatre world to speculate, to invest, to expand, was only a symptom of a wider rush to invest in all other sorts of industry. The great pioneer days of mid-Victorian personal endeavour were finished. Now finance, and financial combination, were the profitable thing. Railways were amalgamating, banks combining; the foundations of Unilever and Imperial Chemical Industries were being laid. And so too in the theatre, these big new ventures were by no means all the work of single adventurers. On the contrary, they were mostly undertaken by syndicates – groups of business men with money to invest, seeking a reliable, shrewd chairman with a knowledge of theatre finance.

The body running the Comedy Theatre in 1892 is typical: Mr Hawtrey, an actor; Mr William Fladgate, a theatrical lawyer also interested in amateur theatricals; General Sim, a retired Army Officer; and Mr Clifton, an architect.[14]

So with even the Theatre Royal, Drury Lane. That august house was now being run by Arthur Collins, who had been superintendent of productions under the previous lessee Sir Augustus Harris. But he worked to a committee with a capital of £125,000, mostly, he himself said, found by his friends.[15] In 1892 the Prince's, Manchester, was sold to a syndicate of brewers.[16]

John Hollingshead, who combined theatre management with theatrical journalism, gives figures that show some results of these commercial ventures. The speculative builders had everything their own way. They exacted from a manager not only a quarter's rent in advance, but a deposit banked against dilapidations. Hollingshead was the first manager-tenant of the Gaiety Theatre, when it opened in 1868. It had cost £15,000: the rent was £3,500 with no prospect of an offset from profits on bars and sales, which being retained by the owners, brought them a further £1,000 a year. A net dividend of some 33 per cent their investment brought in, for they also retained two proprietary boxes in the auditorium, which might well add £500 a year.[17] In the year 1893, which was a 'slump' year, the Gaiety Theatre company declared a net profit of £3,116 for its shareholders, who included the manager George Edwardes. By 1891 theatre values had increased so much that the owners of the Court Theatre, lying out in Chelsea, and half the size of the Gaiety, were able to ask a rent of £4,000.[18]

In addition to high rents, the unhappy tenant bore the costs of rates, taxes, insurance and even land-tax. Hollingshead had to go very carefully, with the capacity of the Gaiety limited to 1,360. Since the innovations of the Bancrofts, London audiences were accustomed to luxurious fittings, carpets, upholstered seats, house lighting, and other such amenities. No manager dared have anything but the best, and in good condition.

The public expected star artists, and spectacular shows: the only possible channel of economy, therefore, was the salaries of supporting players; for their names would not by themselves fill those dearer stalls without which the weekly expenses could not be covered, and it did not much matter who they were. Small wonder that Terry (Edward O'Connor Terry, that is, the one who married Sir Augustus Harris's widow, and was himself steeped in the traditions of the Shakespearian clown)[19] earned a reputation for parsimony in this respect. By nature, and in his private life outside the theatre, he was anything but parsimonious.[20]

High pre-production overheads are the quickest method of imperilling a theatre's finances, however sound these may look on paper. The higher they are, the less chance there is that a success can pay for a failure. But when there is no alternative, a clever manager will assure to himself a fairly steady and faithful audience by finding a special line of theatre-produce and never trying out anything beyond it. Such specialisation duly occurred. In the eighties, to quote Julia Neilson:

> at Drury Lane Augustus Harris presented spectacular drama; at the Savoy were D'Oyly Carte's light operas. The Gattis provided melodrama at the old Adelphi; the Haymarket was known for light comedy during the Bancroft management; at the St James's Hare and Kendal provided domestic drama, a policy which George Alexander continued. Vedrenne and Granville Barker were at the Court. At the Criterion the name of Wyndham stood for drawing-room comedy, and last but not least, there was the Lyceum with Irving.[21]

Between the stars and the small part player came the rank of supporting star, whose salary no actor manager could afford to reduce for reasons already considered. When the Bancrofts abolished the ignominious custom of benefit nights, they paid their leading supporters (if the phrase may be excused) as much as £60 a week, or even £100 for a special star; compared with the £5 or £10-plus-benefit which had obtained hitherto.[22] They afforded this by abolishing the old-style pit and filling the space with ten shilling stalls, an action which at first caused a riot, but ended by becoming the regular thing. So regular, in fact, that the owners increased the rent proportionately.

True, actor-managers were not crippled by any financial burden of leading roles, since they played these themselves; and they could always supplement their weekly balance, if this was not big enough, by engagements at evening parties. In those days of ostentatious hospitality in high places, it was nothing for the Duke of Newcastle to fee Seymour Hicks and Ellaline Terriss at 100 guineas for a few recitations.[23] But economic forces were at work all the time, and against them; and the only possible channel for them also, to economise, was the pay of the small-part player. It is not surprising if they struck hard bargains. What is surprising is that they struck so few of them. For indeed, even the commercial managers were finding finance difficult. Horace Sedger, who besides managing the Lyric Theatre, was a director of the Automatic Rifle Syndicate Ltd., writes in 1895 a most revealing and interesting letter to *The Pelican*:[24]

During the last four years at the Lyric I have either been more or less in the hands of certain capitalists who desired, for interested reasons, certain pieces produced, or the capital has had to be borrowed at as much as 150 per cent, which would kill anything or anybody. I have as we all know survived the ordeal, although the Lyric Co. Ltd. was, very unwisely for the creditors, liquidated by an irate gentleman, whose costs I refused to pay.

In other words, backers, whom Seymour Hicks described with witty bitterness as 'a large body of gentlemen not entirely surrounded by money',[25] are here seen at their worst. Not only did they insist on high returns; they controlled the choice of play and policy to ensure this. From there, it is a short step to forming a syndicate of backers, not for a particular artist or manager, but for a specific show. This process, so familiar in our own day, now began, greatly helped by the plethora of theatre premises, into the high rent commitments of which not every actor dared tie himself, however much he might wish to be his own manager.

Such syndicates assembled ill-paid companies to perform particular plays for as long a London run as could be squeezed out of them. So soon as a show reached its fiftieth or hundredth night, a touring company was organised, even worse paid.[26] Before long the process extended to large cities outside London for tours that had never seen and would never see a West End performance. The gambling mania spread from top to bottom, from the grand house in the Strand to the meanest fit-up in Alton or Basingstoke. In one case a member of a syndicate of the latter kind was a city tailor, who cadged orders from his own company.[27] In another case a backer was a country squire who had written a one-act play, and for vanity backed a tour to play it as a curtain-raiser to a farce and a melodrama alternately in two-night stands. This piece was so bad that the company had to drop it; and when their backer found out, he withdrew his backing, leaving the players stranded. They had been so badly paid already, that they were sleeping four in a room and smoking fag-ends picked up in the street. They had to pawn their watches to get home. This company was advertised as 'The Comedy-Drama Company of Specially Selected London Artistes'. Nor were such persons above accepting contributions ('part-investments') of sums like £25 from applicants for parts, even in the Strand Theatre. An occasion is on record when £500 was paid by (or for) an 'actress' to play a principal part. Horatio Bottomley entered into theatrical transactions, in order to advance a colour-printing business he was interested in.[28] In this way the narrow path, which in later years was to become a busy highway, was cut through the theatrical jungle.

It was only to be expected that with some fine exceptions, like Wilson Barrett the elder and Frank Benson, the standards of the London Tour, which the theatre-starved provinces had welcomed so eagerly, should drop swiftly and deep. 'An Actor', writing to *The Stage*, 6 July 1893, says that companies were sent on the road 'virtually stage-manager-less', by which he meant that there was little attempt at direction, or, as we would say, 'unproduced'. Touring companies were produced, if at all by one of the acting company who drew a slightly increased salary, or even by the music director – for companies generally included a so-called 'small orchestra'. The account given in this letter is confirmed by an editorial the following week.

Even when a provincial tour did receive any preliminary instruction, it was only to ensure that it should hold as much mimicry of the London original as the players could be forced to learn. 'The country players' (which term by now meant London actors and actresses who could not get any engagements in the West End, and welcomed even this prostitution of their abilities) 'parrot every tone, gesture and bit of business inserted at the original production.'[29]

Now it is a natural thing in every art, and indeed wholesome, and for that matter necessary, that a beginner should in his or her style show signs that the technique of an admired master has been studied for its secrets. The artist who in extreme youth shows no influence whatever of any senior, tends when he grows up to atrophy; whereas the artist who in his maturity has style and understanding unique to himself, is generally the one who in his youth can almost pass off his work as a minor work of some established master. So it is in acting, too. Squire Bancroft, certainly an original performer, made his first reputation as Lord Dundreary at Plymouth, because he 'reproduced in facsimile' that character as E. A. Sothern created it.[30]

But that is a very different thing from compelling a girl to imitate the well-known little sob and moan of Mrs Pat Campbell when you are preparing *For the Crown* to tour. It is a very different thing from engaging a young player specifically to imitate a star, and re-engaging him because he is likely to do as well in the same star's next part, and the next, and next. Seymour Hicks said that in the

restaurants at the east end of the Strand, you could easily identify
the actor-manager for whom each youth threading through the
tables was working. 'Lyceum youths had the halting gait, the
muffled tones, the long hair, the drooping hands of their great
chief': Olympic youths, like Hicks himself, were like Willard, with
hair brushed away from left temple, chin out, 'and the deadly
frown of the famous heavy man shadowed my quite inoffensive
face'; while Wilson Barratt's boys 'had curly hair falling in well
arranged, impromptu-looking clusters with bunches of gold seals
on their fobs, and staccato voices'. Of course they did! It was not
only identification of self with hero; it might also get them a better
job.[31]

But even when they got such a job, the pay was disgraceful.
Ellaline Terriss as understudy in *David Garrick*, one of the
Criterion's greatest successes, received at the age of nineteen one
guinea a week. When her principal was ill, she played for six weeks
at that price. Wyndham came to hear of his own meanness quite by
chance, and, smitten with shame, gave her a ruby and diamond
ring – a flamboyant gesture of contrition, and a singularly un-
imaginative one.[32]

Seymour Hicks in his youth went on tour as assistant stage
manager playing also quite important parts, at thirty shillings a
week, and his living expenses on a level just above starvation were
twenty-three shillings. After three and a half years in 1890, he
managed to rise to £6, by joining the Kendal's American tour.[33]
But this was so rapid a rise as to be almost unheard-of, and was due
to his own fascinating personality and talent. By far the great
majority of young people, of whom we do not hear because they
are not important enough to publish reminiscences, stayed on the
lower level. Managers who had such disregard for their employees
had as much contempt for their public. Hicks was once sent to
Ryde, knowing nothing of the stage, to get by hook or crook a
scratch company there to perform a nautical drama with com-
plicated sea effects which he had to improvise from any material
lying about. The managers had overlooked a date booked for
Ryde when the real touring company was engaged elsewhere.

Let me give some actual, general, salary figures, taken from a
long letter to *The Stage* of 26 October 1893. In Number One
touring companies from London, the leads were paid £10 or £15 a
week, and utility men and women £2. In Number Two and Number
Three tours from London the usual terms were £7 and £6 for

leads, thirty shillings for utilities. But there were many companies, playing the same dates as the last, which were organised from places other than London; in these the rates were seventy shillings for leads, and a guinea for utilities. In fit-up tours, pay – unguaranteed – fell as low as a norm of forty and fifteen shillings respectively.

Artists classed as 'utility' were by no means the dregs of the stage. Many of them were middle-aged folk with a life-long experience and a richly developed technique, who could be relied on, like that of their successors in many a present-day repertory company, never to give a bad performance. Stage production, then and now, would be impossible without them. Many had families to support. The reason for their humble status, in many cases, was that when young they had lacked the face or the figure to play romantic juveniles, had never caught the eye of any manager, and had for economic reasons fallen into a rut from which now it was as impossible for them to escape as for a blinded man to navigate by the stars.

For husband and wife to be together in the same tour was no saving. On the contrary, their joint pay was a reduction of what they would have got separately. Nor was a long engagement in this side of theatrical life altogether a boon: touring managers reduced the pay in proportion to the estimated length, though they reserved the right to cancel the tour without notice or compensation whenever it suited them. Matinees seldom brought any extra money to the people who played them. When they did, it was never more than half an evening's pay; this might amount, in a tour organised from outside London, to three shillings and sixpence. But in fact even these figures are deceptive; for they are weekly figures, and it was very improbable that any one player would be in work for more than forty-two weeks in any year: his actual annual earnings might amount to £104, and no more.

Let us now examine the minimum expenses. Gone were the comfortable days when the theatrical family arrived, less on tour than on circuit, at its usual howff – or haunt – in a familiar town, with the landlady giving a friendly welcome to old friends, or appraising looks to a new member of the company. Landladies were confused and dismayed by hordes of strange and often down-and-out-looking 'theatricals' seeking lodgings, sometimes at 11 p.m. on a Sunday night, grubby, hungry, and disagreeable after a fourteen-hour journey in an uncomfortable train with exasperating waits at places like Crewe. If they had charity, they had civility; but often they had neither.

The profession sometimes, it must be admitted, deserved its reputation. The demoralisation of unmerited poverty, the need to live on one's wits to live at all, the insecurity, the frustration, and sometimes the recklessness which long bad luck may distil from that mercurial temperament which is in us all – these and other causes made many a poor player turn anti-social, take to petty theft, minor dishonesties, vicious gambling, or drink. For it is hopelessness and loneliness, in the last analysis, that causes crime; and not any abstract evil entering the human heart.

But landladies, pressed as closely as they, cared nothing for such subtleties. In many cases they were hostile; in most, suspicious. Because actors make for the immediate neighbourhood of their place of work, the lodgings would generally be near the theatre; and commercial speculators generally built their theatres in neighbourhoods where the ground was cheap. So that the landladies too were poor folk, living on a narrow margin and therefore on their sharpness of wit. The sanitation of the rooms they let out, the smells, the bugs[34], the dirt, the absence of even a hip-bath, made them a byword in an era of wretched lodgings. But even so, they had to be paid for.

Costs varied from fourteen shillings a week for a couple or ten shillings a week for one, to nine or ten shillings for a couple and six shillings for one. But the latter class of lodging was best occupied in extremity only. By 1893 these costs, with no improvement of accommodation at all, had advanced by 25 per cent and in some cases 50 per cent.[35] A fairly well-paid actor might thus have £2 a week from which to save for his out-of-work weeks, and pay for food, clothing, stage clothing except period costume, make-up, tips at theatres, porterage of his basket, to say nothing of any medical expenses, and such additions as a family requires, baby-clothes, education, apprentice fees.[36] An unskilled labourer in the countryside may well have been better off with his pittance of eighteen shillings; for as long as he behaved himself and gave no trouble to his boss, he would have a roof for nothing, and quite an amount of edible food as perquisites. The human humiliations of the two trades were about equal.

However, according to another *Stage* correspondent, in the issue of 9 November 1893, claiming fifteen years' experience in the profession, very few actors averaged even £2 a week actual; not ten per cent of his acquaintance he says, for years past, even those lucky enough to get pantomime engagements. According to some figures published in the *Sunday Times*, and quoted in *The Stage*'s editorial column 'Chit-Chat', out of some eight or ten thousand actors and actresses, not more than half were in work at any given time.[37] And yet there was this boom in tours. As many as 150 of them left London in a single autumn.[38]

Is there an explanation of this extraordinary contradiction? There is; and it is almost as incredible as the facts it explains. For the sake of quick returns, commercial organisers of touring companies were giving parts on a big scale to inexperienced amateurs of independent means, who were eager to play for nothing.

It was not in one or two freak exceptions. It was the rule, it was widespread. Article after article, letter after letter, in the theatrical press, mentions it; volume after volume of reminiscence recalls it. One letter in *The Stage* (30 March 1893) from an actor of six years' professional experience reports that a manager had offered him a touring part at seven and sixpence a week, saying that if he didn't accept it, the manager knew he could get an amateur for nothing. Nor is there anything on record to contradict it. On the contrary, its prevalence was notorious. The right word for the glut of amateurs, says *The Stage*, on 30 March 1893, is 'appalling'. Small wonder that Seymour Hicks and others of his generation bore to their graves an implacable and bitter hatred of amateurs. For the amateurs were not only taking away the livelihood of the professionals; they were also debasing the prestige of acting. They did not know how to act. In some cases they did not even trouble to memorise their words.[39] The good taste, and good sense, of audiences outside London caused attendances to drop; people began just to keep away from the theatre altogether. Maybe this accounts for the non-theatrical generation that followed, which, when it finally did go to places of entertainment, went to the movies. Maybe we are suffering still from the long-range effects of it. In London too the amateurs were debasing standards. For they were depriving the London stage of the best training for newcomers.

Under the new commercial touring system, the acquiring of experience would have been difficult enough without the amateurs to block it. For the best way to learn acting is to be on the book when fine artists are rehearsing. In the old tours, which were in effect travelling repertories, one learnt well and quickly. Sydney Blow said he learnt more from Madge Kendal in one tour than in his previous four years.[40] But in these protracted tours of single plays there were no rehearsals after the opening night, no changes of characters, no handing on of hints and tradition. The unfortunate beginner might find himself studying some conceited young rake with even less knowledge than his own. One could, of course, pay fees and study under Vezin, or Lacy, Genevieve Ward or Fred Terry; plenty of elderly actors took pupils in such a way. But thereafter there was no certainty of employment. It was possible to get an excellent training at Sarah Thorne's 'pupils' repertory' at Margate. Gertrude Kingston did.[41] But numbers were limited; and so were subsequent jobs. There was no recognised training school at this time. The stage got its fresh blood by accident, sometimes through the very freshness of that blood, bursting impudently and with charm into private houses of leading players, as William Terriss did in 1868.[42]

In London indeed the positions of amateur and professional became reversed. The amateurs would hire theatres for matinees and themselves play the leads, while experienced professionals took gratefully the fees paid for their assistance in *Othello* and *Hamlet*. One such recital of *Hamlet* cost its strutting young socialite £500 in salaries alone; it was so ridiculous that it was all but laughed off the stage by an audience even of friends and relatives.[43] Disappointed authors of the same type did the same. A little coterie of unemployed minor stars appeared frequently, sometimes in four such try-out plays within one week. The plays seldom came to anything, but they made a welcome break after a long run of payless months.

Apart from the amateurs, however, there were worse conditions yet. Even employment, even prosperity, had their dangers. It is noticeable, in reading through old stage papers, how many, many gifted young artists died too young, from pulmonary or more often gastric troubles. The reason for this lay in the filthy condition, not so much of lodgings, as of dressing-rooms.[44] There had long been complaints about this, but the truth came to light during the investigations of a Select Committee on Theatres and Places of Entertainment set up in 1892. There was no intention of investigating sanitary conditions. The terms of reference included only methods of preventing outbreaks of fire, questions of censorship, and other matters affecting licensing, which at that time had no concern with sanitation. The officials giving evidence before the Committee had had no intention of raising the question, either, nor had they any information, when questions were asked; they had to go and find out.

In the previous year a paper had been read[45] to a Congress of Hygiene by a throat specialist named Lennox Browne, whose wife was a keen amateur actress, in which he had observed:

> Dressing-rooms are often quite inadequate, faulty in situation, in air-space, in ventilation, in the number (of) windows, and in water-supply. Water closets and urinals are frequently placed in improper situations, bad forms are used, and sometimes the workmanship is at fault. They are often ventilated into dressing-rooms, refreshment rooms, lobbies, staircases, and even on to the stage.

The majority of these defects were of structural origin, due partly to old fashioned and partly to hasty or parsimonious designing. He went on:

> The effects produced on the health of the audience were theatre-headache and theatre-diarrhoea; and of the actors were sore throats, loss of voice, typhoid fever, so-called rheumatism, and habits of intemperance.

The picture of a tumbledown old actor, wheezy, crippled and drunken, so popular with humorists of that time, thus takes on another hue. But the learned expounder did not stop there. Theatrical industrial disease, as it would now be called, was his special study. He undertook a special tour of investigation of London theatres for the purpose, and published his findings in a series of five articles in the *British Medical Journal* (1893, March, May, June and July), which always suggested simple remedies for the ills he found. In fairness to the proprietors it should be stated that almost every one allowed him free access and hastened to set matters right to his wishes, sometimes at considerable expense. The conditions varied, as might be expected; and it was generally the older houses that were the worst offenders. Some important details are given also in articles of 2 April, 30 April, 1887, and 30 November 1889, and 22 November 1890. Among things noticed were rat-droppings in Terry's Theatre, and a date in the North of England to which a certain company always sent a messenger in advance with perfume and disinfectants.

> Certain theatres are recognised in the theatrical profession as risky places to play in from the liability of illness being engendered.

Recognised by part of the medical profession too, evidently! But not by the Law. An actress under the terms of an agreement she had signed was directed by her management to play at a certain theatre notorious as a source of typhoid. She was already a patient of Lennox Browne, who warned her of the danger; and she used his professional advice as a plea to be released from her agreement. Her employers held her to the bond. The case went to the High Court. The Judge observed that he did not see that a medical man was called upon to give an opinion until his patient had actually suffered.[46]

One or two individuals in Local Government may have been aware of such sources of disease, but they could do little about it. Thomas Blashill, Superintending Architect of Metropolitan Buildings, informed the Select Committee that his duties related specially to matters affecting danger from fire and panic; 'also to reasonable ventilation and for sanitary arrangements so far as the Council (i.e. *The London County Council*) may have any power, which' he added reassuringly 'I do not think is very far.' He always accompanied the inspection committee on its rounds. Never in his experience had it increased the stringency of any requirements on his advice; quite the contrary, it had 'very frequently' relaxed them, after having interviews with theatre proprietors.

Mr Blashill had not heard of any complaints about Covent Garden, and the Council never surveyed the dressing-rooms there; but he went off to make inquiries, and stood before the Committee a week later with scandalous information.[47] At Covent Garden, it appeared, there were nine dressing-rooms in the basement, of which only half had fireplaces or windows, and these latter ventilated into basement areas; the rest were just cellars without any light or ventilation. There the 'supers' (that is, the non-speaking parts, chorus, *corps de ballet*, and so on) dressed. On the ground floor there were about the same number, all having windows, but half of these were blocked by the Floral Hall. On the other floors were five more dressing-rooms, divided by moveable partitions. There were only twelve closets for the entire company and staff of the theatre, not more than three of them having light or ventilation; and the 100 or more people in the nine dressing-rooms and 'vaults' were expected to share a single one.

'The Council', Mr Blashill explained, 'has never had anything to do with such matters, but I have no doubt that under the Public Health Act of last year, it will have power to act in case of default by the vestry.' (The vestry, or district board, did have as much power to insist on proper sanitation in a theatre as in a private house if it threatened public health or convenience, but it never exercised this power, or very seldom.) No Council either would take action in those days under any law, unless a complaint were lodged; and 'no complaint as to these dressing-rooms had been received by the Council'.

This again, was no isolated example. It was prevalent. In Toole's Theatre – and J. L. Toole was a humane and generous man – the dressing-rooms were once flooded with half a foot of water from the mortuary tanks of Charing Cross Hospital next door.[48] If such were the conditions in the fine West End of London, it can be imagined what they were like outside. Thomas Shelmerdine, architect and surveyor to the Corporation of Liverpool, reported that when a sub-committee of Liverpool Justices of the Peace inspected theatres there in 1887, the size and sanitation of the dressing-rooms had some attention, 'but I may say that the justices at that time had regard more particularly to the safety of the audience and to the safety of actors than the sanitation'. Perhaps he meant to the safety of their own reputations, in case anything started a panic and the local press could level charges against the licensing body before the next election. The burning of the Queen's Theatre, Manchester, in 1890 was not regarded with very great concern by the profession. Two or three years previously an actress returning from the stage to her dressing-room there had found rats eating her grease-paint, hare's-foot, and powder puff.[49]

There was no compulsion to think about the actors. They were not local electors. They did not even work in a factory, over which government inspectors were getting a little more control. If they consented to work in conditions that were dangerous to life, that was a matter of their individual freedom, with which no local government ought to tamper; still less with the freedom of an employer to create such conditions. People were contracting such diseases; and dying of them. Insanitary conditions were the primary cause, and insufficient pay the secondary cause. They were glad to run the risk if only they could get work. There were many other risks, wrongs and injustices which they were glad to overlook, if only they could get work; about this we will be dealing as the occasion arises. 'Free Trade in the Drama' was the cry of the managers in *The Era* and other papers. Free Trade seemed the best and most up-to-date theory in every business; and in Free Trade by jungle law the weakest goes to the wall. Many a victim on their way thither still praised Free Trade.

A glance backward, now, at the general pattern that had brought the profession to this point. Out of the London stars came the break-up of the old stock companies and the success of the actor-manager. Out of the success of the actor-manager came the speculative building of theatres and the new touring system. Out of the latter of these came the speculative manager in the provinces, and out of the former the syndicate in London. Out of all these growths, each inevitable, and not all without their merits, came evil and suffering for the rank and file of actors and actresses, tied up in a knot that nobody seemed able to untie.

Nobody accepted responsibility. The rank and file blamed the actor-managers; the actor-managers blamed the touring managers; the touring managers blamed the provincial proprietors: and all these blamed the actors. Professionals blamed amateurs; and for all I know, the amateurs may have blamed the professionals for being hidebound, insincere or careeristic, as they sometimes do today. Complaint of a nuisance or a scandal, even to a competent authority, even of something forbidden by law, might earn the complainant a name for being a trouble-maker, or malcontent, or possibly an 'agitator', though the time for that term had not yet come: that would make employment harder than ever to find. Indeed it would have been as hard to find the individual source of the trouble. It was in the air, in the times, in the very system; reform seemed possible only piecemeal, in small pockets of kindliness and goodwill.

Now in any industry when an evil is so widespread that no individual can remedy it, there are only two courses by which it can be remedied. Either the Government can step in, whether of its own initiative or compelled by opposition pressure, which is the political way; and several actor-managers, notably Sir George Alexander, were public-spirited enough to work in local government, and even, as he did, contemplated entering the House of Commons. But in the main the hours and labour of the theatrical life do not, or did not then, encourage such individual activity; and as for prodding political parties, the profession as a whole was practically disfranchised.[50] For it was continually on the move; and no M.P. could regard its members as more than very casual and uninfluential constituents. But even when resident it was scattered; there was no 'actors' quarter', as one might speak politically of a 'working-class district' at election time; so political action was negligible. Or else there is the industrial way: action by combining; collective action.

A few saw this alternative, and tried to organise and plan it. But they could not act until they had power; and collective power demands collective feeling; the group, or community, must feel that it is a group or community. The question therefore was; would the theatrical profession feel that it was a profession at all? With that, went a second question: Would it see that everybody in it was involved together? With that, went a third: since thousands of different people, however much they may agree, need leaders, spokesmen, representatives, to give their actions voice and direction, would the theatrical thousands find a means to empower such leaders? With all these questions, and most critical of all: would the people who seemed about to lead, prove the right kind of people to do so?

For some thirty years, these questions went largely unanswered; indeed, almost unasked. The people in our profession were too preoccupied with personal struggles and fears to see themselves as a profession at all. They were content, separately, as actor and as actress, to take life week by week, engagement by engagement, since this they had to do. The future, wider view, was limited by favourable press-cuttings that might lead to something better; by Green Room gossip about possible casts; by the way other people played a part, better or possibly worse than oneself.

Three principles only governed the morale of the stage, three virtues or superstitions, according to how they have to be viewed: there was Faith, there was Hope, and there was Charity. Faith in one's talents and techniques; Hope in one's luck and life-line; and if this last showed signs of breaking before the others had come into their own, then in old age, Charity – mostly from outside.

Notes and References

1. H. G. Hibbert, *A Playgoer's Memories*. London, 1930, p. 230.
2. *The Stage*, 6 January 1893, and 6 July 1893, p. 9.
3. H. G. Hibbert, loc. cit.
4. *The Stage*, 17 August 1893, p. 9; 24 August 1893, p. 7; and *Dramatic Year Book, 1891*.
5. H. G. Hibbert, op. cit., p. 222.
6. *The Pelican*: 14 November 1896, p. 7.

7. *The Stage*, 11 January 1893 and 9 February 1893. £90,000 then would be a huge fortune today.

8. *The Theatre*, 2nd N.S. Vol. I, p. 61, 1 January 1883 and Vol. III, 1 May 1884.

9. Ibid., 2nd N.S. Vol. I, p. 101, 1 February 1883 and Vol. II, p. 197, 1 October 1883.

10. *Dramatic Year Book, 1891*: and information from Messrs. Howard and Wyndham. This Wyndham, of course, is not to be confused with Sir Charles Wyndham, the lessee of the Criterion Theatre, London, who built Wyndham's Theatre in 1899, and to whom he was not related.

11. *Dramatic Year Book, 1891*.

12. *Report of the Select Committee, etc.* 11 May 1892. Evidence by Thomas Shelmerdine, Architect and Surveyor to the Liverpool Corporation: 3717. And Appendix No. 2 B (1) and (2). One is tempted to suppose that if the phenomenal figure of Liverpool Music Halls is not an error, it must have included a number of places that might better be called 'Penny Gaffs'!

13. *The Players*, Vol. I, p. 146, 26 January 1892.

14. Ibid., Vol. I, p. 135.

15. *The Theatre*, 2nd N.S. Vol. XXX, p. 46. 1 July 1896. Also: *The Green Room Book, 1906, or Who's Who On the Stage*, under Collins. The details in the majority of entries, according to the editor of this work, were either supplied or revised by the subjects themselves.

16. *The Players*, 13 May 1892, quoting *The Umpire*.

17. John Hollingshead, 'Theatrical Bricks and Mortar', *The Theatre*, 2nd N.S. Vol. XXVIII, pp. 73–7. 1 August 1896. Also, *The Stage*, 14 September 1893. 'Chit-chat'. Hibbert, op. cit., p. 222 gives the possible yield from bars and other extras as £2,000 a year; but I do not know his sources, nor how reliable his figures are.

18. *The Pelican*, 19 March 1892, p. 363. This was a society weekly founded by its editor, Frank M. Boyd, in 1889. It willingly cast unpleasant hints at the virtue of actresses but objected to passages in Ibsen's *Ghosts* as 'nasty' and 'suggestive'. It is a trustworthy guide for the scholar to *fin de siècle* and Edwardian gossip.

19. This Terry was not related to the famous family to which Ellen and Fred and the others belonged.

20. Hibbert, op. cit., p. 89; and *Green Room Book 1906*.

21. Julia Neilson, op. cit., p. 259. The authoress has confused her dates a little. The Vedrenne-Barker management did not exist before 1904. Also it is not quite true to limit Alexander to 'domestic drama' when his authors varied from Stephen Phillips to Anthony Hope. 'Romantic drama' would have been a better description, if this had not been the speciality of the charming Julia Neilson herself, with Fred Terry. But the general picture of specialised houses is true.

22. Julia Neilson, op. cit., p. 30.

23. Seymour Hicks, op. cit., p. 211.

24. *The Pelican*, 28 December 1895, p. 8.

25. Seymour Hicks, op. cit., p. 45.

26. George Alexander, 'On Theatrical Apprenticeship', *The Theatre*, 2nd N.S. Vol. XXI, pp. 54–5, 1 January 1893.

27. Harold Child, *A Poor Player*, London 1939, pp. 33, 36, 56, 60, and also an

advertisement in the *Financial News* inviting subscriptions to a production of a new light opera at a West End theatre. Prospectus available. Quoted in *The Pelican*, 18 April 1891.

28. Ibid., p. 56. And *The Pelican*, 18 April 1891, p. 468: and 18 July 1891, p. 726.
29. *The Theatre*, 1 January 1886. *Our Omnibus Box*.
30. *Plymouth Telegraph*, 6 September 1862, quoted in *Mr. and Mrs. Bancroft*, p. 69.
31. *The Theatre*, 1 September 1897, p. 237.
32. Seymour Hicks, op. cit., p. 172.
33. Ibid., p. 40.
34. Letter to *The Stage*, signed Charles Boult, 13 April 1893.
35. Letter to *The Stage*, signed G.E.B., 2 February 1893.
36. *The Pelican*, 21 November 1896, p. 6.
37. *The Stage*, 21 September 1893.
38. Ibid., 24 August 1893.
39. Ibid., 25 May 1893. Letter from J. Reynolds, one of several writers. *The Stage*, 27 April 1883, gives names of three amateurs who received leading parts at Drury Lane, the Haymarket, and the Court, and subsequently on tour.
40. *Green Room Book 1906*, p. 33.
41. Gertrude Kingston, *Curtsey While You're Thinking*, London, 1937, p. 122. Although Gertrude Kingston's gifts as a society woman and a picture-painter, together with her political interests, prevented her to some extent from concentrating on a career as an actress, she was none the less an instructive figure in the late nineteenth and early twentieth-century theatre history. Wilde and Pinero admired her acting. Shaw wrote *Great Catharine* for her in 1892; and she claims that when she founded the Little Theatre, London, as a house for chiefly feminist plays, it had – what would seem to be – the first cyclorama in Britain, designed for her specially by Max Reinhardt's engineer in Berlin; and what certainly was the first dimming outfit in British stage-lighting, newly imported from America.
42. *Mr. and Mrs. Bancroft* (Squire Bancroft's narrative), p. 126.
43. Seymour Hicks, op. cit., pp. 27, 28.
44. 'Half a dozen deaths quite recently of well-known actors and actresses, all clearly traceable to bad drainage', *The Pelican*, 13 December 1890, approving a letter by Matthew Brodie to *The Stage* on the same subject.
45. Reported in *The Times*, 13 August 1891, and quoted in evidence before the Select Committee by T. G. Fardell, Chairman of the L.C.C. Licensing Committee, pp. 107–8.
46. Reported in *The Players*, Vol. II, p. 135, 17 June 1892.
47. *Report of the Select Committee*, 1643, 1646, 1648, 2513–20.
48. Seymour Hicks, op. cit., p. 138.
49. *Select Committee, etc.*, 3707. See also Edward Terry's evidence, 3417. And *The Pelican*, 30 August 1890, p. 878. Cyril Maude, *Behind the Scenes with Cyril Maude*, London 1927, pp. 73–5, describes the filthy conditions at the Vaudeville in the 1880s and says that at that time Tom Thorne, its lessee and manager, was fairly prosperous.
50. *The Stage*, 19 October 1893. Letter from Dora Langlois.

CHAPTER THREE

Charity, Hope and Faith

> *The noblest charity is to prevent a man from*
> *accepting charity; the best aims are to show*
> *and enable a man to do without aims.*
> The Talmud

In the comfortable prosperous middle-class of the nineteenth century there were many decent folk whose consciences were uneasy when they saw that their well-being depended on the misery of others. There was an outburst of philanthropy, which was seldom hypocritical, and never half so cynical as are some of the clever little wits that try to debunk it nowadays. If the Victorians never questioned their divine right to be prosperous, they did their best to alleviate suffering when they could without any such question. Compared with the flint-hearted individualism of Regency times and the decadent affectation of Edwardian, the middle of the century was positively angelic.

The social origins of stage folk might range from the mill-girl who called herself 'Adelaide Neilson' and in the words of the *Dictionary of National Biography* 'had no English rival as a tragedian', to Earl Cowley, who earned his living in the chorus.[1] But when they got successful they settled down, or up, to the manners and outlook of the upper middle-class. Like the upper middle-class they tried to relieve the distress of their less lucky fellows; even managers did so. In so doing they revealed a truth which was not very pleasant. 'The reports of the various charitable dramatic institutions', wrote an anonymous journalist about the poorer actors in *The Saturday Review* of 21 November 1885, 'show indeed that there is an appalling superfluity of them, and that but for the well-directed workings of a Society nobly led' (he meant a certain corporate body, not the high-born indwellers of Belgravia) 'a terrible number of provincials would be without bread as well as without engagements'.

He might have gone farther. Charity discovered to her consternation that even when an actor was in work his margin between life and starvation was as thin as his blood. Pantomime time was the actor's 'harvest of the year'; but at Walsall once, when a pantomime actor named Diggory lost his way one dark night and was found next morning drowned, a local subscription had to be raised to save his parents from starving. The contributions ranged from £1 4s. to sixpence, each gratefully acknowledged in the local press; they sufficed.[2]

Theatrical charities were not new; neither was the need for them. Drury Lane and Covent Garden had had their own benevolent funds more or less since their foundation, when companies were lifelong. That at Covent Garden grew very rich down the years: it seems to have been some kind of tontine, and in the nineteenth century, as one by one the beneficiaries died off, it was said there was one survivor, awaiting his windfall of £60,000. But public opinion, led by *The Stage*, stepped in; the fund was placed in Chancery; and the interest was administered for the benefit of two less limited theatrical charities. The one at Drury Lane still exists, and still has its pensioners; though how the qualification of three consecutive seasons' service is assessed in these days when there are no seasons but only interminable runs, I do not know.

Other theatres followed their example. The Lyceum under Irving had its charity fund. The Strand, thanks to Edward O'Connor Terry, founded its fund in 1875: it was partly contributory, and partly charitable;[3] a small affair in size, but well supported. Its annual dinner was chaired by the Lord Mayor of London, and attended by such as the Duke of Beaufort. Nor were such funds unknown in the provinces, one of the late funds being at the Theatre Royal, Birmingham, founded by Philip Rodway in 1926–7.[4] Edward O'Connor Terry who left £44,000 behind him was much concerned with charities and contributory benevolence. He was Treasurer of the Royal General Theatrical Fund, President of the Theatrical Fire Fund, and one of the first Trustees of the Actors' Benevolent Fund. Indeed, according to himself, the last-named was a copy of his own fund at the Strand.[5]

Bewildering in their number, these theatrical charities! But our chronicle must make a survey of them; for there was a feeling in Victorian times that charity was all the unlucky stage artist was entitled to and this feeling is the background to the story our chronicle tells.

The Royal General Theatrical Fund was founded as early as 1839, to provide old-age pensions for a limited number of deserving players. If during their working years, old-timers had contributed to a Friendly Society, they would find themselves with annuities of £20, £40, or £60. The object of this fund was to raise these pitiful allowances to more than double, to £1, £2 or even £3 a week, a reassuring sum for very modest living. As the capital was £100,000, the fund could do much good; it was administered with understanding. Small hardships were smoothed away: a gap between death and the next quarter-day payment of death benefit was filled in and a year's bonus granted; if a contributor died before reaching pension age, those he left behind received all he had paid in. And Society patronised its money-making dinners, as they sipped the Veuve Monier Special Cuvée 1884 of the Hotel Metropole, and Ben Davies sang.[6]

Although inside this there was a 'Samaritan Fund' for relieving special cases, there was no money generally available here if an actor fell sick or was incapacitated before pension age; and poverty wears out the health quickly. So in 1855 a new Fund was launched, to include artists of the opera, the ballet and the circus, under a somewhat clumsy title: The Dramatic, Musical and Equestrian Sick Fund Association.[7] Its dinners also became social events. Though they were encouraged to open their gold or silver chain purses in private, ladies were not in those days allowed to partake of public banquets. They sat in the gallery at Willis's rooms, and watched their lords feasting, and listened to their lords toasting them – until 1862, when a social revolution occurred. The open-hearted Mrs Stirling was allowed to reply for the ladies; which she did, very wittily – so wittily that she continued to speak for them every year till 1880, and ladies were then allowed to nibble a croquette and sip from a glass. This was only right, and was fashionable too, since about this time it was being legislatively conceded that they really did own their own property.

Ash Wednesday followed Ash Wednesday, a good evening for a theatrical dinner, since the Lord Chamberlain closed all theatres that night. But the funds dwindled; in 1883 the income had dropped to £320. No accounts were being rendered; actors and actresses were reluctant to contribute. It is now many years since this fund was wound up, and its capital distributed among various charities.[8]

The staple charity of the profession, the Actors' Benevolent Fund, was founded in 1882, at a meeting in the Lyceum of the principal actor-managers of the day: Irving, Wyndham, Bancroft, Kendal, Hare, Barrett and Toole, who promised an initial sum of £1,200.[9] It covered many ills of poor stage folk: sickness, bad luck, old age. By its help aged players could avoid the dreaded Workhouse, for which, as a sympathetic phrase in the appeal leaflet put it, 'many of them are temperamentally totally unfitted' – as indeed would have been you or I. Those who run it have always been theatre folk; and the stars have always helped to expand it. Sir Charles Wyndham gave the proceeds of £2,400 from a special performance that celebrated his twenty years of management on 1 May 1896.[10] He, Irving and Alexander used to close their theatres in order to attend its annual dinners, thereby to draw in bigger attendances and collect bigger sums.[11] When in 1896 the management of the Covent Garden Fund was called in question, it being said that little of the available income was being paid out and that only to favoured applicants, Chancery took and held two-thirds of that income for the Actors' Benevolent Fund, which was able to do very much more thereby.[12]

However, it did not always prosper. In spite of Irving's proud words at the annual general meeting in January 1892, that 'actors were drawing more and more together and becoming a corporate body', the figures showed that they were not. They were not – as a body – even supporting their own Benevolent Fund. The principal contributors were wine-merchants, lawyers, doctors, journalists, soldiers and publishers:[13] only a small handful of prominent actors took any interest in it. 'If it were not for Mr Irving, Mr Bancroft and a few other generous-minded actors, the Actors' Benevolent Fund would cease to exist', wrote that sprightly, smart, scandalous, and not very pleasant journal The Pelican in January 1890. It shows how few were the stage figures available, when in

1892 Squire Bancroft had to cancel his chairmanship of the Actors' Benevolent Fund Dinner on 21 June, because he was also booked as Chairman of the Royal General Theatrical Fund Dinner on 26 May, and could not ask his friends to support theatrical charities twice in so short a time.[14] Lady Wyndham, who was continually helping the A.B.F. and other charities, suggested that after every 100th performance all London managers should give it a Benefit Night. Du Maurier, its president, Matheson Lang, and a few remaining actor-managers did so; but the commercial managements did not, and as they superseded the actor-managers the custom lapsed.[15]

It was the same mere handful of men and women who founded the Actors' Orphanage in 1896. In those difficult and decadent times there were many theatrical orphans. Some had fathers who had abandoned unwed actress mothers, not by any means all men of the stage. Others had lost one parent or both through what was almost an industrial disease: tuberculosis. Hitherto many such parentless children had been the responsibility of the Actors' Benevolent Fund, who had lodged them with a famous London Orphanage at Watford. But general orphanages then were no very good beginning to life; and not all the children were ever discovered by the Fund or sent anywhere. 'I suppose', Irving said in an eloquent speech in 1891,[16] 'the living legacies of dead actors go to the workhouse, or are got into charitable institutions which have no connection with the theatrical profession, which, by the way, is about the only trade or profession or pursuit which does not possess asylums for its destitute and sick members.' It is to Irving's credit that the stage came to respect itself and compelled society to respect it as a noble profession. 'A blot it is', he added, 'on a profession, which, taken altogether, is not, nowadays, characterised by poverty.'

One or two members, also seeing the blot, responded. The most energetic was Mrs Kittie Carson, herself an actress, married to Charles L. Carson, founder and first editor of *The Stage*. With her worked Mrs Clement Scott, wife of the most assertive dramatic critic in an age of assertive dramatic critics, who had suggested using the Covent Garden Fund for such a purpose. There was also Compton Mackenzie's mother, Virginia Bateman. Mrs Carson gathered a nucleus of other hard workers for whom she acted as secretary. In 1896 a huge bazaar was held in 'the large and small Queen's Halls', with stalls staffed by actresses and shows given by the profession. John Passmore Edwards, a newspaper proprietor and editor, offered a big sum. Barrie, with Harrison and Cyril Maude, gave a matinee of *The Little Minister*. Later Bernard Shaw wrote for its benefit *Passion, Poison and Putrefaction*; and the Theatrical Garden Party was instituted to provide an annual income.[17] A house was found at Croydon and its door opened wide. Destitute children not only of actors or actresses, but of any member also of the vaudeville profession, were 'boarded, clothed and educated and fitted for useful positions in after-life'.

So they still are; at Langley Place in Buckinghamshire where the institution moved in 1915: over eighty of them at a time, of whom many have had successful academic and other careers. Sir Gerald du Maurier was its first president (his aunt Isabel was Clement Scott's first wife): and later Noël Coward, suitably typifying both legitimate and variety stages. Prosperous it was and efficient; even if it lost part of its income when the collecting boxes vanished with the vanishing of the touring system.

Kittie Carson, not sparing herself, did not stop there. No charity helped the women who work in theatres but do not appear on the stage: cleaners, wardrobe-assistants, dressers, wives of the stage staff – the very ones who from time to time had financial chasms their narrow living-margin could not bridge. Often they lacked food, fire, blankets, clothing; lacked them when they most needed them, at child-birth. So Kittie Carson in 1891 organised a Theatrical Ladies' Guild, whose members would make such articles as they could out of materials themselves had provided, in regular Sewing Bees, once or twice a week in her sitting-room at Great Russell Street. By the following year she had enrolled as many as 300, including actresses as famous as Fanny Brough, (whom Violet Vanbrugh succeeded as President, followed by Athene Seyler). The original dozen chairs increased to sixty; and the ladies worked long and hard in the afternoons, with a short interval for tea. They spread into the dining-room; they had to hire a hall; they moved to Wellington Street, then to Russell Street, Covent Garden; and finally returned to Bloomsbury, to the self-same street in which they started.[18]

Not long ago they were relieving people in distress at the remarkable figure of 12,000 a year. Mrs Carson's health gave way in 1907, under all the work of distribution, and they had to get a new secretary; but the work went on, and so did Kittie Carson, health or no. She founded the Theatrical Christmas Dinner Fund.[19]

More and more charities started. To mark the Coronation of King George V, a gigantic Gala Performance was held at His Majesty's Theatre with all-star casts in scenes from six classic plays, including a crowd of 250 in the Forum Scene from *Julius Caesar*. Sir Herbert Tree, director and host, said he would devote the proceeds, which came to about £4,600, to start a new fund inside the Actors' Benevolent Fund, because there was no means then of providing pensions for well-known artists who had become incapacitated. It is not known why he changed his mind; but after an interview with the King, he announced that His Majesty had consented to give his name to a special independent fund for this purpose, and that each year the proceeds of a special Royal Command Performance would be given to it.[20] These began in 1913; and the takings varied from £460 to £2,000. In 1929, when the King's illness prevented the event, as a Thanksgiving for his recovery £10,000 was given by Lord Rothermere.

So King George's Pension Fund for Actors and Actresses came into being. The standard of artistry, that a claimant must have reached if he or she is to qualify, is a high one, and at least fifteen years must have been spent on the stage. In six years since the 1939–1945 war there were some fifty-two beneficiaries receiving £150 each. Some other charitable and public bodies, of which I have heard, might well study the administration expenses of this one, which then totalled no more than £10 a year.

Next came the happy notion that aged and lonely players should have some place where to end their days in comfort, companionship, and security. As early as March 1858[21] a rich gentleman named Henry Dodd, who had, as he said, been so much 'delighted and mentally recreated and improved by the Drama' that it pained him to think of popular favourites ending their days in poverty and the Union Workhouse, accordingly wrote through his legal adviser to the Secretary of the General Theatrical Fund, offering two and a half acres in Buckinghamshire (oddly enough at Langley, in the same locality as the Actors' Orphanage was to be), together with a hint of a big endowment, to build twenty almshouses and a common hall, the whole to be known as 'The Dramatic College'.[22]

Prominent actors and literary figures like Dickens, Buckstone, and Wilkie Collins, met and elected a committee. The Queen's patronage was intimated, if the necessary public support were secured. A constitution was drafted and agreed. Over £800 was collected in cash. Then negotiations fell through. The generous offer had been received by the Theatrical Fund with a good deal of shilly-shally. 'I regret to observe', wrote Mr Dodd's lawyer with more professional rebuke than professional tact, 'how supine and indifferent you are upon the subject of this handsome offer', though it is only fair to add that in a longer and later letter he says he has no complaint of neglect.

Maybe Mr Dodd was not a supine sort of person, and disapproved of such a quality in public bodies. Maybe he was offended, and not without just cause, when the Secretary of the General Dramatic and Equestrian Sick Fund coolly claimed to have suggested the gift originally.[23] Certainly he decided that this was not the charity nor the channel for him. He refused to make conveyance of the land and left unanswered the committee's inquiry whether he would build them a central hall. So that project came to nothing.

However, there were other donors at hand. Other land was obtained at Woking in Surrey. The Dramatic College duly took shape but fell into a state of lethargy.[24] Despite a legacy of £2,000 in New Three-per-Cents from T. P. Cooke, which was gradually sold off; despite benefit performances by Phelps, Ben Webster, Mrs Stirling, and others; despite what Mrs Charles Calvert called 'rather vulgar Dramatic Fêtes' at the Crystal Palace every year, there was no steady course of income. The profession as a whole did not care about it. The very inmates did not care very much. They were comfortable enough, at least at first, with £1,500 a year being spent on them. But despite visits from the assiduous good-natured Mrs Stirling with half-pound packets of tea in a big bag, they were lonely and unhappy, and had no stage doors to drop in at for a crack with younger or luckier fellow artists. Never were the little homes full. They became emptier as the money dwindled (and with £400 being spent annually on keeping the grounds in order, it soon and swiftly dwindled). In 1877 the Dramatic College was wound up, the premises sold, for less than cost, to the Crematorium, and such income as remained was administered through the A.B.F.[25]

Forty-eight years passed before any similar scheme was tried; and then it was the work of one man. Mr Alfred Denville, of Nottingham, deserves two niches in theatre history. First, having started as actor and comedian in Nottingham and with Herman Vezin, and thence proceeding to produce his own pantomime, it is his claim that he founded the first repertory theatre in Great Britain as early as 1900, at Morriston, a suburb of Swansea; that would predate him long before those so credited hitherto. Secondly, he founded in 1925 Denville Hall, at Northwood, Middlesex, a haven of rest for aged members of the theatrical profession. This, though there was an impressive list of vice-presidents, he went on to administer himself – very much so. The fifty residents, who were to contribute what they could afford, got good value for their money, including joint rooms for married couples – who had been segregated at the Dramatic College – in a handsome house where Garrick once abode, whose rooms became named now after various great performers.[26]

Many other schemes for relief there were. There was the Adelaide Neilson Fund, in memory of the mill-hand, children's nurse and barmaid, who thrilled all London and the U.S.A. with her Juliet in the 1870s and died suddenly in Paris when she was just thirty – what a theme for radio or film.[27] There was the Rehearsal Club, anticipating our own little Equity Club, a place where players that lived for cheapness in the suburbs could meet and rest before or after performing. Alexander presided over its inaugural meeting, at Londonderry House; he had just been staying with the Londonderries of that time in Ireland; the Duchess of Teck came to the meeting. There was a proposed home for actors on the French Riviera, where players not able to pay could convalesce or holiday free of charge, of which the acid *Pelican* observed that there ought to be no difficulty in filling it several times over.[28]

We cannot here give account of the many Variety charities or Christian Missions; there was a chaos of them. So confused were both public and profession, that a case is recorded where an actor applied to the A.B.F. on the grounds that he had for years in affluence paid annual subscriptions, but was found to have been paying in to the Actors' Orphanage.[29] The confusion was to the benefit of some: others were jealous. In May 1897, when Wyndham suggested that they should all be merged in one huge common fund embracing all their purposes and covering all the profession's needs, his proposal was at once attacked by the Drury Lane Fund, as threatening its own interests.[30] Reply was difficult, because this fund did not publish any financial details. Although it would be improper and untrue to impute hidden motives to so august an institution, it is a fact that both Augustus Harris and Arthur Collins did regard the pension-like character of their Fund as an advantage to be offered to an actor with a slightly lower salary than he might otherwise have accepted.[31]

Some failed. Some never materialised. Others are with us still.

The very multitude is a symptom that something was felt to be wrong, and that nobody knew what to alter. The slow growth, in all but a few cases – a growth quite out of proportion to the growth in stage folk's needs – is due to one cause, and to one cause only: the apathy of most actors and actresses. For to almost all the charities mentioned in this chapter, apart from the handful of prominent players, most of the money came from outside. It was the Rothschilds, and the Rothermeres, who helped the Knights of Lyceum, Criterion or St James's. The bulk of the profession, those very ones who might some day be grateful for help, scarcely stirred a finger. Forethought for the morrow means money put aside; and money put aside means money spared. Sometimes it proves extravagant to be economical. Two chorus girls were leaving the Gaiety Theatre after work. One got into a hansom with a young man, the other went home by tram. 'There', said a moralist, 'go the two extremes of the profession: the one who lives for the moment, and the other who stints for the future'.

'Yes', said his friend, 'but which is which?'

Notes and References

1. Archibald Haddon, *Green Room Gossip*, London, 1922, p. 188.
2. *The Stage*, 19 January 1883. A leading actor would get £10 a week in pantomime, a supporting actor £5. See 'The Salaries of Players', *The Stage*, 17 July 1885, quoting from *St James's Gazette*.
3. *The Stage*, 21 July 1932, article by Lionel Carson, 'Our Charities'. Also *The Stage*, 19 May 1882.
4. P. R. Rodway and L. Rodway Slingsby, *Philip Rodway and the Tale of Two Theatres*, Birmingham, 1934, p. 448.
5. Hibbert, op. cit., pp. 230–1.
6. *The Pelican*, 3 June 1893.
7. Percy Allen, *The Stage Life of Mrs. Stirling*, London, 1922, pp. 172–5.
8. *The Stage*, 3 March 1882, 4 April 1882, 9 February 1883. And Walter G. Gray, secretary of the Actors' Benevolent Fund in conversation with the author. £500 of the capital was reserved for this last, being distributed through the Theatrical Ladies' Guild. See below.
9. *The Stage*, 16 June 1882.
10. F. T. Shore, op. cit., p. 48.
11. *The Pelican*, 4 November 1896.
12. Ibid., 1 August 1896, p. 8.
13. *The Players*, 26 January 1892, p. 137. *The Pelican*, 9 November 1889, p. 168 and 11 July 1891, p. 706.
14. *The Players*, 29 March 1892, p. 338.
15. Walter G. Gray in conversation with the author.

16. *The Pelican*, 30 January 1891, p. 251. At the Council of the A.B.F. If the attitude of society toward living and virtuous actresses was as it has been shown to be in the Fitzwilliam Peerage case, there is small difficulty in imagining what the fate of an actress's fatherless child in such institutions were likely to be, even if it were legitimate.

17. *The Pelican*, 14 March 1896, 15 May 1897, 18 December 1897. *The Green Room Book: 1906*, p. 307; *The Stage*, 21 July 1932.

18. *The Stage*, as in note 17. *The Players*, 17 June 1892, p. 125 and 20 May 1892.

19. *Stage Year Book 1909*, p. 52 and photographs; *The Stage*, 17 October 1907.

20. Walter G. Gray in conversation; and *The Stage*, 21 July 1932. The A.B.F. has a copy of their letter to Sir Herbert agreeing to his original suggestion.

21. *Daily Telegraph*, Thursday, 22 July 1858, a 3-column article headed 'Dramatic College'.

22. MS. copies of the correspondence are in the possession of the A.B.F.

23. Advertisement in *The Times*, 17 May 1858.

24. Printed letter from William Cullenford, Sec. Gen. Th. Fund. A copy is in possession of A.B.F. Part of the endowment was made by T. P Cooke, who had made a fortune out of Douglas Jerrold's nautical drama *Black Eyed Susan*. Printed balance sheet of Royal Dramatic College, for the year 1876.

25. Mrs Charles Calvert, *68 Years on The Stage*, London, 1911, pp. 51–5. Walter G. Gray in conversation.

26. *Who's Who*, H. Chance Newton, *Denville Hall*, a souvenir brochure, n.d. (about 1926).

27. Adelaide Neilson was engaged to Compton Mackenzie's father, Edward Compton. See C. M. *My Life and Times* Vol. I, p. 27.

28. *The Theatre*, 1 April 1897, p. 236; *The Pelican*, 9 January 1897, p. 6.

29. Walter G. Gray in personal conversation.

30. Ibid., 15 May 1897, p. 13, and *The Stage*, as in note 17.

31. I publish this statement by permission of Mr Horace Collins, brother of Arthur, and a well known figure in the London theatre, who told me in conversation.

CHAPTER FOUR

The First Attempt

*Actors and actresses take all their knocks lying
down in the most charming manner.*

Sir George Alexander

How could it be expected that actors should attempt by themselves
to better their lot? In law, as actors they scarcely existed. In society,
despite a few knighthoods or marriages into the Peerage, the great
majority were little better than outcasts, friends of Society's secret
hours, unacknowledged in daylight. In business to make a public
complaint might prove not only bad theatrical policy. They kept to
themselves, and grew resigned to their lot, and drew what consola-
tion they could from the applause and love which rewarded them –
and asked no questions.

Public complaints have always been rare in theatre history. In
1641 a *Stage Players' Complaint* was published about the miseries of
unemployment in time of plague. But that clever and entertaining
little piece of propaganda was less an attack on the structure of the
profession than appeal to the public against the Puritans, who were
trying to put down the Stage, together with Monopolers, Projec-
tors, Star Chamber and Bishops. Nor was the sequel, the *Actors'
Remonstrance*, which appeared two years later less political in its
ironical, cogent, and unavailing reply-direct to the Puritan purge.[1]

In 1710 Colley Cibber and Wilks and others induced the Lord
Chamberlain to tie up Drury Lane with a silken rope, so that Rich
should have no chance to defraud his actors of their benefits or

other sharings. But the Lord Chamberlain's interest was limited to the proper administration of the censorship. In Victorian and in Edwardian days this personal representative of the monarch would have as little to do with the welfare of actors as a Field-Marshal. Indeed, in 1743 it was the Lord Chamberlain himself who, when the twenty-seven-year-old Garrick sought his protection against the dishonest exactions of Fleetwood, snubbed him by saying he was overpaid already. It was only because Garrick and his fellow-sufferers could afford to be 'out' for some time that they could band themselves in a limited kind of boycott. Even that was of dubious effect, except that it made a scapegoat of poor Macklin.[2]

In 1800 the 'Glorious Eight' at Covent Garden made a stand against financial exactions by their managers Harris and Lewis. Sir St. Vincent Troubridge has told[3] how they took their grievance, with the first overt solidarity of action of its kind in theatre history, to the Lord Chamberlain for arbitration. They got small satisfaction from him, at a time when the French Revolution was still causing Privilege all over the world to tremble and protect itself against rebellion however small. This splendid and daring gesture was an isolated one, and the treatment it received did not encourage others.

In the days we are discussing, a strike of actors, indeed any collective action, apart from being in psychology unthinkable and as a social instrument preposterous, would have taken effect only if it could have been made complete throughout the profession. This as a policy was impossible. It was impossible policy in any trade or profession at that time. According to G. D. H. Cole, the trade unions themselves, the backbone of the theory of collective action, 'in the struggles of the seventies represented, and could with their methods and policy represent, only a fraction of the whole working class'.[4]

Now though many players were of humble origin, they did not feel themselves as a body at all connected with working class methods or movements. They did not connect themselves with any movements. They were innocent and uninformed about any such things as 'movements'. They did not even have a trade paper to tell them what interests they had in common, apart from the shop that was talked when they met together. They could have no idea of bettering their lot until they had such a regular reading place devoted to stage matters and people. At first even this would be concerned more with forthcoming or rumoured productions and companies and a means of keeping the name in the eye of potential employers. Such was *The Stage Directory*, founded in 1880. However, in 1881 this turned into a regular weekly called *The Stage*; and it was fortunate for all of us today that its founder and first editor had the knowledge and vision, and indeed initiative and courage, to stimulate his readers' minds not only about future engagements but also about the right of actors and actresses, under any decent system of law, to decent conditions of work and engagement.

Charles L. Carson is one of the names that should be written in letters of gold on the walls of our National Theatres, if we ever have any. Although he was not an actor except for some experience of the operatic stage when young, and although his name does not appear in the *Dictionary of National Biography*, week after week for twenty years he served the profession quietly, wisely, and with full consciousness of what he was doing. Without nagging or sanctimoniousness, he made our theatrical fathers and mothers aware of themselves as members of a true profession, almost as public servants; and when they had grown used to that thought, the mere reporting of abuses, unobtrusively but firmly, was enough for them to know that these ought to be remedied. When he died in 1901, his son Lionel Carson carried on that tradition and policy, and it was pursued by S. R. Littlewood, when he took over in 1943. As early as 26 May 1882, Charles L. Carson suggested, in a leading article which dealt with absconding managers, that an Actors' Protective Agency should be set up which would list by name the black sheep among the swindling managers, as was being done in chambers of commerce and other mercantile circles; and so, for a small fee, a scrutiny would tell at once whether any would-be employer were financially sound.

This article was followed up by something only to be described as 'exciting'. In the issue of 30 June 1882 Carson published a letter signed 'Unity is Strength'. It is a very long letter, occupying a column and a half, and is printed in an unusually small type, so that it could be inserted unabridged. The heading is *An Actors' Protective Association*, and it is plainly the product of a clear, far-sighted and unprejudiced mind.

The first evil attacked is what it called 'bogus and swindling managers', explaining that the laws of defamation prevent exposure in the press; this was true; the press had to be careful. A provincial manager once brought an action for defamation against

the mere allegation that his theatre was insanitary.[5] Members of
the Kendal company were cited as witnesses; and it became clear
that actors and actresses had to be as careful as the press, even when
they had been stranded by the defalcation and disappearance of
their ex-employer. 'The reluctance or inability of individual artists
to seek the protection of the law', the letter continues 'enabled such
swindlers to snap their fingers at consequences'. This also was true;
it is often recorded that managers who had absconded promptly
proceeded to form new companies.[6] The writer goes on:

> But it is not against bogus managers alone that artists need protection.
> Encroachments on their rights and liberties are daily becoming
> greater, owing partly to the reluctance and inability of professionals to
> combine for resistance, partly to the proverbial professional ignor-
> ance of the law and un-business-like habits.

Here spoke something new. Few players knew they had 'rights'.
Their horizon of human intercourse was bounded by friendship,
public approval, and good luck. As for 'resistance', and 'combining' in the cause of 'rights', you might have with equal
probability suggested that ducks should combine for resistance
when their pond was frozen.

Next the letter analyses the other evils the profession suffered
from: unnecessarily – and uneconomically – protracted Sunday
journeys; bad dressing-room accommodation; 'frequent unfair
advancement of inexperienced amateurs and "outsiders"'; 'the
increasing difficulty of obtaining engagements legitimately and
without recourse to agents'; and 'the one-sidedness, unfairness,
even illegality, of many of the present code of managerially-
instituted "rules and regulations"'.

All these would be agreed at sight; everyone on the stage knew
them. What many did not know, or did not know how to regard,
were the two remaining evils: 'the present deterioration of salaries
in the face of increasing commercial prosperity', and 'the growth
of unhealthy monopolies'.

With these words a broader view and a wider grasp were given to
the small utility-man, studying his copy of *The Stage* in his gas-lit,
plaster-damp, stinking cellar at Wolverhampton, and to the out-
of-work chorus girl in her dismal anxious Brixton lodging. There
could be no question that there was a boom in Theatre. Every
newspaper and fashionable magazine had begun to carry critical
stage articles or gossip paragraphs about shows and show-folk.

High Society flocked to every first night. Though prices of stalls went up, so did House Full notices. But workmen's wages were rising, and with them the price of goods. It was costing more to live; yet the pay of the ordinary actor and actress did not rise. On the contrary, one had often to accept an engagement at a salary less than one had been receiving – Why? The writer explains why:

> In short, to my thinking, the entire present business relations between artist and manager are most unsatisfying and unworthy of noble profession and would be none the worse for a thorough overhauling. This can only be taken in hand by some combination or association, for so long as dramatic artists remain in their present disgraceful, unprotected and disorganised state, unparalleled, I should think and hope, in any other calling, so long will managers successfully continue to exercise an unfair and excessive authority; and those few who manfully show solitary resistance, after all are only selected for worse suffering, thanks to the cowardice or laziness of their degenerate comrades.

So he suggests a line of action. A society or combination should be formed 'to be called the Actors' Protection Association, or some similarly significant title' of all professionals with more than twelve months' stage experience; and there should be a small entrance fee and annual subscription of ten or fifteen shillings. It should have an office in London with a permanent salaried secretary, 'a man of business besides being well acquainted with all theatrical customs and habits'. Periodical meetings should be held in the big cities other than London.

The functions of such a society were to be wide indeed. The writer hints at functions which only years later the Actors' Association was to fulfil; functions that later still only Equity could fulfil; functions that even Equity has not yet begun upon. But the first enemy was the bogus and swindling manager; he must be brought to justice, and a fund raised to assist his victims. The writer admits with serene cheerfulness that this would be expensive 'at first'.

Then there must be proper sanctions to disputes between actors and managers. Should the latter remain obdurate, 'and no doubt many would' then 'such legitimate pressure and power as the Law affords' might be used. Test cases, for example, in the courts could very soon settle the matter of Sunday journeys. (It is no lawyer writing!). Next, a standard contract: 'some more definite and binding form of engagement'. Members' engagement forms might receive the *stamp* of the Society. There could be many amentities: a reliable Dramatic Agency; a bureau for forwarding letters; even, perhaps, a school could be started for amateurs to enter the profession on a proper basis. The ideas are plentiful. One less happy idea gave offence to the Actors' Benevolent Fund; it was found to be false in its innuendo and was withdrawn in a later letter. But the culminating vision still haunts our own future: the Society should set up Commonwealth companies on thorough business principles, which would help to break down 'certain pernicious managerial monopolies and rings'. Finally the basic structure of the profession is found faulty. 'It is to the travelling system', the letter concludes, 'that the profession owes nearly all the evils I have cited, more especially bogus managers. Sweep these away, and a heavy blow will be dealt at the system itself; or remove the system first, and they would quickly follow'.

The authorship of this letter is not known, but two arguments may identify it. Firstly, on internal evidence, there is a similarity of prose style between this and the usual leading articles. Secondly, the phrase 'bogus managers' should be noticed. Hitherto such persons have been called 'swindling' or 'absconding' managers. Now the term 'bogus' is not quite accurate: it was an American word, meaning 'sham'. These gentlemen, however, were not 'sham' managers; they were real ones, making money out of management, but making it dishonestly and without scruple. Nevertheless, the term 'bogus managers' passed into currency; and eleven years later,[7] when its meaning was called in question by a managers' apologist, the editor claims that *The Stage* invented the term. If this is the case, then the writer signing himself 'Unity Is Strength' and Charles L. Carson were one and the same.

However that may be, composing the letter or not, Carson certainly supported it in no hesitating manner; and that alone would give his name a pioneer's glory. The editorial of that issue welcomes the letter's proposal, and throws the columns of *The Stage* open to discussion of it. This was the best way to get such an association going. Press letters of approval can be anonymous. Faces and voices at public meetings are liable to be recognised, and remembered, by employers.

This was the first reasonable analysis and appeal to stage folk on record. Its facts, arguments and conclusions were beyond question. Only by such corporate action could the profession hope to improve its lot. But whether its individual members could, or would dare, commit themselves to public approval, was, unhappily, very questionable indeed.

The opened columns stayed empty. Next week an astute manager pseudonymously suggested that in any such association managers ought to be included. The writer of this letter himself, he said, had been 'cruelly had' by persons calling themselves actors; managers too needed protection. But nobody replied to this manager next week; in fact, there were no letters on the subject at all.

The following week another anonymous manager (or it may have been the same one) took a stronger line: there were many 'bogus actors', he said; managers should combine, 'assume a code and adhere to it', and any infringement of it by an actor should justify immediate dismissal. It should be for the manager or lessee to be their own umpires, too. If actors did not like this, they could seek employment elsewhere. Here was a sign that the managers at any rate were alert to the benefits of combination. One would have expected a storm of protest, or at least an alarum, a single bugle tentatively tongued from under closed canvas. But not a bit of it; both managerial letters were disregarded. Only one brave actor, signing his name, gave an example of one more bogus manager in his experience.

The fifth week there were no letters on this subject whatever; and the sixth week, the same. In the seventh week, Edward O'Connor Terry, describing himself at that time as 'only an actor in London although a provincial manager', wrote that having been abroad, he had only just seen the original letter, and sympathised with much of it, but could not see any managements taking any notice of a society that represented one side only. There should be an arbitration board of actors and managers, elected annually. This was not an unreasonable letter. It ended with an offer of five guineas a year to any protective association 'saving our poorer brethren from swindling managers', from whom Terry himself had suffered.

Next week 'Unity Is Strength' answered Terry. He asserted boldly 'artists are socially and intellectually the managers' equals and superiors'. There was no need of an arbitration board. If there had been a Protective Association fifteen years previously, the travelling system could never have arisen.

Maybe there were puzzled pens being put to paper at that very minute, which such outspokenness shocked and dismayed. At all events nobody wrote anything to this in the ninth week; nor, apart from an example of touring managers defrauding the public by false publicity, was a word written in the tenth. But in the eleventh week a certain 'F.K.' from Great Yarmouth expressed surprise at the lack of any reactions from stage folk. Terry's letter, he explains tactfully, was a guarantee that the scheme was not 'a rebellious gathering against managers, but a necessary safeguard against unprincipled adventurers, and a protective weapon against encroachment on our liberties'. He proposed a general public meeting.

Next week 'Unity Is Strength' replied. He had been hoping that Terry's letter would bring in other 'artists of position'. It had not; but he was biding his time. The tone of this letter implies that its writer knew the columns of *The Stage* were always available to him.

By now it was obvious that actors and actresses as a whole were not going to move of their own accord. In the thirteenth week, a letter was quoted in the 'Chit-Chat' column which demanded that somebody should give a lead, and suggested that the right person would be the Editor of *The Stage*. To this the Editor expressed his willingness to start such a society, and opened a list for those who would join. This was misunderstood. Next week the same column assured its readers that the Editor had never intended to publish names, merely the total numbers. But he gave no numbers yet, and awaited further letters. He received none.

It was in June that the original letter from 'Unity Is Strength' had been published. On 1 October 1882 the list was opened. By 10 November the result was announced: forty-one actors had been enrolled, and thirteen actresses: fifty-four in all; 'and some gentlemen decline to have their names published unless something definite be arrived at'. It was estimated that about this time there were some 20,000 people on the stage.[7]

This reluctance cannot be altogether ascribed to apathy, nor certainly to fear. I think our forebears of the stage were bewildered. Never had they connected the theatre with industrial disputes; and the very phrase 'Unity is Strength' had a militant, trade-union like, ring to it. 'Dealing a blow at the system itself'? For *The Stage* to contemplate such a thing was as shocking then, as if the editor today were to open a list of those willing to organise soviets of theatre-workers or occupy Piccadilly Circus with tommy-guns. Many of its readers must have felt about the proposal as one imagines South Americans feel about *coups d'etat*: if they succeed, they are respectable and their adherents are richly honoured; if they fail, they are high treason, and their adherents are quickly executed; but in neither case need the ordinary citizen concern himself until government is government.

Nor could they regard all managers as tyrants, or even as their natural enemies. On the contrary, the leading actor-managers in London, and such decent men as Wilson Barrett whether in it or outside, were highly respected. All that the ordinary actor wished was protection against abuse and exploitation. Small salaries for minor players were neither of these. They were part of the scheme of things, requiring undignified haggling and bluff and the recital of past good press notices if managers were to be impressed into improving them.

But the scheme of things was unalterable. If it was not un-alterable, then it should be altered only by those whose job it was to alter it: politicians, or judges, or whoever made the law. Indeed it might be better, perhaps, if the scheme of things remained un-altered. An actor depends both for personal satisfaction and for personal existence on the approval of the theatre public. Today the theatre public is heterogeneous, from all social classes. Then it was mainly upper-class. Even matinees, which were often try-outs of new plays not performed at night, were attended by leisured and titled persons. To be 'in' with the upper-class meant success in your calling and freedom from insecurity. To be 'out' with it meant banishment and poverty. So that, without being snobs, most of the profession were socially conservative.

But the best way to get 'in' with Society, was to be 'in' with the actor-managers, who hob-nobbed with Society. To decry these openly, or even to disapprove of their methods in secret, might be very foolish. So without being inartistic, most of the profession were also artistically conservative. From both angles, they looked to the actor-managers as their friends and advisers. It might, without undue extravagance, be held that if the Actors' Protective Association was still-born, the blame lay less on its parents the players than on the actor-manager for not attending as family doctor.

Certainly when Carson, a year later, kindled and stoked up interest in a Theatrical Mart, or Exchange, where engagements could be made without agents, the flagging of this may well have been due to the action of Irving. He had signified his approval of the idea, and Carson in good faith published his name as an ap-prover. Irving reproached him for doing so, and made him retract it; and the scheme ultimately perished.[8]

Granville Barker

Charles Carson

Lewis Casson

Norman McKinnell

So things went on, bogus managers still stranding companies, touring managers still using amateurs or under-paying professionals, and the London theatre managers gradually getting into more and more treacherous water, as we have seen. The lot of ordinary actors grew worse and worse. Exploited and abused, they became restless. Slowly they came to see that unless somebody made a move, the whole profession would perish.

Even so, it was not they who made the first move toward that Unity which was Strength. It was the managers – toward their own strength.

Notes and References

1. A. Cane, *The Stage Players' Complaint in a Pleasant Dialogue between Cane of the Fortune and Reed of the Friers'*, etc. London, 1641. Reprinted in *The Old Book Collector's Miscellany* (Ed. Hindley), London, 1873, Vol III, No. 14. *The Actors' Remonstrance or Complaint for the Silencing of their profession and banishment from their Several Playhouses*, etc. (The full title fills the title-page. London 1643.) Reprinted as the above.
2. Percy Fitzgerald, *The Life of David Garrick*, London 1868, Chap V.
3. Sir St Vincent Troubridge, *The Glorious Eight: forefathers of Equity. Film and Theatre Today: the European Scene*. London, 1949. pp. 32–4.
4. G. D. H. Cole, *A Short History of the British Working Class Movement, 1789–1927*. London, Vol. III, p. 11.
5. Elisabeth Fagan, *From the Wings, by the Stage Cat*. London. 1922, p. 229.
6. *The Stage*, 2 June 1882.
7. Ibid., 20 April 1893.
8. *The Stage*, 22 July and 12 August 1883.

CHAPTER FIVE

Actors Associated

When bad men combine, the good must
associate; else they will fall, one by one, an
unpitied sacrifice in a contemptible struggle.
Edmund Burke

In 1889 a number of touring managers founded an association to look after their joint interests.[1] Some such combination would obviously strengthen their hand in dealing both with provincial lessees and proprietors, and also with any possible trouble from an occasional public-spirited player. Undoubtedly it was a prudent move: combination was in the air. If Professor J. H. Richardson was right in saying that employers' organisations appeared after, and as a counter to, the appearance of trade unions in their particular industry,[2] this statement certainly does not apply to ours: the touring managers struck first. Not that there was any threat of trade unionism at that time among actors; far from it. But the great depression of the 1880s, with its evils of unemployment and destitution, was goading all kinds of inoffensive people into offensive action.

Among employers of all industries, as Adam Smith detected, there is a kind of freemasonry of understanding and fellow-feeling. Before the end of that year two more managerial associations had been formed: the provincial managers, who owned or controlled the buildings which received and part-profited by the touring companies, banded themselves in the Provincial Managers'

Association; and the London Actor-Managers formed a Committee. In many respects the interests of these three organisations had for some time been in conflict. Each would find salvation in being able to apply a 100 per cent all-over pressure to any local point of disagreement: but also they all in this way acquired an offensive weapon against their common adversary the actor – weak, self-divided and unconscious though that adversary at present was.

The sharp-eyed editor of *The Stage* at once saw the implications. Again he took the lead in an editorial of 15 November 1889, calling on all actors to form a protective combination of their own in reply: this time he could cite a precedent. At the beginning of that year American actors had founded an Actors' Order of Friendship with the mild programme of charitable activities, elevating the character and promoting the interests of the profession, and checking what it called 'imposition and tyranny' in the pursuit of the histrionic calling: 'Honour, Union and Justice' was its motto.[3] The Order of Friendship was a defence against the same process of combination in North America, where the greater number of large cities had already resulted in much stronger and more ruthless chains and circuits of managers, heading shortly to become the Theatrical Syndicate. In Britain the pressure was less, but the process was the same; and both countries were feeling a new stir and restlessness which, though economic in origin, may best be called spiritual. The words 'rights' and 'liberty' were in more common use than they had been previously on the lips of ordinary folk.

Sidney and Beatrice Webb have shown, in the important Chapter VII of their *History of Trade Unionism*, how the despair and industrial chaos of the middle 1880s brought into even the old-fashioned and conservative trade unions a new faith, a new spirit, socialistic in direction, which turned from polite and ineffective industrial action to action more purposeful and forceful because political in form. But even industrial action was succeeding beyond all hope; for it was receiving sympathy, and indeed active, monetary, support from the general public.

The impulsive strike of the match-girls in July 1888 had roused public indignation against the conditions that forced them to it. 'It was a new experience', say the Webbs, 'for the weak to succeed because of their very weakness, by means of the intervention of the public'.[4] A similar strike by certain London gas-workers in August

1889, declared by their union which had been formed only in the previous May, achieved the eight hour day and a small increase of wages almost without action of any kind. But it was the great Dock Strike of the same month that most impressed ordinary folk. So great was public sympathy with the strikers and against the employers, that not only did public disapproval hinder the companies from hiring blackleg labour to break the strike, but a public subscription of nearly £50,000 helped to finance it.

As a result, workers in many other industries took heart and recognised that after all they too had rights which respectable people recognised: new unions and societies sprang up all over the country. Public opinion soon saw that this was an organic thing, not the result of discontented 'agitators' with sinister designs. Trade unionism became, if not respectable, at least respected.

Now it would be untrue to say that many actors or actresses at all identified themselves with dockers or gas-workers. But against such a background they were slowly influenced with the idea of collective action, but action that would have to be worthy of the stage as an art and a profession, and so not strike threats nor boycotts, but still collective in some way.

Other kinds of workers in the theatre were more militant. In August 1890 the stage operatives, including stage-hands, limelight men and so on, met at the Bedford Head in Maiden Lane, London, and founded a union of their own, with sixty branches in the metropolis itself sending delegates to an inaugural meeting later the same month.[5] The actors were not so prompt, although some managers saw that an actors' combination would be to the good of everybody. J. H. Chute of Bristol, the best of the remaining actor-managers in the provinces, pleaded for a general theatrical union; or rather not a union which suggested controversy of class, but an 'association'. Managers took financial risks and must be considered. W. S. Penley, a successful comedian not yet possessed of the fortune brought him by *Charley's Aunt*, agreed.[6] In *The Stage* Carson indefatigably coaxed and cajoled and argued and sought sympathetic opinion from leaders of the profession. He ran a series of articles; he sent out questionnaires; he prophesied and warned. At last towards the end of the year he found the right field and the ripe moment.

Pantomime was still the province of the legitimate actor; and at pantomime time in the larger cities more of them were gathered together within speaking distance than at any other period of the

year. This was therefore the best moment to organise a meeting:
not to the direct sound of Carson's trumpet, but definitely playing
his fanfare, such a meeting was called by a number of optimistic
members of the profession, at Manchester, on Sunday, 1 February
1891.

The circular that called it gave ten articles of aims, nine of which
were resolutions that would be put to the meeting. As'this was the
first formulation of grievances or proposed reforms that the acting
profession had ever made, it is worth considering in detail. The
following were the nine resolutions:

1. The failure of any manager to pay the salary due to a member of the
   Association shall be instantly reported by such a member to a committee (which shall be appointed *at a general meeting of the entire
   profession*); and that such committee shall be authorised to take
   whatever steps they may deem necessary to enforce the neglected
   payment, or to prosecute and expose the defaulting manager.
2. The existence of any insanitary dressing-rooms, or of a theatre so
   constructed as to be a real source of danger in case of fire or panic,
   shall be instantly reported to the aforesaid committee by any
   member of the Association to whom such sources of peril shall have
   become manifest; and that the committee shall be authorised, in
   every such case, to take whatever steps they may deem necessary to
   induce or compel the management of such theatre to convert it to a
   safe and healthy condition.[7]

The third resolution reads a little oddly in this context. Evidently it
was put in to show that managerial interests were not being
overlooked. It provides that if any member of the Association is
found drawing or writing on the walls of theatre dressing-rooms,
he shall be compelled to make good the damage; and for a second
offence be expelled from the Association. But we should not be too
ready to smile: it is not very long since the B.B.C. has had to put up
notices in certain studios asking artists not to 'doodle' on the
acoustic screens.

4. That the terms 'playhouse pay' and 'no play, no pay' which now
   figure in most agreements between managers and artists, shall be
   superseded by a more definite phrase, providing that an artist's
   salary shall be stopped only under the following circumstances, as
   (1) an illness depriving the management of his or her services, (2)
   upon Good Friday, Christmas Day, and upon occasions when the
   theatre must be closed owing to a Royal Demise, public calamity or
   fire.

5. That six performances shall constitute one week's work and be paid as such.
6. That artists are entitled to payment for rehearsals attended before the initial performance of an engagement.

The next is rather clumsily worded, and is another sop to the managers.

7. That while the Association is determined to crush the infamies of bogus managements, it is also most anxious to enforce honest conduct on the part of its members – i.e. to compel the honourable fulfilment of their responsibilities to managers, landladies of lodging houses &c., and to stamp out, as far as it is possible, those instances of reckless or fraudulent action whose scandal reflects disgrace upon the whole profession; and that all cases of dishonesty or gross inattention to business charged against members of the Association shall therefore be investigated by the committee and dealt with at their discretion.
8. That the foundation of an actors' Orphanage shall constitute one of the aims of the Association.
9. That all disputes between managers and members of the Association shall be settled by arbitration.[8]

A little reflection will show that this somewhat school-boyish effort was no sort of foundation for a great professional organisation. Resolution 3 could be a bye-law: Resolutions 4, 5, 6 and 9 could be bargained for, but as soon as they were won other objectives would have to be formulated; they are hardly aims of a new permanent society. Indeed, coldly considered, most of these resolutions were mere matter for an indignation meeting and were merely reforms that were required. However, they were something to discuss and centre upon, and they raised much interest and expectation.

Of those circularised, 430 declared their intention to join as soon as the Association was formed. There was a 'good attendance' at the Manchester meeting;[9] and with their consent the society was duly formed under the title of the Actors' Association. All the resolutions were carried, except some that were referred to the committee for further discussion.

In the chair sat Robert Courtneidge. He had been one of the signatories of the circular. Indeed, he may well be called the founder of the Actors' Association, as Benson later gave him main credit for being; he was undoubtedly its leading spirit in the early days.[10] Father of Cicely Courtneidge, he was once described as 'a Scotch boy with the glimmering of an Auld Licht guiding him still',[11] who ran away from home to join a theatrical company and suffered all the vicissitudes the stroller can know. In the early 1900s he became a manager, and 'made a kind of showman's progress up Shaftesbury Avenue', beginning at the Lyric and arriving at the Shaftesbury in 1909, where he produced the celebrated musical comedy *The Arcadians* with his daughter, little more than an infant, making her first appearance.[12] His strict upbringing remained with him all his life; he was a stern figure, but a reliable one. As a manager he was always on the lookout for new talent, and 'one of the few managers taking a real stimulant interest in his chorus'.[13] He was always a believer in collective bargaining, on both sides.[14]

If the circular was vague and amateurish, this sturdy figure was neither. He made quite clear the lines on which the Association would run. It would remedy evils which all members of the profession ought to wish to see stamped out. It would avoid all controversies likely to damage relations between actors and managers. It would include actor-managers; and, later on, perhaps commercial managers too. In fact, the provisional committee recommended that the Executive Committee when it came to be appointed should be composed half of actors and half of actor-managers.

This was, in short, not an actors' union at all; and certainly very far from the militant protective association Carson had asked for. It was rather a self-chosen legislative assembly, electing from its own ranks a benevolent oligarchy for the better government of the histrionic realm. Collective bargaining is difficult when the bargaining channel is lined jointly by partial representatives of both sides. However, the first step of a new government, especially a self-appointed one, is to make sure of the support of the strong men of the kingdom. This was duly taken by the provisional committee, which consisted of Foster Courtenay as Secretary, Courtneidge as Treasurer, Frank Benson as Chairman, and Messrs. M. R. Morand, Payne, Hatchman and Brodie.[15]

Frank Benson, who had been active in the ill-starred Actors' Exchange and Mart, had managed to get up to Manchester that Sunday. He was empowered as envoy to enlist the support of the London actor-managers, especially Irving; but he found that great, if not very intellectual figure, very ill-disposed to actors' organisations. There had just been a meeting of London managers, of whom Irving was President – that very morning, in fact. To them Irving had denounced the new association as

'revolutionary', 'a trade union', 'subversive of managerial
authority' and 'destructive to our best traditions of comradeship
and understanding'.[16] This sincere if ignorant indignation
probably represented Irving's true sentiments better than the sanctimoniousness of the well-known 'Let us be artists, not artisans'
argument. Benson, to whom Irving had given his first professional
engagement, and who had already founded his own famous
Shakesperian company, persuaded him to change his mind. The
new organisation was intended, he said, 'to avoid the establishment of a trade union in the ranks of our art'; it had the same ideas
as Irving, and wished to launch itself officially at the Lyceum
Theatre, with Irving as its first President.

On hearing that, Irving consented within two days; and as
Benson and his fellow-envoys had had equal success with Barrett,
Hare, the Kendals, the Bancrofts, Edward O'Connor Terry,
Wyndham, William Terriss and Lestocq, they were able to ensure a
high-class meeting at the Lyceum on 5 March 1891, to which 400
people came.

Irving was without question elected president with four Vice-
Presidents: Barrett and Edward Terry, as actor-managers, Lionel
Brough and Ellen Terry as players. The council was divided
between players and actor-managers, and included Benson,
Courtneidge, Fanny Brough, Penley, and J. L. Toole. H. S. Tyack
was appointed permanent secretary. But the body that received its
constitution at the Lyceum by no means corresponded with the
body proposed at Manchester. The statement of aims reads like
that of a quite different society:

1. To further in every way possible the best interests of actors and
   managers.
2. To furnish means for the expression of the public opinion of the
   profession, upon such occasions as may seem advisable.
3. To organize and assist all schemes that tend to benefit the profession
   in general.
4. To do its utmost to put down bogus managements.
5. To protect artists from the dangers and discomforts to which they
   are often exposed from insanitary dressing-rooms.
6. The Association thoroughly approves of the principle of arbitration
   in all disputes between actor and manager, wishes to facilitate such
   arbitration and to arrive at a clear understanding on those points
   upon which disputes most frequently occur.

Later there were included under aim 3 such amenities as an office for forwarding letters, a library, an insurance and sickness benefit fund, and a dramatic school.

The first General Meeting took place, also at the Lyceum, on Wednesday, 29 April, and another on 24 July. Benson presented a report.[17] Qualification for membership had been fixed at two years' professional experience. The Council was drawing up a model contract. Difficulties had already been met in dealing with bogus managers, because there were too many people willing to go on at any price under any management, however dubious; and the law of defamation demanded great skill and care. A free actors' agency had been started, through which some members had already secured engagements. At 6 Duke Street, Adelphi, there was a room for interviews, and it was hoped to provide a bigger one for callisthenics, then all the rage, and fencing lessons; a lodgings list was in preparation; a legal reference file was being compiled. The Council wished it to be known that the Association was not a mere debt-collecting agency. It hoped that membership of the A.A. would become a guarantee of trustworthiness, and expulsion from it a serious penalty. The income was £332, and the current balance £223 14s. 11d.; some 154 new members had joined the original 320.

This was not very inspiring, perhaps; but not, on the other hand, very wrong, to all appearances. Little irksome details were being smoothed out of the actors' life. For good or ill, the Actors' Association had been launched and was slowly gathering way: whether she were seaworthy or not, or how she would behave in a storm, nobody could tell; very likely nobody anticipated any storms. There had never been anything like her before, and they were pleased to have her, for more comfortable travel if not for a luxury cruise. She was unique.

Indeed, perhaps her uniqueness would prove her failing. In every other industry at this time, in almost every other social grouping with a distinction between persons employing and employed, relations were growing more and more strained. There was a bitter war on; and she should have been a battleship. But the theatre profession sincerely believed that though among them were employing and employed, they were not as other men; that no stage employer would use the last two words of aim 3, 'in general', to checkmate any benefiting of the employed. Whether such a thing did happen, it is the task of this chronicle to record; but at present there was no question even that it might. They were all just a band of artists, employer and employed alike, united in common loyalty to 'the show'; if, of course, they were lucky enough to be in a show.

Notes and References

1. *The Stage*, 25 May 1893.
2. Professor J. Henry Richardson, *Employers' Organisations in Great Britain*, in an American symposium *Industrial and Labour Relations in Great Britain*. New York, 1939, p. 139.
3. Alfred Harding, *The Revolt of the Actors*. New York, 1929, p. 5. The Theatrical Syndicate was founded in 1896.
4. Sidney and Beatrice Webb, op. cit., pp. 401 seq.
5. *The Stage*, 29 August 1890.
6. Seymour Hicks, *24 Years of an Actor's Life*. London, 1910. p. 48.
7. *The Stage*, 25 April 1890 and 23 May 1890. The assumption in the phrase I have italicised is admirable, but unfortunately unjustified.
8. The referance to 'playhouse pay' and 'no play, no pay' explains itself. The former provided that an artist would be paid only in respect of such days and nights as the particular theatre was open for public performance under that particular management. If for any reason the scheduled theatre were not available and a performance took place in some other building, it was managerial practice to invoke this clause and pay the artist nothing.
9. *The Era*, 7 February 1891.
10. Sir Lewis Casson in conversation with the author.
11. H. G. Hibbert, *A Playgoer's Memories*. London, 1930, p. 177.
12. W. Macqueen-Pope, *Carriages at Eleven*. London, 1947, p. 184.
13. H. G. Hibbert, *Fifty Years of a Londoner's Life*. London, 1916, p. 199.
14. H. R. Barbor, *The Theatre: an Art and an Industry*. London, 1924, p. 4.
15. *The Era*, 21 March 1891.
16. Frank Benson, *My Memoirs*. London, 1930.
17. See *The Era* of Saturdays following these and other dates in this chapter. One bogus manager actually joined the A.A. and was appointed to the provisional committee. An actor wrote to *The Era* complaining of the treatment he had received from this manager, and the manager had to resign. The new Association repudiated the defaulting manager as widely as it could, but irreparable harm was done to its prospects from the outset by this sudden fall in credit.

CHAPTER SIX

Actors Limited

Heich hooses is affn toom i' the tap storey
Perthshire Proverb

The Actors' Association settled down to several years of solid routine reform; in a small way, much good was done. The range was not limited to London; meetings were held in Liverpool, in Glasgow. After some time spent in discussions between actors and actor-managers about suitable clauses, a model agreement was drawn up and sent to various managements; the idea was that these managements would adopt it as a standard, though the ordinary members of the association were not consulted about what the standard should be: but in any case, no managers so accepted it. That may have been a good thing; for it contained loopholes from which any astute management would have profited while still keeping to formally agreed standards of satisfaction. For example, no engagement was to be terminable at less than two weeks' notice. This meant, as *The Stage* pointed out,[1] that on a ten-week run an actor might still be paid for only eight weeks, provided that at the end of six he received a fortnight's notice.

Relations between *The Stage* as the conscious voice of actors and actresses and the A.A. as that of actors and managers in combination, had grown bad, even bitter. The Council of the A.A. had decided to start its own newspaper *The Players* and had created a limited liability concern to run it; the Actors' Newspaper Company. Carson called this ungrateful: *The Stage*, he argued, had started the

A.A. He might have gone farther; it had made the profession industrially conscious. But Frank Benson, dominating a somewhat uneasy meeting at Glasgow on 7 February 1892, denied that *The Stage* had played any such part. 'We cannot consent', he announced, carefully and clearly rounding off each word in his elocutionary way, 'to be regarded as the creation or creature of any one paper or any one individual. Those responsible for promoting the Newspaper Company have no wish to make *The Stage* either their *model* or their foe.'[2] This declaration of independence was greeted as all such declarations are: with enthusiastic applause.

The impression was given, though not the statement made, that the Newspaper Company and the Association were quite unconnected; as is the usual gambit of financiers and statesmen. But in fact Tyack was secretary to both, which caused some questioning at the A.G.M. in the Lyceum Theatre in March 1892 – questioning, but nothing more; for the matter was adroitly 'soft-pedalled' (to use the metaphor used by soft-pedallers) by an influential speaker into silent acceptance. 'A threat of criticism on this and other themes was not fulfilled, partly owing to the able speech of Mr. Lestocq, which put those responsible for the work in such a strong position that attack would have been idle and dangerous.'[3] This account, frank almost to naïvety, given in the actors' own Newspaper Company's own paper, shows that even in its first year *The Players*, and the Association itself, were content to be run by the governmental tricks used by skilled politicians in any party.

William Lestocq described himself as a 'junior touring manager'. He said at that A.G.M. that he had himself already benefited by advice from the A.A., since he didn't know all the rules. He especially approved of arbitration and declared his capacity with that of the entire association to trust the ladies and gentlemen on the platform; and he alluded to the 'little minds' of some professionals who refused to join the A.A. because there were too many managers in it. There were, he said, only seven managers out of a Council of twenty. This was, of course, true arithmetically, but did not allow for their prestige and influence, nor those small words and tones of voice that inevitably affect councils, and hence counsels.[4]

It was less as actor or manager than as politician that Lestocq got his way, after the manner of all magnetic politicians especially with folk so impressionable, not to say sentimental, as stage folk. They knew how hard he worked for the good of the actor, how ardently he prodded members to report abuses. He bewildered them with reasonable charm. When he had finished, there was a silence. The report was adopted unanimously.

All the same, *The Players* was a propaganda organ, a suspicious product. It threw open its pages to A.A. spokesmen and concerned itself with their words of wisdom far more freely than an independent journal would have done. The *Evening News* was right when it said *The Players* belonged to the A.A. It not only belonged to the A.A.; it tended to stress the angle of the managers, which reflects in its turn on the A.A. itself. The editor, W. E. Chapman, who used the pseudonym 'Ithuriel', was one of a syndicate of four called Theatrical Trust Limited formed with a capital of £20,000 to carry on the business of theatrical proprietors, agents, etc. This was openly announced in the third number.[5] But Benson had said at Manchester in February that if they found *The Players* were a mere imitation of *The Stage*, it would cease to be published: this was just what it turned out to be, only not so comprehensive in coverage, and not so progressive in outlook. The last number appeared in November, not quite completing a weekly run of one year.

The members of the A.A. used the reading room in Duke Street so much that bigger premises were needed; in July 1892 a move was made to 'a capital suite of rooms in a handsome red-brick building' in St Martin's Lane. Pinero gave a cheque for some new furniture.[6] The members were loyal to the association: but in spite of that, its growth was slow and uneven; in spite too of powerful publicity; in spite of the inducement of a Friendly Society scheme whereby through the good shrewd kindly offices of the Ocean Accident and Guarantee Corporation any actor or actress whose stage card appeared in *The Players*, while it existed, would receive in their estate £500 if killed, and in their person £3 or fifteen shillings a week if totally or partially disabled, in a railway accident.[7]

In 1893 the membership had not risen above 1,050. In 1895, after four years' work, it was only fifty more.[8] The reasons were partly financial: not everyone could afford to join; fifteen shillings a year takes a lot of getting together out of an income of £2 or £1 a week.[9] But there was also another bad slump in theatre at this time. Only Irving and Tree had crowded houses, and their audiences were mostly aristocratic, with incomes derived from land rents independent of business crises. Indeed, in one West-End house the audience had actually paid one evening only nine shillings all told. Some managers lowered their prices, but without effect. The business community of London and elsewhere was giving the theatre a miss for the time. This slump, however, did not stop the commercial company which ran the Gaiety Theatre from presenting its theatre manager, Mr Charles Abud, with a silver dessert service; but it bore very hard on the rank and file actors, whose faith in their Association was put to a stiff test and did not in every case survive the ordeal.[10] Many managers were lowering salaries.

The Council could do little about that. They had not foreseen such a thing. Individually the more sympathetic actor-managers, whether on the Council or not, kept wages stable enough to make it worth while for doubting impresarios to go on staging plays. The trouble was that the Council did so little else. In 1893 the Annual Report referred to a few cases of insanitary theatres which members had brought to the Council's notice; these had been dealt with by writing to the manager concerned or to the sanitary authority which ought to have been concerned. A few debts had been recovered for members, though again Mr Benson had to plead that the Association was not a mere debt-collecting agency. A member of the Council rose to deplore the apathy of people toward the Association. Another rose and said how important it was to have Mr John Hare as Chairman of that meeting; and Mr John Hare, recalling how in days when he himself had had to dress in a cellar he would not have confined a dog in he had made a vow one day to have a theatre of his own with decent accommodation for his company, announced with complacency that this he had now fulfilled. This was very likely true of the Garrick, which had been virtually built for him by W. S. Gilbert four years previously, and it was certainly to his credit; but it was hardly of much interest to the 19,950 or so people who were not in his company.

The account of that meeting observes: 'No business of special importance was transacted.' Yet in that very week a company was stranded at Warrington, and had to beg thirty shillings from the local magistrates out of the poor box, the court missionary being instructed to see that at least they got a good meal.[11] At that time deaths or serious damage to health through typhoid or poisoning from insanitary theatres were being frequently reported in *The Stage* and elsewhere. Even the cruel, superficial *Pelican* pours scorn on the A.A. Council for being so feckless.

Other branches of the profession were taking more active steps, seeing all too clearly that their interests and those of managements were in conflict. In January 1892 the stage hands, scene-shifters and lime-light men at the Criterion went on strike a few minutes before the curtain was due to rise on the Saturday evening performance of an adapted American play called *Brighton*. They got the worst of the battle: Wyndham was not impressed; he had served in the American Civil War. To quote his lady biographer, he 'summoned his personal staff and various members of the company on to the stage and himself working as vigorously as any one of them, directed the putting up of the scenery. Mr Henderson recalls with amusement that they set the scenery and changed it between the acts much quicker than the ordinary stage hands were in the habit of doing, in spite of the fact that every obstacle had been put in the way, even to the removal of the stage screws.'[12] Mr Henderson's amusement was shared by the society and conservative newspapers, one of which rejoiced that the game was certainly with Mr Wyndham and the strike leader would have to sing smaller for a week or so. The 'actors' own' paper, *The Players*, recommended that Wyndham's example should be followed by any of his brother managers who found themselves in the same fix.[13]

The stage staff had already founded their own union, affiliated to the T.U.C. This, the National Association of Theatre Employees (later to include cinema workers of the projection-men and usherette grades, and known as N.A.T.K.E.) was started in 1890 with branches in Birmingham, Bradford, Oldham, Newcastle, Middlesbrough, Stockton-on-Tees and Greenock. It included stage managers, and later, when it was large enough, founded a subsidiary in 1902, called the Heads of Departments Association. As a trade union it was also a friendly society with a benevolent fund; and this side, but only this side, of its activities was encouraged by the presence of rich actor managers at its annual dinners.[14] In the same way some of the theatre and opera chorus, pressed even more closely and in greater danger than even the poorly paid straight actor, decided to organise. A Theatrical Choristers' Association was formed in January 1893, formulating needs that in some ways resembled those put at the actors' first meeting at Manchester, but with the excellent request that engagements should be for the run of the piece. Chorus members, especially girls, often found that after they had done all the work shaping a show, unpaid at rehearsal, they were suddenly displaced by some pick-up of the management's.

This union started briskly enough, having got a claim settled for one of its members before it had been in existence more than a week or two. But it never grew. Although in 1896 it was given a benefit matinee which was patronised by Lord Rothschild, and although its president was D'Oyly Carte, its first year's income was only £76; and its numbers were never impressive enough for management to take much note of it. It was a gesture of appeal more than a trade organisation; and it disappears from the records as quietly as it came, leaving the problems of the chorus to be tackled, if at all, by the long-lived but stiff-jointed A.A.[15]

The Council of this body seemed to be working hard. It met regularly, and members attended conscientiously, an allegation to the contrary by a Canadian-Scottish character actor named Cremlin being disproved and withdrawn. This little incident is interesting because it shows the faith of the members in the organisation itself. If anything was wrong, it must be due to the personnel running it, not to any aspect of its policy, methods or structure. Indeed, this same Canadian Scot wrote to *The Stage* the following August appealing for openness and publicity for the Association's doings. 'There are some managers who think we are working against them. Yet all we work for is the safety of our lives, and the amicable settlement of disputes. There is no better friend to the manager than the Actor's Association. If this were not a vital part of our creed, hundreds of us would leave tomorrow.'[16] There can be little doubt this was the view of the great majority of members. Without the goodwill of managers (or an entire change of the financial system towards state intervention, or some kind of socialism, for which few of the profession were ready), the small-part actor and touring lead would perish together in those days of crisis and depression. Yet even with the goodwill of the good managers, little was being done against the bad ones.

This same year an Italian named Moro staged a light opera called *Peterkin* at the Royalty Theatre, London: it flopped; and having no money to pay salaries, Moro decamped to Italy. As usual a public fund was raised to help the victims; but the A.A. said it could do nothing. No County Court could reach Moro, even if it were worth proceeding at law against a penniless wretch; in any case, the *Peterkin* company were not members of the Association. Yet this very point might have been used as publicity to get more members and avoid repetition of such disasters; but no move was so made. When the news arrived that Moro had been given a sentence of twelve months in Italy for defrauding a waiter, the profession began to blame the A.A. for not preventing such adventurers from having anything to do with the stage.[17]

As the principal society of the stage in name at least, it was not showing up very admirably. Always so jealous for the reputation of his beloved profession, Irving was finding that. Whether trade union in character, or a safeguard against trade unions, it had one duty, and that was to be well run: it was not well run. Presiding at the Annual General Meeting on 1 March 1895, Irving suggested that a better body would be a Chartered Institute of Actors, similar to the Royal Academy of Painters, with a proper training school; nothing seems to have been done about the dramatic school that the A.A. was to organise. It was not the first time he had made such a suggestion. The far-sighted, sincere, somewhat lofty-toned address in which he had first adumbrated this, was given to the Walsall Literary Institute the previous November, when he was discussing the then unheard-of idea of municipal theatres paid for out of the rates. It is worth quoting his final words: 'It may be that in years to come our countrymen will scarcely understand how, in our times, so potent an instrument for good or ill as the stage, was left entirely out of the sphere of public administration.'

All this was connected with Irving's desire to make the stage more respected than it ever had been; and also with his demand – for that is the right word – that the acting profession should have at least as much access to the Sovereign as a furniture shopkeeper. Of course this was closely connected with the knighthood conferred upon him within four months.[18]

The proposal for a Corporation of Actors was not new. It had been made by a Professor Jenkyn at a Social Science Congress in Edinburgh and taken up by W. E. Henley in 1880.[19] Irving's wider revival of it was now supported by Clement Scott in his dramatic magazine *The Theatre*. But it did not come to anything: very likely this was just as well; for its achievements could have been little more than academic, useful in their kind though these may be. Actors are not like doctors or painters, who deal with their clients direct without being as a rule divided into employers and employed. Nor are they like accountants or secretaries or other professionals who receive fixed salaries all their lives through. Actors are employed by managements, whatever source these may derive their finance from. All the good that such a Corporation could have done for the ordinary actor would have been to ensure that entrants to the profession were properly qualified in a theoretic sense before they began to draw salaries. Even that would not have prevented managers from exploiting them, and through them, experienced actors entitled to higher pay.

Meanwhile, however, the managers were forming a non-Royal Corporation of their own. In June 1894, the provincial managers and the London managers met together to form the Theatrical Managers' Association under the Presidency of Irving. Carson wrote in *The Stage*: 'The managers will now have a giant's strength, but, of course, they are not the men likely to use it tyrannously', a comment worthy of the Outer Hebrides for its capacity to warn without defaming. There was no sign that the A.A. noticed the event. It was busy holding a matinee in aid of its funds. The funds were at no time too healthy; neither was the membership. In 1896 there were 1,250 members; in 1897, 1,553; in 1898, 1,732. But then the numbers dropped. In 1899, 1,669; and at the end of ten years' work it could count only 1,600 full members, little more than a twelfth of the acting profession. Nobody knew how to get new members. Canvassing only elicited the reply: 'but what is it doing, laddie?'[20] The confession had to be made, it was doing very little.

In 1895, true enough, at the plea of a special committee of the Council, headed by the new Secretary, Fabian, the Railway Companies consented to reduce fares for actors by one-quarter on a single journey and to a fare and a quarter for a return. By this, undoubtedly, the Association made things a little easier for touring companies when they were stranded, or had a week 'out' between dates in a tour, as frequently happened. But it would have been more valuable to remove the sources of these evils. In any case the privilege was extended two years later to managements; for in January 1897 Alexander, on behalf of the managers, handed a richly decorated testimonial for his services in securing this concession to – of all people – Charles L. Carson of *The Stage*!

In the natural course of things, or rather in the man-made course of economics, the general and theatrical slump gave way to better times. There was a theatrical boom: more and more theatres were built; the Diamond Jubilee of 1897 gave a boost to entertainment. But this boom was not reflected in the association's funds or membership. The only benefit secured was that a number of medical men undertook to attend actors and actresses free of charge. The blatant causes of ill health went hardly recognised. According to Lionel Brough[21], when a complaint was lodged with a local sanitary authority about a faulty theatre, the answer was delayed for three months; it was then discovered that the chairman of the authority was proprietor of the theatre complained of. Matters were so bad that in 1897, a leading actress, Agnes Hewitt, nearly died of poisoning due to the insanitary Brixton Theatre.[22] In that same year, Judge Bacon of Bloomsbury County Court said: 'I have never heard that bugs were injurious to health.'[23]

In that same year theatre rents soared higher than ever: £44,000 was paid for an eighty-year lease of the Comedy Theatre, which ten years before had changed hands at £10,000 for ninety years.[24] The next year Irving transferred the Lyceum to a commercial company: the hauling down at nightfall of the colours of the old actor-managers. Commercialisation grew wilder. Fat little Buddha-smiling Charles Frohman, who had smiled his way across the Atlantic as a front-of-house man and was destined to smile his way to death in the *Lusitania* in 1915, had in that year shows running at three different theatres besides being in association with Edwardes and the Gattis. Soon he was to have interests simultaneously in five theatres and five plays in London alone.[25] His manager was William Lestocq, a life member of the A.A. Frank Curzon, interested as much in his racing and shooting as in his theatres, by 1903 controlled eight London houses: the Avenue, the Camden, the Coronet, the Prince of Wales's, the Comedy, the Criterion, Wyndham's and the Strand.[26] His real name was Deeley, an oil-merchant's son. George Dance, a reporter, owned a number of Drury Lane dramas, together with twenty-four touring companies. He was also the 'Westby and Co.' who made a fortune from theatre bars. Macqueen Pope says he had the poorest opinion of theatrical art; his object was to make money.[27]

Managers and the syndicates they represented did make money. In 1898 the Drury Lane drama *White Heather* cost £15,000 to produce; it took £40,000 and yielded a net profit, apart from profits on tours, of 90 per cent to the shareholders.[28] More and more actor-managers were going in with syndicates who with their accountants controlled and dictated policy. With rising rents, they had to; with middlemen appearing between owners and impresarios, they had to; and this process was now widely used. Cyril Maude was financed by a £30,000 syndicate at the Garrick in 1896.[29] Seymour Hicks enlisted under Frohman or the Gattis for his own plays at the Vaudeville; and when he was proprietor of his own theatre in 1905, Frohman was lessee and manager.[30]

The actor-manager in fact was no longer king; his chancellors could depose him. Ethel Irving at the height of a successful period in managemenet at the Criterion in 1905, was thrown out by its owner, because her lease was expiring. She had to tour the suburbs till another theatre came vacant.[31]

Anyone could speculate in theatre, not for the theatre's good but for their own. An Etonian traveller (Herbert Sleath), a Dublin hotel-keeper's son (Frederick Mouillot), a Melbourne solicitor (George Musgrove), a newspaper-manager (Louis Calvert), attracted by this method of making a fortune, together with others who had already seen the inside of a theatre in box office or front-of-house: these were now the rulers of taste and policy in tours and in the West End of London.[32] Nor is that remembering the thousands of smaller figures investing an odd thousand or two in a show instead of in rubber or in diamonds. Soon enough they did not need even to do that. Many saw an easier and quicker way yet. They possessed themselves of a theatre building for a term of years, and sold their interest as a sub-lease to the highest bidder over the sum they paid.

In a sense, against such men, the actor-managers for all their faults had been a protection to the actors. On them still to some extent, therefore, depended the future of the A.A. It was little wonder that the humble player looked to them with loyalty as to men of the same art as themselves. It was little wonder, either, that the actor-managers looked upon the A.A. as a safeguard against the commercials. As long as they themselves kept the rank and file quiet, the actor-managers could give at least a livelihood to some. To the actor-manager the A.A. was as essential as it was to the actor. Nor was it any great wonder if as early as 1892 voices were raised at the A.G.M. against so many managers running the association. Time proved them true: the managers did run it, because they had to. They even lent it money in debentures to keep it going.

Notes and References

1. *The Stage*, 8 September 1892.
2. *The Players*, 9 February 1892, p. 177.
3. Ibid., 8 March 1892, p. 254.
4. Ibid., 4-page supplement, devoted to a report of this A.G.M.

5. Ibid., 6 January 1892, p. 72.
6. Ibid., 13 May, 20 May 1892.
7. Ibid., 20 May, p. 46; 1 July, p. 166.
8. *The Stage*, 16 February 1893. *The Theatre*, 1 May 1895, p. 255.
9. *The Stage*, 6 July 1893. Letter signed 'A Provincial Couple'.
10. *The Theatre*, 1 February, 1 June, 1893. *The Era*, 21 March 1891. *The Pelican*, 6 February, 22 April, 1 July 1893. Charles Abud's interests ranged from swimming baths to proposals for importing an entire Chinese theatrical production as a novelty. *The Pelican*, 18 July 1891, pp. 728 and 907.
11. *The Stage*, 16 February 1893.
12. Florence T. Shore, op. cit., p. 76. The N.A.T.E. appears to have done nothing about backing these men. Mr Tom O'Brien, General Secretary of N.A.T.K.E. (into which this Union has since developed) tells me that there is probably no official record of the incident, which would today be called an 'unofficial strike'. The subject of dispute, he thinks, will very likely have been a demand for higher wages.
13. *The Era*, 2 January 1892. *The Players*, 6 January 1892.
14. *Stage Year Book 1909*, p. 136.
15. *The Stage*, 2 February, 20 July, 1893. *The Pelican*, 7 November 1896.
16. *The Stage*, 22 June, 29 June, 6 July, 13 July, 27 July, 3 August 1893.
17. Ibid., 5 October, 16 November 1893.
18. *The Theatre*, 2nd N.S. Vol. XXIV, 1894, pp. 216–20; Vol. XXV, 1895, pp. 125–8, and 255–7. Irving made his demand for 'access' in March 1895 at the Royal Institution, and was knighted in July of the same year.
19. W. E. Henley, 'A Corporation of Actors', *The Theatre*, N.S. Vol II, 1880, pp. 274–9.
20. Reported by Frank Cremlin at the A.G.M. See *The Stage*, 13 July 1893.
21. Giving evidence on behalf of the A.A. at the Select Committee of 1892 already referred to. 3503.
22. *The Pelican*, 29 May 1897. The Brixton Theatre had been opened only the year before, 21 September 1896, and was regarded as a modern, and even luxurious building. For this information from the *South London Press*, I am indebted to the Librarian of Lambeth Public Libraries.
23. *Cripps v. Philipps*. Reprinted in *The Pelican*, 30 January 1897.
24. *The Pelican*, 20 November 1897.
25. W. Macqueen Pope, *Carriages at Eleven*, pp. 132–5.
26. Ibid, p. 147.
27. Ibid., pp. 124–5.
28. *The Pelican*, 1 January 1898.
29. Ibid., 28 March 1896.
30. *Green Room Book 1906*, p. 174.
31. Ibid., p. 182.
32. Ibid., under biographies.

CHAPTER SEVEN

Breakaways

> *What is wanted is not an Association in the professions, but the profession in an Association.*
>
> Charles L. Carson

The epigraph at the head of this chapter is perhaps the wisest thing that ever was said about the British stage as a group of human beings. Carson wrote it in *The Stage* in July 1893, but until 1903 there was not the slightest sign that anyone in the profession had read it, no sign that any significant number of people understood the need it expressed. The evils continued: bogus managers still thrived; dressing-rooms still poisoned; and although a model contract was drawn up, it was never applied. The Association at this period continued to do very little.

The matter of actors' parliamentary votes was taken up in 1894 by its legal adviser, T. H. Bolton, who was also an M.P.: but nothing came of that. Granville Barker stated that good provincial actors should not be displaced in London by amateurs; but that point was not pursued far. Proposals were made for tightening the standard of membership, so that members might have a better chance in castings; and for tightening the finances by a general private one per cent tax on the salaries of everyone in work; but they remained proposals. A request was made for the long promised dramatic school; and Irving went to talk to Squire Bancroft about it: it remained talk. However, the Council was not altogether idle. It found new, more commodious and much more expensive premises at 10 King Street, Covent Garden, altogether more worthy of the association than the Regent Street offices it had occupied in 1900. As a result the A.A. ran into debt to the sum of £300, which, with a total membership of only 1,600, was not nothing.

Something was plainly wrong; and several members were getting uneasy. This time, however, there was no Lestocq to hypnotise them into obedience. On the contrary, it was the uneasy ones who had the hypnotist, in Granville Barker. Harley Granville Barker was the nearest British approach to Stanislavsky. At first taking part in 'experimental' and 'literary' groups like the Stage Society and the Elizabethan Stage Society, he was making a name as a fine actor in Shaw's plays before these became popular, and he was a quite outstanding producer.[1] In 1904 he joined in management J. E. Vedrenne, who had worked managerially for Benson, Forbes-Robertson and other good class actor-managers and was a person of quite a different type: with a gift for casting and finding new talent; driver of a very hard bargain; inclined to view his employees as possessions. Vedrenne was among the first managers to allow his artists to appear 'by permission'. But when he found young stars, he paid them well; it is to his credit that he never paid a 'walk-on' less than £2 a week.[2]

These two gathered round them young actors and actresses who were finding a want in the old-fashioned Edwardian stage and wished to appear in worthwhile plays, not in trash translated from the French which had so long enriched managers and impoverished audiences. In a sense their venture at the Court Theatre, out in the suburb of Chelsea, was an echo of the old 'Independent' Theatre of J. T. Grein in the 1890s; but it was built more firmly, and sought a new British drama. It was here, at the Duke of York's Theatre, and later at the Savoy, in pursuit of that drama, that Granville Barker became a famous 'producer', as the director of a show was now coming to be called;[3] and the ideas he put into practice were in many ways like those Stanislavsky had practised since 1898; sincerity in acting, truthfulness in presentation and meaning in the content of the play. These required an understanding of things beyond the oldfashioned actors' technique; so that men and women interested in this kind of art would tend to be alive to matters and questions outside art. Thus it was that the names which began to shine from out of these three theatrical ventures were the same names that began to shine with a new light in the Actors' Association: J. Fisher White, Lewis Casson, Donald Calthrop, Sybil Thorndike, Sidney Valentine, E. W. Garden, May Whitty and many more.

Barker himself electrified the A.G.M. of 1904 by putting forward, from the floor, a motion that was considered revolutionary. Why should not the Council, he suggested, insist on the following concessions from the managers: that all salaries be paid on a weekly norm of six performances, with every performance beyond that paid at one sixth of the weekly salary? That special salaries be paid during rehearsals? and that no actor or actress be employed in a West End theatre in a speaking part, other than as an understudy, who was not qualified to be a member of the A.A.? This was a wild ideal in those days. But there was a wilder sting in the tail. Barker actually challenged the manager members of the Council to pledge themselves to this programme.

At last, an attack at the managers from a member of the Actors' Association! The actor-managers took it as an attack on them, but Barker assured them it was not so; they were essential to the Association's work, he explained. Only he asked the managers to take the Association a bit more seriously. Seven-tenths of the leading actors and actor-managers in London, he counted, were members of it. Between them there was no reason why common working rules should not be arrived at.

Lawrence Grant, a name not known to me, but evidently some kind of manager and also a dramatic author,[4] replied that this was making the Association equivalent to a trade protection association for unskilled labour – he would seem to have been a little uncertain in his knowledge of trade union history and conduct; and he added some remarks about rehearsal pay which were offensive to a number of members. When he went on, with unconscious self-revelation, to warn them that if engaging an A.A. member was likely to lead to litigation later on, managers would say 'You are an A.A. member, and we cannot employ you', 'Don't they do so now?' called voices from all round him; and the meeting became noisy.

At that Edward O'Connor Terry, now a fully fledged actor-manager and proprietor of his own 'Terry's' Theatre, intervened in suave sorrow that such a delicate subject, touching the profession they all loved so much, should be openly discussed at a public meeting. But he was no Lestocq; and the floor of the house was too

angry to be taken in by this attempt to discredit Barker's good taste
or manners. He was not allowed to go on, and all he could do was
to move the reference back of Barker's proposals, which meant
that they would be shelved. Only thus was the customary calm of
the A.G.M. restored.

Such incidents, however abortive they may seem at the time, are
seldom without sequels. Granville Barker was elected to a vacancy
on the Council in June of that year. Doubtless he found it a hard
struggle to maintain the rights of the ordinary actor before the
managers on the Council, who, though still in an arithmetical
minority, were virtually industrially without opposition. Another
financial depression had hit the country; the theatre, as always, was
the first to feel it. There was unemployment again in all trades; and
on the stage as badly as anywhere.

That is perhaps why Barker kept rather quiet for a year or two.
But also his position was difficult. He was in effect an employer
himself, though one who had taken up the side of the actor, and in
so doing had let his own side down. In the absence of minute books
it is impossible now to say how deliberate the Council was in its
policy. But even with his presence at the A.G.M. in 1905,[5] the time
was mainly spent in discussing the foundation of a London
equivalent to the Comedie Francaise; and at the following A.G.M.
even *The Stage* observed that the bulk of the members was not given
latitude enough to voice their complaints or make suggestions.[6]

In any society supposed to be democratic these are the
symptoms of ossification. Much disaffection resulted. It was given
a strange lead, in terms not easy to define even at this interval of
only forty-five years. In March, H. B. Irving, then thirty-five
years of age and fresh from a double triumph as Hamlet and as
author, joined Seymour Hicks, who was a year his junior and one
of the most successful comedian-author-producers in the country,
in issuing proposals for a rival organisation, to be called the *Actors'
Union*. The exact purpose of the move is obscure, indeed baffling.
H. B. Irving had been for a long while, and still was, Chairman of
the Council of the A.A.; nor did he resign before bringing out the
manifesto, which was called *Will You Join the Actors' Union?* The title
of the new organisation had no connection with the trade union
movement; but Hicks did not make things any more clear by
writing in *The Referee* that it would 'bring us all into closer contact
with the managers.' What contact closer than that already established at A.A. Council meetings? Further, this reassurance of

managerial approval was the less necessary in that Hicks himself was firmly enough settled in management to have his own theatre, the Aldwych, then building.[7] Further yet, their aims did not differ very greatly from those of the A.A., except that they opposed its financial dependence on the managers. This presumably refers to the debentures, most of which were held by managers; a fact which itself argues the closest possible contact with them.

It may have been a mere *démarche*, or an attempt to win more power than was possible at Council Meetings, or a thermometer test of the feeling of the rank and file. Both leaders are dead; and I have found no evidence that throws any light on their motives. At any rate the proposal was dropped, and left little trace, except that some members tended to accuse the two would-be leaders of disloyalty. The rank and file remained uneasy, but all the more loyal. In a questionnaire issued by *The Stage* in December 1905, out of 3,000 replies only six objected to an Actors' Association as such. The reasons for the general lassitude emerged as (1) the size of the subscription and (2) the inclusion of managers.[8] The minor points of the 'Union's' manifesto were taken up by the A.A. Council without need of a rival organisation;[9] but the rank and file were not impressed. They had no idea what was wrong; and little idea what they wanted. But outside events were pressing on them; and though as a profession stage folk did at that time tend to be isolated in a more or less make-believe world, with which economic troubles had, or should have, no connection, nonetheless all of them were affected, if only vaguely, by their public background.

It cannot be repeated too often that most stage folk had no conception of the help trade Unionism might be to them. They talked of their art as 'business', but the overtone of that was money, big money if possible; certainly not 'trade' in the sense of men minding machines or making boilers. That had been a general attitude of the middle class. But now something of a change had occurred. In the General Election of 1906 the Liberal Party had ousted the Conservative by a big majority, and the Labour Party was established as an effective, if small, Parliamentary force. One of the first acts of the new government was to reverse the harsh decision of the Taff Vale Case which had made trade unions to all practical purposes illegal as soon as they became active. By the Trade Disputes Act now passed, trade unions were no longer legally liable for huge sums in damages to employers if they called their members out on strike. Effective action by a trade union, so long as it broke no criminal laws, was now not only permissible but respectable; and this is important sociologically. As a result there was an enormous jump in membership of the Labour Party and of all the trade unions.

Undoubtedly this government action agreed with the unexpressed feelings of the nation, with that unreasoning sense of justice beautifully expressed by the Cockney phrase 'Taint right, somehow'. Respectable people, though still afraid of working men when discontented, felt the change of the times and many, perhaps most, approved. So did ordinary stage folk. The sense of the time was ready to admit, in some alert stage heads, even that actors were an employed class, and the laws which applied to other employees might possibly apply to them too. It needed, however, a forthright personality to say so. This personality now appeared: Cecil Raleigh. He will come closer to the camera in later pages.

From time to time social meetings were held in the 'cosy little salon' at King Street; somebody would give an informal talk on a theme of interest to the profession, and a short discussion would follow. At one of these, on a Friday afternoon in January 1907, Cecil Raleigh gave such a talk under the title 'Counting the Cost'. It was pure trade unionism, even anticipating the day when actors would be able to enforce a 'closed shop', that is, to ensure a hundred per cent trade union membership in every company, so that blacklegging would not be possible and that what the union decided was necessary must be conceded by employers. The strange thing about this informal meeting was that in the discussion speaker after speaker rose and agreed with Raleigh; in fact, nobody disagreed. Women are supposed to be as a sex anti-trade union, or were then so supposed. But these social meetings were largely attended by women; and three of them, Rose Matthews, Italia Conti, and Gladys ffolliot wanted action. Raleigh was asked to write up his notes in pamphlet form for distribution among members.[10]

Other artists of the stage were far in advance already. In 1896 a young theatrical journalist had founded a Music Hall Artistes' Railway Association, which managed to get railway fares reduced for parties of five or more. Music hall artists were even more concerned with fares than legitimate actors were; and by 1905 this society numbered 11,000.[11] But fares were by no means their only grievance; music hall artists were being shamefully exploited by purely commercial managements, and only collective action could

redress this. An attempt by the famous Charles Coborn to found a
Music Hall Union in 1903 had fallen through; but in January 1906
at a joint meeting of representatives from the Water Rats and other
Variety clubs and societies, the Variety Artists' Federation was
founded, and adopting full trade union principles affiliated itself
to the Trades Union Congress, an act which stood it in good stead
the following year when it became involved in 'The Music Hall
War'.[12]

In the variety world there was no equivalent of the actor-
manager; and the issues were therefore quite clear. But variety folk
are made more individualistic than actors by the very conditions of
their trade. It was stirring, therefore, to see them organising
themselves so quickly, so thoroughly and with such firm
businesslike determination. Stage folk proper, though many of
them held the music hall and its performers in some contempt as
practising what they considered a lower form of art, could not but
be influenced even if only a little and at the very secret back-end of
their minds.

The new V.A.F. showed that the thing was possible in another
form of theatre art. If the Actors' Association was too supine to do
anything, a new organisation must be formed which would. There
was a feeling, a stir, among artists of the legitimate stage. That it
was organic and general is shown by the fact that action was taken,
quite independently, but on the very same day, in London and in
Manchester.

An actor called Fred Bentley had for some time been critical of
the A.A.: 'initials', he said, 'which had about as much value as the
bought degrees of foreign universities'. Finding that the profession
outside London was much oppressed by twice-nightly performances which were paid for at once-nightly salaries, and that there
was a need for matinee and rehearsal pay and a minimum salary of
at least £2, he organised an open meeting of the profession at
Manchester on Sunday, 8 February 1907. Relations with the
Variety Artists were cordial. They sent a deputation to give what
help they could, and organised a benefit performance for the
purpose. The attendance was mostly from Manchester and the surrounding district. It was enthusiastic and unanimous; and resolved
without delay that a rival organisation, of a character determined
and tireless, must be started. It was to be called the Provincial
Actors' Union.[13]

Simultaneously, a London actor named Arthur Bawtree, who

had spent most of his nineteen years' stage career in India, North America and the Dominions, called a meeting of those in London who were dissatisfied with the A.A. Cecil Raleigh was to have taken the chair but could not do so. At this meeting quite a number of people pleaded for action inside the A.A., notably Rose Matthews and Lawrence Grant, and on a later occasion Lucy Sibley. But the fifty or sixty present decided that only a new organisation could be expected to achieve anything, and this was duly founded 'for John the actor and Jane the actress'.[14] As the aims of this and the Provincial Actors' Union were identical, the two groups amalgamated almost at once, calling themselves first the Dramatic and Musical League, but later reviving a previous suggestion, and using the title abandoned by H. B. Irving and Hicks: the Actors' Union.

The aims were drafted with great skill and elasticity. On the surface they were restrained and moderate, covering all the troubles that the A.A. was neglecting: the question of actor-managers; unity of action; abolition of *all* abuses (and not just those that were comfortable to handle); death-legal- and old-age-benefits; a trade paper; and so on. But careful consideration soon reveals that they could be made also to cover not only strike action, but a fund for strike pay, and no need of a referendum for calling a strike.[15] The body was registered as a trade union on 8 October 1907, its membership at the end of the year being 637. But it had no intention of 'officially connecting itself with trade unionism', which meant that it would not affiliate itself to the T.U.C. It did however send a representative to that body in 1907, in the person of Frank Gerald, and it did work with local trades and labour councils, thus making, as Gerald said, an approach to the working class, who were the Pit and the Gallery.[16]

One major fault in its constitution was that by a small minority vote (72 to 67) it excluded women from its Council, although the first signature at the inaugural meeting had been Gertrude Kingston's, and other actresses had joined at once, Phyllis Broughton doing so by telegram. A Ladies' sub-committee was permitted; but the major exclusion gave the body an old-fashioned air. Women's Suffrage was becoming a question of the hour; and many male privileges were being broken down in other professions and groups. Indeed, in 1910 an Actresses' Franchise League was to be formed, with Mrs Kendal as president, seven first-class stars as vice-presidents, and over 300 members including Ellen Terry, Fanny Brough and Lilian Braythwaite. Secondly, although Cecil Raleigh was continually writing letters to the press advocating a more militant policy by actors, the aims of this Union were a great deal too militant for many of its members. Thirdly, in the actual handling, the methods were dictatorial. 'In the first year of the Union,' says the *Stage Year Book 1910*, 'they made an order which practically prevented the affairs of the Union being discussed by its members in the Press. Publicity among those interested was accordingly denied the Union, with the inevitable result.' A similar action taken by the Actors' Association Council in 1909 had earned the same criticism in the Press,[17] Lewis Casson being among those who objected to such narrow rulings. In an old body such bottling of opinion was bad enough; to a new one it was among the faults that proved fatal. The Union never caught on. It got into debt. It held several meetings with the A.A. to discuss amalgamation, at which it agreed to sink its trade unionism(!); but its socialistic leaders could not reconcile to their conscience the A.A.'s financial dependence on the debentures, and on November 16, 1909 at Hammam's Hotel, it was wound up. Henry Bedford, a member of its committee, sadly suggested that the inscription on the gravestone should be 'Killed by the apathy of the Actor'. Most of the members joined or re-joined the A.A., exempt from entrance fee.[18]

As a bid for power it had failed, but it served one vital purpose. It showed that, however remotely trade-unionistic, a trade union of actors was possible; and it started some people thinking that maybe if it had been a full trade union, having the potential backing of others, as the V.A.F. had, it might have made more of a mark. It might perhaps have survived.

Eleven days after the two meetings in Manchester and at Bedford Street, the A.A. was itself in its own home shocked by the same new sense of the time. It was known that for some time a Reform Group inside the A.A. had been agitating for a more active attitude to the everyday problems of the plain actor. The centre of this Reform Group was Granville Barker. Now at the A.G.M. at the Playhouse Theatre on 19 February 1907, he and eleven other Reform apostles were elected to seats on the Council by very large majorities.[19] They had stood for election on a specific ticket: to put the Association on a sound financial footing, and to obtain from the managers an agreed minimum salary of £2 a week. There could be no doubt about the meaning of their election victory.

The Reform Group did not consider themselves bound to

regard their mandate in any narrow way. They held a meeting on their own at Bedford Street to decide whether managers should be allowed to remain as members of the association at all. With young Lewis Casson taking the chair (his abilities in this respect had apparently already been noticed), Granville Barker, with Henry Ainley supporting him, urged that the influence of the actor-managers might not always be obvious, but it was always there, 'an unconscious influence perhaps, and certainly to be deplored'. If they allowed such men to remain, they were running counter to the objects of the association, which was for actors. He even proposed that if an actor became a manager, even for a short while, he should be suspended from membership as long as his management lasted.[20]

Although Henry Ainley subsequently resigned from the Council, the other members of the Reform Group agreed with Barker, and pressed the Council on the point. They got few concessions from it, and had recourse to a stratagem. The A.G.M. had authorised the Council to call a special general meeting of members and get the association's approval to reduce the statutory number of Councillors to twenty-four, who should be elected entire each year, and not by a third retiring annually. The important request was also made that this special meeting should consider excluding from election to the Council members who were in management at the time of election.

In the present temper of the members, there was little doubt that these would all have been passed, and the older members of Council would be out of office within a twelvemonth; for this reason, or so one supposes, the Council refused to call any such meeting. Now that they were Councillors themselves, the Reform Group put into action the machinery designed for the purpose in No. 27 of the Articles of Association, namely, an application, which was signed by H. Athol Forde, Frederick Forde, Edith Wynne Matthison, and Lewis Casson, followed by a requisition, which was signed by 120 members.[21] Obedient to this, a Special Meeting had to be called, and duly took place on 5 May 1907 at the Passmore Edwards Settlement in Tavistock Place.

Several questions were put to the assembled members, besides those raised by the Reform Group. But the vital one was quite clearly defined: were managers to be excluded from the association or not? The voting also was clear: in favour of excluding managers: 164; against their exclusion: 136, a majority of 28 in

favour out of a total vote of 300. But for an alteration of the constitution a majority of three quarters of the total membership was
required; so this resolution was ineffective, and managers were not
in fact to be excluded.

Stalemate might have resulted, if the actor-managers had not
made a clever move, at the same time reasonable, modest and
honourable. When the Council next met, on 14 May 1907, they
stated that the figures at the Special Meeting were tantamount to a
vote of no confidence; and resigned, in a body.[22]

The Association was now legally governed by the Reform Group
alone; and on Counsel's opinion, decided to remain in office until
the end of the society's year. Their chairman was Lewis Casson. It
was a brave decision and no doubt they all knew how difficult the
circumstances were; probably few guessed how desperate they
were to prove. Being actor-managers, most of the leading
members of the profession were now out of office. These had been
at least an indirect source of revenue and financial security; even
with their help, the budget looked bad. By March 1908, unless
drastic economies were made, the deficit would be £303, despite all
the donations, legacies and other unexpected single payments that
had been made, and which ought under orthodox financial rules
to have been placed in reserve.

Making what estimates and economies they could, the new Half-
Council resolved to sublet part of No. 10 King Street, which was
ostentatiously large. They set their canvas and stores for a stormy
and hungry passage. The withdrawal of the actor-managers had a
good side as well as a bad. Now that the Association was purely a
body of wage-earners, its only hope was the chance given by the
managers' withdrawal to adopt a full trade union policy. After
much heart-searching argument, several doubters were converted
to the view that in the growing public knowledge and valuation of
trade unionism, this course might well result in an increased
membership, which would ease the finances. The decision was
taken.[23] But almost at once this view was carried away by the wind;
the committee appointed to examine and advise upon the financial
situation reported that it was beyond hope.

In all unhappy bodies whose finance is difficult, there may come
a time at which examination of figures and balances reveals that
only a miracle can stop the rot. In some cases to allow the rot to
continue in trust of a miracle is not only folly, it may be fraud.
Then the honourable man cuts his losses and pulls out leaving

Cecil Raleigh

Ben Webster

J. Fisher White

Sidney Valentine

behind him only a fraction of the damage he might otherwise cause.

Some such hour had come to the Actors' Association. Dismally the triumphant Reform Group listened, watching all their hopes float away before their eyes. The Association they had just won power to save was insolvent beyond recovery; it was a bitter moment. But the only honourable decision was bitterer still; they issued notices summoning a Special General Meeting of members, to recommend that the A.A. go into voluntary liquidation.[24]

At this meeting the position was explained to the thirty members who condescended to turn out that September day. They had been living beyond their means; they had lived on money borrowed mainly from their more prosperous members, who were the seceding actor-managers. At any moment, and with perfect justification, any of those might request repayment, and it was unthinkable not to honour the Association's word even to some extent. To go on incurring public debts with these interior ones hanging over their heads, would be embarrassing and probably unethical; nor were there other reserves of any kind. Sadly the thirty agreed; and a statutory meeting was called for 14th October, when the Association would receive its quietus.

It certainly looked, and one or two unscrupulous people were muttering this, as if the Reform Group by its very keenness had condemned to death the body it had sought to serve. But the actress Lucy Sibley, who had acted in shows as different as those of Gordon Craig, Brandon Thomas and Ben Greet, wrote songs and adored the theatre, was not going to capitulate to a mere budget. She rose, proposing that the necessary £300 he raised by voluntary contributions, and the Association continue in being. Her vigorous manner and determined faith were infectious; the meeting rallied. Lewis Casson undertook to get a card printed, for the circulation of all members.[25] Others joined in with suggestions and help. An appeal was launched for sums to reach £300. But alas! the results were pitiful. Those who supported the association best were the very ones who could not even afford a guinea. Only £189 was forthcoming; and that in itself was a fine sum, for it was composed largely of amounts from £1 to sixpence. There was plenty of will to contribute but nothing to give. It seemed the calm water was only the heart of a hurricane.

Now a small gleam showed on the horizon: Edward O'Connor Terry, always ready to help misfortune of this kind, renounced his claim to his debentures. But this was only a little light, from an almost irrelevant lightship. The 14th October came, and the members duly met, more of them this time; about sixty or seventy. Some were angry and some were rude. Little William Lestocq manipulated his usual eloquence, seeking to blame the Reform Group and their trade union aims for the present plight. But for once he did not hypnotise his audience. They knew the facts and recalled them. It was not the Reform Group Half-Council that had caused the extravagance; but the Full Council for years before, when there was no Reform Group on it. But argument over and everybody having had their say, there was still nothing to do but propose the winding up of the great venture, pass this resolution and go home. This was duly done.[26] The staff received its notice; steps were taken at once to get rid of the premises.

But the appeal was not yet closed, and it was not altogether inconceivable that hard work and personal canvassing might not yet save the day, or at least postpone the end for a few months. Little by little the money came trickling in, till the £189 rose to £200. Two-thirds of the voyage covered! Members kept dropping in at the slowly dismantling offices to tap the financial barometer; slowly it rose. The staff and the Council went about their work in alternate moods of despair and desperate hope. 24 October, £220: another eighty pounds to find. Surely this was not beyond imagination? Desperate hope became desperate expectancy. More and more people called for news. Another big effort was made. Again the money trickled in, now in slightly larger sums. The barometer rose more quickly. So did the spirits of the unbelieving Council – till on the 26th October the total not only topped £300 but went on to over £320.

The notice to the staff was revoked. Another Special Meeting was called at the Bijou Theatre in Oxford Street. The motion to liquidate was annulled. Thanks, as the Treasurer Arthur Applin explained, to the tireless efforts and example of a few strong spirits, especially Lucy Sibley and *The Stage*, the premature death of the Actors' Association had been averted.[27] That is to say, the apparently fatal disease had been arrested, at least for the time. There was a chance of recovery and of a long and useful life. But the patient was still very, very weak, and would need careful nursing, doctoring and diet. Whatever happened, it would be a long time before it could do what it planned to do and go about its work as it wanted.

In the meantime, it had enemies and ill-wishers, among the very ranks of the poorer actors it wished to help, who would delight to see it perish, if they did not indeed go so far as to plot that it should.

Notes and References

1. 'Experimental' in those days meant the opposite of what it means today. The innovators sought reality in detail and truth in conception. The 'literary' play is best described by Bernard Shaw: 'The "literary" play is a play that the actors have to act, in opposition to the "acting" play, which acts itself.' *Our Theatres in the Nineties*, Vol. I, p. 116.
2. W. Macqueen Pope, op. cit., p. 194. And statement at a weekly meeting of the Actors' Union, 3 March 1908, reported in *The Stage*, 5 March 1908.
3. 'Producer' was still a fairly novel term in 1909. See *The Stage*, 22 April 1909.
4. According to a letter in *The Stage*, 16 March 1905, p. 11.
5. At Arthur Bouchier's theatre, the Garrick. *The Stage*, 2 March 1905.
6. At His Majesty's Theatre; Irving had died and his place as President was filled by Sir Squire Bancroft. *The Stage*, 22 February 1906.
7. *The Stage*, 9 March 1905.
8. 7 December 1905.
9. Ibid., 20 April 1905.
10. Ibid., 24 January 1907.
11. Ibid., 30 March 1905.
12. A full contemporary account of the Music Hall War is given in *The Stage Year Book 1908*, pp. 54–72.
13. *The Stage*, 14 February 1907.
14. Ibid.
15. *Stage Year Book 1908*, pp. 31 and 62.
16. *The Stage*, 10 October, 24 October 1907. See also Gertrude Kingston's article 'Trade Unions and the Censor', *Stage Year Book 1908*, pp. 9–11.
17. *The Stage*, 30 December 1909.
18. *Stage Year Book 1910*, p. 94. *The Stage*, 27 June, 8 July, 26 August, 2 September, 1909.
19. Ibid., 21 February 1907.
20. Ibid., 21 March, 23 May 1907.
21. Ibid., 4 April, 11 April, 25 April, 9 May 1907.
22. Ibid., 16 May 1907.
23. Ibid., 13 June 1907.
24. Ibid., 19 September, 26 September, 3 October 1907.
25. Ibid., 10 October 1907.
26. Ibid., 17 October 1907.
27. Ibid., 24 October 1907. Letter from Lucy Sibley, and 31 October 1907.

CHAPTER EIGHT

'The Struggling Mass'

> *It appears inevitable, alas! that in any*
> *calling there should exist a struggling mass*
> *who cannot by the divine right of living ensure*
> *to themselves a living wage.*
>
> Sir Herbert Beerbohm Tree

The slow convalescence of the Actors' Association was further delayed when in the normal way of stage life it lost more leaders. From 1907 on Granville Barker really ranked as a manager, because he did his own engaging. It was hardly decent for him to lead a purely actors' association. Although Lewis Casson remained nominally on the Council and kept bringing before it the claims of the extra-London theatre from a distance, he left metropolitan affairs for a while to join Miss Horniman's pioneer repertory in Manchester. So did Sybil Thorndike; and others had to go about other professional ploys.[1] Those who remained in the lead were a kind of second theatrical generation of Reform Group-ers, apt on occasion to criticise their predecessors for as much lack of business method as the old Council these had ousted. They put into practice drastic economies required. Having got rid of the entire King Street premises, they took over for three months the much more modest apartments of the Playgoers' Club in the Strand; and subsequently meetings were held in the Adelphi Rooms.[2]

They also went to work on the managers, trying to induce the Theatrical Managers' Association to set up jointly with them a committee to standardise the business relations of employer and player. They thought it prudent, for an appearance of unity, to promote another committee of six, half from the A.A. and half from the Actors' Union which was still in existence, although the new spirit of the former really made the latter unnecessary. As long as it lasted, this was a standing committee.[3]

The Chairman of the A.A. in 1908 was Cecil Raleigh, whom we must describe more closely. An amusing person and a fluent speaker, his real name was Abraham Rowlands, and he was the son of a sporting doctor who took a practice near Epsom. He had started in a comic opera chorus, had stage-managed *Ghosts* at the Royalty in 1891 and had played various small parts in various shows, until he deserted the stage for theatrical journalism. By accident one day, being asked to write a scenario for a ballet staged by Sir Augustus Harris, he turned playwright and became the author or joint author of many pantomimes and the chief dramas at Drury Lane during this period. He was a man of agile mind and very wide interests, often saying of himself in his droll way, that it was having appeared at the age of eight in an amateur show with H. M. Hyndman that had made him a convinced socialist ever since. At one time he had been a jockey, however, and managed to combine socialism with horsiness by wearing a pin with the word 'Labour' formed in diamonds.[4]

He had always been active in the Reform Group; and an article of his in *The Stage Year Book 1908* called 'Socialism and the Actor' shocked those many members of the profession still in the mental habits of the 1890s, by whom the very notion of socialism was regarded ethically as pernicious and socially as vulgar. But it carried some weight. For Socialism whether approved or not, was very much to the fore; and the article was written simply and sincerely by a man not without position and influence in the dramatic world. Anyone interested in the theatre could see at once the difference between socialism and trade unionism and the importance of both to actors.

So here was something new: a man of the theatre not only deeply concerned with principles of behaviour outside, not only conversant with the laws of economics, but also able to express himself clearly and compellingly on the subject both in print and in person. His very first remarks as Chairman sounded a new note, determined and stirring. First, the Association must get new recruits, hundreds and thousands of them. Then it must establish a

minimum wage; further, and this was new too, it must enforce the
minimum wage by insisting that all members refuse to appear with
anyone accepting less. The figure of a minimum wage which
Raleigh asked the Association to adopt was £2 a week. It was based
on the results of inquiries into a typical Actors' Budget – scientific
inquiries, another new thing.[5] This Actor's Budget, from even so
far off as today, is a moving thing to read:

Clothes (renewing wardrobe)	per year	£10	–	–	
Boots (2 pairs @ 18/-)	,,	,,	1	16	–
Two hats	,,	,,	1	–	–
Two pairs of gloves @ 2/6	,,	,,	–	5	–
Re-covering umbrella	,,	,,	–	6	–
Bedroom (lighting and firing @ 5/- a week)	,,	,,	13	–	–
Washing @ 2/3 a week	,,	,,	5	17	–
Postage and Stationery @ 4d. a week	,,	,,	–	17	4
Bus and Tube @ 1d. a day during Resting	,,	,,	–	8	6
Baggage (collecting and carting for 35 weeks on tour)	,,	,,	1	15	–
Tips to dresser for 35 weeks	,,	,,	–	17	6
Make-up	,,	,,	–	3	–
Haircutting once a month @ 6d.	,,	,,	–	6	–
A.A. Subscription	,,	,,	–	15	–
		£37	6	4	

The total received, if the actor were lucky enough to have thirty-
five weeks in work, at a minimum of £2, would leave £32 13s. 8d.
for food: one and ninepence a day; say sevenpence a meal. I would
ask my readers to take this list as their own for a minute, and fit into
it such luxuries as tobacco, an occasional drink, and occasional
newspaper, or a bar of chocolate. Out of expenditure on food, of
course, would come such necessities as tooth-paste or bottles of
medicine. The experiment will, I think, leave them with a sense of
compassionate uneasiness amounting almost to shame.

Without difficulty, therefore, this minimum was adopted by the
Association, and laid before the managers. But it was not accepted
by the managers, neither touring managers nor those in the West
End; not in August 1908, nor in 1909, nor in 1910; nor indeed for
eleven years: and much had to happen before even the principle of
a minimum wage was agreed, as we must now show; although even
if it had been so accepted, it would not have overcome all the

difficulties facing the actors' organisers. There would still be players, as Frederick Morland quoted in a Sunday evening lecture to the members,[6] who would actually go to managers and underbid each other for the sake of getting employment. More beneficial indeed than a minimum wage would have been a minimum engagement. Even toward a minimum wage, therefore, as it now seemed to many besides Cecil Raleigh, a strong drive for membership might well be useless unless the strong membership, when achieved, acted on trade union lines. Many members at once went to work to achieve both.

A benefit matinee for the Association was organised by 'The Play Actors', a scratch company of considerable talent limited to members of the A.A. It was to be given at the Scala Theatre under the management of Rose Matthews in June 1908. But for one reason and another this fell through, and Rose Matthews gave a recital by herself.[7]

It is good when a Council Member takes a stand on principle. It makes the whole council feel the rock beneath them. But it is frequently bad, too. It makes other council members apt to take a stand also, on an opposite principle; and it is not every council that is scientific enough to see the conflict as other than just a clash of opinion. So with Cecil Raleigh. His socialism gave him a twinge when the council proposed to repay the rich men their debentures in full and at once. He, Edmund Gurney and Lucy Sibley, held that the rich men could afford to wait. The rest of the council opposed them just as firmly. So no sooner had Raleigh defined the best direction for the Association to take, than he had to resign on this question of the debentures. Thus the council lost two men and a woman of a kind it could ill afford, although Lucy Sibley reappears before long; Raleigh continued from the roadside to pipe his flock forward by continual and compelling articles in the Press.[8]

But there was now no lack of firm spirits: Frederick Morland, Fred Grove, Cecil Brooking, Clarence Derwent, Rose Matthews. These ardent spirits were sincere in their concern for the general welfare of ordinary actors; but the managers were stubbornly against the A.A. as long as it made demands. To some, therefore, it seemed that a more reasonable attitude could only be induced among the managers by winning them over to methods of co-operation. With Raleigh no longer bodily present, this easier route seemed more attractive, perhaps, than it really was. Clarence Derwent put the view forcibly to the A.G.M. in January 1910. He had come to the unalterable conviction, and he said it with no hesitancy and not without careful consideration, that no form of trade unionism, or anything faintly approximating to it, could ever be successfully applied to the conditions of their profession.[9]

This meeting, at Terry's Theatre on 25 January 1910 was a divided one and somewhat disturbed by charges of lobbying and doubtful behaviour on the council, which Raleigh had levelled in a letter to *The Stage* on 6 January, three weeks before. He alleged that when the Council was considering whether it should recommend to the A.G.M. that the managers' co-operation be invited, which meant inviting them to rejoin the A.A., a document was suddenly produced with signatures approving just such an invitation, which had been secretly obtained by the pro-managerial party on the Council, unknown to the others; and that Haydn Coffin had previously taken this document to Sir Herbert Tree, who had turned it down.

The rights and wrongs of this unhappy incident do not now very much matter. The question had been brought into the open, and good came of it. Many candidates for election as officers at the A.G.M. wrote to *The Stage*, declaring themselves as candidates for or against readmitting managers. Basil Dean, Lewis Casson (though with growing doubts whether the A.A. would ever achieve anything), sixteen in all, stood for once more excluding them: on that issue they were all re-elected. But other candidates would allow managers into the society though not to be Councillors; and yet others were for the managers unreservedly. These also were re-elected. The Council having already decided to recommend the re-admission of managers without limit to their activities, put a resolution to this effect, which was carried with only fifteen votes against; and Rose Matthews' resolution that managers be debarred from serving on the Council was rejected by eighty-eight votes to twenty-six. About 130 members were present.[10]

So there stood the Actors' Association, back where it had been before the Reform Group had tried its hand. But the time had not been lost, and the circumstances were not quite the same. In the first place, the question of a trade unionism policy was now familiar to members, whether they approved or not: and secondly, the aspect of the managers in general was altering, and hardly for the better. In February 1909 the Theatrical Managers' Association reorganised itself. This joint body included the West End Managers' Association; the Theatre Alliance, which was mainly composed of managers of the growing suburban theatres;[11] and the Touring Managers' Association. To bind these sometimes conflicting bodies tighter together, the territory was enlarged. Four divisions were created inside the joint body: The London; the Suburban, with six members; the Provincial, with twenty members all resident outside London; and the Touring. But the last division contained one member only, Walter Melville. The Touring Managers' Association was practically an independent body, all the more militant against organised actors from the existence of the token rival Touring division inside the joint body.

It is quite possible that under these conditions, to re-admit the better disposed type of manager to the A.A. was a prudent step, even if it seemed a backward one at the time. Certainly something had to be done, and the majority of the profession could not be otherwise enlisted in the numbers required for a stand-up fight.

All that the A.A. sought was what *The Stage* called 'an actors' working system'.[12] There were bogus managers everywhere, even in London. The collapse of *Dorothy* at the Waldorf Theatre, the Marie Dressler fiasco, the failure of Robert Hilton's *Richelieu* in February 1910, were all due to small managements, or in Hilton's case small actor-managers, having insufficient initial funds and trusting for support to verbal promises from people who had more: and 'for one fiasco in town, there are a dozen, a score, in the provinces'.[13] Such men were a threat to the genuine manager as much as to the actor; and re-admission might have led to stronger action against such defaulters at least. But it did not: all that the council did was to warn members to satisfy themselves of a management's soundness before signing (as if they could!); and elect Tree as their President.

Tree's return to the fold had been expressly conditional on the Council abandoning all thought of a trade union policy. His letter to this effect was published in *The Stage*, 24 February 1910, and contains the sentiment printed at the head of this chapter. He was perfectly sincere in expressing it. It never occurred to him that it was the divine right of managers which prevented the struggling mass from securing a living wage. He was uninformed on that subject; he was uninformed about his own actions on that subject. A good, kind, and considerate employer, as actors whom he employed confirmed, he never paid a speaking part less than the £2 that the A.A. required. When William Johnson, the secretary of N.A.T.E., two years later stated that the conditions at His Majesty's

were in some respects the worst in the West End, Tree at once expressed 'regret and sorrow' at the rates he had just found out he
was paying his stage hands. In future, he said, he would certainly
pay them the minimum rate – provided they left the Union![14]

On the same conditions of Council behaviour, Alexander re-
joined, and Martin Harvey; but not Hawtrey nor Cyril Maude, who
said that the A.A. was no longer 'representative'.[15] The 'struggling
mass' appeared to approve of re-admission. The membership
rose; the budget was balanced: it remained balanced up to the
Great War. Almost it seemed as if the Association would after all
become that Corporation of employers and employed – or, as its
members would have perhaps preferred to put it, of master artists
and journeymen artists – which Henley had advocated thirty years
before. Only there was a strange apathy about its counsels:
nominations for Council never exceeded, and often did not even
equal, the number of vacancies; meetings and Annual General
Meetings were poorly attended; the deliberations of the Council
itself were apt to weaken when Cecil Raleigh was ill, or abroad, and
could write no provocative letters to The Stage.

Shortly before the A.G.M. of 1911 (that was, astutely, during
preparations for the election of Council) Clarence Derwent, rejoic-
ing that the A.A. was once more representative, wrote to The Stage
to announce a further concession. Tree had agreed to the principle
of payment for rehearsals, at the rate of 25 per cent for salaries
under £5.

Rehearsal without pay was one of the greatest hardships. In
London runs there might be four weeks of work and one of
playing, before any money was forthcoming; and then the play
might fail, leaving – even on a hard-won £2 minimum – a net
income of four shillings a week on which to feed, get to and from
work, and if necessary repair or replace clothing. On tour it was
worse. In 1911 judicial notice was taken in a County Court case,
that there was a theatrical custom by which, although in London
advance notice of two weeks was usual when a play closed down, no
notice at all was necessary for a tour to end.[16] So that the shorter
the run, the more difficult it was to ease the financial strain, or even
debt, incurred during unpaid rehearsal and first-playing weeks.

Tree must have sounded like Father Christmas with his promise
of a minimum ten shillings a week. With Alexander, Benson, H. B.
Irving and Martin Harvey as Vice-Presidents, all the other
managers might well have followed suit, for Tree was also Presi-

dent of the Theatrical Managers' Association and Vice-President of the Society of West End Managers. But most did not. The Secretary of the Theatres Alliance proposed one-third pay for rehearsals, to be deducted from wages paid in playing weeks.[17] Others agreed to Tree's example, but refused to discuss even the principle of a standard contract; they said they already had one of their own. Slightly disconcerted, the Council decided to post a list of such managers as refused to recognise any minimum wage.[18]

There were other questions that roused the decent feelings of the Council: the white slave traffic, for instance, all too common among tours abroad organised not by bogus managers so much as bogus agencies, and sometimes unknowingly by even quite respectable ones. The Danks case[19] is an example in 1908. An actress signed a contract in French, a language she did not know, and was told on arrival at Buenos Ayres that she had sold herself into the absolute power of a very dubious management. Fortunately she was a woman of strong character and challenged this, though it cost her a big sum to get out of the country, which she claimed back from the agents that had caused her to sign. She recovered the sum at law; but the details of the case, only too revealing of worse conduct by agencies, roused a storm in the Press, and involved *The Stage* in a libel action over which the jury disagreed. Good or bad whether the agencies were, the evils they covered were due to a disregard for the human rights of actors and actresses; and this disregard was, in general, founded on ignorance. Democratic ideas were still new, and strange, and not very respectable in Britain; but the spread of them, the forceful but tactful insistence at every turn that evils could be cured only by a new attitude to their root causes, was a policy incumbent on the A.A. Council, not only in the direction of managers, but in the direction also of rank-and-file sufferers themselves.

The Danks case caused a demand for the licensing of all theatrical agencies, which hitherto had only to be registered.[20] Another matter in which licensing was concerned arose from the change in music-hall programmes. Unemployment on the legitimate stage and a failing of material on the variety stage had led to an increasing practice of including long sketches or one-act plays in music-hall bills. These were often unpaid, the actors trusting that their mere appearance would interest managements and win them engagements elsewhere.[21] Now music and dancing licences were granted by the L.C.C., not by the Lord Chamberlain like theatre licences. One way to stop this exploitation would be to have both licences brought under one authority.

In December 1909 the L.C.C. agreed so to unite them, but its examining committee found the project impracticable. The A.A. Council remonstrated with them again in 1911, and also applied for the help of the Lord Chamberlain, who was unwilling to move. Many of the managers favoured single licensing; but the L.C.C. remained obdurate. There was only one course left. The A.A. could act as common informers against any music-hall proprietor who transgressed the law by staging a dramatic show like this, when he had no dramatic licence, as few if any of them had. This the Council decided to do in cases where the actors were unpaid. The test case arose in October 1911, when Moss Empires presented the great French actress Réjane in a play that lasted fifty minutes: a flagrant case; and a successful one.[22]

In prestige, the Association grew big enough to be officially invited to the Thanksgiving Service after King George V's Coronation. Eleven managements granted it the right to have Association notices put on company noticeboards.[23] In democratic methods a small advance was made when Lucy Sibley's proposal to have President and Vice-Presidents elected by the whole membership and not by the Council was carried at the A.G.M. in 1912, despite the objection of Clarence Derwent and mainly because Tree and Alexander approved.[24] In political matters the Association helped to straighten out an absurd tangle over Lloyd George's State Insurance Act. Its drafters having no knowledge of theatrical habits, an enormous number of actors and actresses who earned less than £160 a year and should therefore have benefited, could not do so unless when on tour they gave notice of change of address at every town they came to. Democratic government meant little to our forebears. When Clarence Derwent at an open meeting in 1914 at the Chandos Hall referred to a suggestion that Parliament should be asked to help in a certain matter, he was greeted with laughter – as he intended to be.[25]

In spite of these advances the Association had entered on another period of effete apathy. An investigation into the *Romance of India* failure in January 1914 revealed that this gigantic spectacle had cost £8,000, of which the organising syndicate had only £3,000, and only £1,400 had been really forthcoming. All that the A.A. could do was to carry a resolution that rehearsals should be paid.[26] A stand was made against the growing practice of twice-

nightly performances of straight plays in the provinces. But this
was difficult to win, because not all dates for the same play were
twice-nightly.

It was not entirely the fault of the Council, though they could
have helped more than they did. At the Chandos Hall meeting
there was hardly a famous player present. The 'struggling mass'
came in numbers, because questions like that of Sunday opening
affected their livelihood, but they were not encouraged to do more
than pass pious resolutions, which they generally did with a wistful
and trusting unanimity. Hardly a tenth of the profession were
members of the A.A., and of that tenth barely a fifth ever bothered
to vote at Council elections. This inevitably affected the Council,
whose meetings became routine, dealing only with minor complaints. For the profession in general the Association meant less
and less, as can be seen in the space devoted to its affairs in *The
Stage*. At first nothing below two columns in a prominent place had
been deemed worthy. Now there was less than half a column, in
unimportant positions.

Outside, a crisis was blowing up in a changing theatrical
landscape. Commercial impresarios now outnumbered actor-
managers even in the Society of West End Managers. The Touring
Managers retaliated upon the A.A.'s black-list of uncooperative
managers, by circularising their members with a list of actors likely
to give trouble, a document that led to victimisation and unfair
discrimination.[27] The militancy of the managers this time too was
not unconnected with managers in other industries. It was the era
of the coal strike of 1912, which, even without putting their
employers on edge, also hit the ordinary actor and actress directly.
Sunday travel became more burdensome than ever; the fare concession was withdrawn; audiences in mining and other industrial
districts went thin; as a result, salaries were reduced by many
managers. But the cost of living was rising fast: since 1900 food
prices were up by 14 per cent; real wages had gone down by twelve
per cent.[28]

Other entertainment industry employees were taking action,
and in the process finding common cause with other trades. In
1912 spring, when stage hands in the N.A.T.E. met to discuss the
action of Tree in dismissing union members, there came representatives from associations of Carmen, Cabmen, Compositors,
Machine-Minders and the London Trades Council. William
Johnson, the secretary, said rightly that it was not Sir Herbert they

were fighting, but the commercial forces behind him.[29] Most of the men in this case were reinstated, and the union's pay demands were agreed to, though this latter had not been at issue; and two months later Tree resigned his Presidency of the Theatrical Managers' Association, and Cyril Maude was elected in his place.[30] Variety musicians went on lightning strike in London, with the sympathy of an East End audience; there was unrest among stage hands in Liverpool; the Amalgamated Musicians' Union called its members out at Manchester: all this in the same month, November 1913. At a joint meeting in Waterloo, the A.M.U. and other unions supported N.A.T.E.'s claim for higher wages.[31]

But with all this low-class activity the A.A. had nothing to do. 'Duchesses do not smile at trade unionists', observed St John Ervine in January 1914, accounting with libellous cynicism for the individualistic conduct of the A.A. All that the A.A. could do was to cast appealing eyes once more upon the Managers, and follow Clarence Derwent's suggestion of a joint commission of managers and artists to report on conditions.[32] All they could do, because they knew something must be done, was to set up a Consultative Committee of Members and Non-members, which as good as proclaimed to the world that the A.A. was bankrupt of ideas or responsibility. This created a new society called the Actors' Pay-For-Play League 'to secure payment for rehearsals and all extra performances'. But its only success was that Barker at the Savoy and George Edwardes at the Gaiety granted rehearsal pay, three years after Tree had done so. The new society by the middle of 1914 had only 600 members and a working capital of £55.[33]

So it would seem it was not the *structure* of the A.A. that was at fault. Every ordinary player wanted to see reforms made, and would have backed heart and soul any organisation which looked like being powerful enough to compel them. Now it was clear that only force would do it. Even Clarence Derwent, the convinced anti-trade unionist, had stated at the Chandos Hall meeting that Parliament had only taken up the question of working men's salaries because working men had such great unions and were sending men to Parliament: and there were hints of a similar outlook at meetings of the League in London, and in Glasgow in February 1914.[34]

But no power great enough would come from the profession until conditions were so bad that actors had to see themselves as wage-earners, however artistic they were or however much duchesses' smilees; as people employed by employers and as subject to the same relentless economic pressures as all wage-earners were. That situation arrived during the War of 1914–18.

Notes and References

1. *The Stage*, 6 February 1908.
2. Ibid., 26 December 1907; and letter from Cecil Raleigh in reply to Lewis Casson, *The Stage*, 13 February 1908. Also *The Stage*, 13 August 1908.
3. *The Stage*, 5 December 1907; 14 November 1907.
4. *Green Room Book 1906*, p. 278; *The Stage*, 12 November 1914; *The Players*, 9 February 1892, p. 184; *The Pelican*, 21 March 1891. Also Joseph Knight and W. Eden Hooper; *The Stage in the Year 1900*. London, 1900, p. 72.
5. *The Stage*, 5 March 1908.
6. Ibid., 21 January 1909. Frederick Morland was a provincial actor and a convinced trade unionist. See *The Stage*, 30 December 1909.
7. Ibid., 11 February, 18 March 1909.
8. Ibid., 21 May, 28 May 1909.
9. Ibid., 27 January 1910.
10. Ibid., 27 January 1910, including Editorial article.
11. Ibid., 11 February 1909.
12. Ibid., 18 March 1909.
13. Ibid., 24 September 1910.
14. Ibid., 2 March 1912.
15. Ibid., 10 February, 10 March 1910.
16. *Read* v. *Pilkington, The Times*, 20 October 1911. Cited by Sidney Isaacs in his useful book on *Theatrical Law*, London, 1927, p. 214. When judicial notice is taken of a trade custom, this is read-in as an implied term to any contract that does not stipulate otherwise. Although this was only a County Court case, and not binding on a higher court, it is most unlikely that a High Court Judgement would not have adopted it if it had ever arisen in the High Court.
    Another 'theatrical custom' recognised by the law (in *Cotton and others* v. *Soames*, 1902, 18 T.L.R., p. 456) was the 'Flying Matinee' by which a week's stand in a theatre near London might well be interrupted without compensation to the touring company making it, when a London Star would arrive for a special matinee performance with his entire company and return to London for an evening house the same night.
17. *The Stage,* 19 January 1911.
18. Ibid., 14 March, 23 June 1910.
19. *Danks* v. *Sherek and Braff* (10 and 11 February 1909). See *The Stage*, 18 February 1909. *Also Sherek and Braff* v. *The Stage* (26 January 1910). I have not found these in the Law Reports.
20. *The Stage*, 7 July 1910.
21. Ibid., 14 April 1910.
22. Ibid., 14 April 1910, 5 October, 9 November, 1 December 1911.
23. Ibid., 4 January, 21 March 1912.
24. Ibid., 21 March 1912.

25. Ibid., 15 January 1914.
26. Ibid., 1 January, 8 January 1914.
27. Ibid., 30 January, 10 April, 2 November 1913.
28. Ibid., 21 March 1912, 13 August 1914. Figures from G. D. H. Cole, op. cit., p. 230.
29. Ibid., 4 April 1912.
30. Ibid., 11 April, 13 June 1912.
31. Ibid., 13 November, 20 November, 11 December 1913.
32. Ibid., 13 November 1913.
33. Ibid., 15 January, 22 January, 23 July 1914.
34. Ibid., 5 February 1914.

CHAPTER NINE

How the A.A. became a Trade Union

> *Now no one went and told the workers to form Trade Unions.*
>
> John Strachey

The war of 1914–18 cut across many industrial troubles. Despite the opposition of a few conscientious socialists, convinced that the British ultimatum to Germany meant no more than the internal struggle of one pack of capitalists against another, most of even the militant trade unionists and social reformers were swept away on a current patriotism in 1914 and postponed all industrial conflicts whatsoever. The Liberal government of the time was thus spared many unpleasant headaches.

Among actors there was the same spirit. A few like Miles Malleson and Harold Scott, who were friends of Clifford Allen and followers of Bertrand Russell, held war to be in all circumstances ethically indefensible, said so courageously, conducted themselves accordingly, and paid for their uprightness, many with long terms of imprisonment, others with less official but no less painful penalties.[1] But the majority wholeheartedly placed themselves at the disposal of the war authorities. Many left promising careers in order to join up, despite ill-natured allegations to the contrary by a certain Robert Vansittart, whose identity was obscure until *The*

Stage pronounced him to be 'the author of one or two plays which managers produced but the public did not rush after'.[2] Joining up was a new thing; but this was a new kind of war. It involved more and more classes of people, unlike the wars of the past, which had been fought by professional soldiers keen for promotion, or amateur ones keen for adventure.

At first it seemed as if the theatre would not be wanted in wartime, especially when the 'reduced lighting' which London had to adopt to escape the notice of prowling Zeppelin-airship commanders, kept the public from its West End at night.[3] Nevertheless actors and actresses remained at their trade, and threw themselves into service of the national emergency with the generous, impulsive, uninformed and sometimes ill-advised openheartedness that is characteristic of them. Many managements took financial advantage of this. In London, for example, there were fewer evening performances and more matinees. At His Majesty's, the Haymarket and the Criterion there were six matinees and only two evening performances each week. By contract at that time players lost a proportion of their salary if there were no evening performance, and they received nothing extra for matinees.[4]

Touring Managers told their companies, not always with justifying cause, that if there were to be any performance at all they must accept reduced salaries. They did so, to the extent of a 20 per cent reduction, and in some cases by a third.[5] In one of the latter cases a touring manager was overheard by his victim, an artist of twenty years' experience, claiming credit for his patriotic action in keeping artists from starvation and at the same time boasting that he had not made so much money since the last Christmas boom. It must be hastily added that this manager was not typical, though he existed. Because of the rush to the provinces to book in light shows there, lessees and resident provincial managers had hardened their terms, and a touring manager's position was not so happy as it had been. But many provincial lessees were organising their own provincial tours, so many that they were said now to comprise most of the Touring Managers' Association;[6] possibly the gentleman overheard in his hypocrisy was one of these.

Here again the A.A. could do little. Though it had many friends, it was running out of guides and philosophers: Cecil Raleigh died of cancer of the throat in November 1914; Clarence Derwent had gone to America; men of ideas and force like Lewis Casson were already on active service as volunteers. Malcontents had to be careful; over speech too free hung the blackmail of patriotism. All the Association could do was to call upon the profession somewhat plaintively to 'combine against the unscrupulous use which is being made of the national calamity in certain quarters'. Part of that unscrupulous use was the exacting of free services for relief funds.[7]

As the war went on, normal hours were resumed in London, but reduced prices continued. So did reduced salaries. Both in the provinces and in London one-third or one-half of pre-war pay was now the norm of contracts. But there was prosperity in box-office takings. Soldiers on leave sought relief with their wives and friends in gay shows of many kinds; they besieged the theatres. The twice-nightly habit reached London.[8] Now was the chance of the Association to stand up for the rights of the exploited actor, one might think: public opinion would have favoured so just a cause, even in wartime. But no; the affairs of the Association were not happy. Finance was difficult: the reserve funds were all used up to get through the financial year; a war Emergency Fund had to be set up to help members who had suffered as a result of war. In 1915 the number of new members joining had dropped to fifty; but the Government told the Managers' Association that the A.A. was the only stage organisation that they recognised, with the result that there was quite a rush of actor-managers to re-join. This included so many celebrities like Hicks, Godfrey Tearle, Lilian Braythwaite and Kate Cutler, that from their example the total next year went up by 300 or more.[9] There were also personnel difficulties. Unhappy revelations made a new secretary indispensable. In Adnam Sprange a good one was found, a character actor who had been a business man and a business manager.

Some good, though, the A.A. did succeed in doing. The boom in light entertainment offered easy prey to Mr McKenna's budget in 1916. The Entertainments Tax was invented and imposed, purely as a wartime measure, of course, like the hours of liquor licences. Managements complained, but it is doubtful if they suffered by it, except for a slight increase in staff to deal with fragments of tickets and filling up returns. It hit the young actor and actress hard. Players depend on knowing what is going on in their trade: they have to visit new shows, at matinees if they are themselves in work; that is why they have always been entitled to complimentary tickets. Those who drafted the Budget did not know this. They saw no reason why the tax should not be paid on complimentary tickets too. This would mean that managements would curtail the issue of them, if they did not abolish it, for there were few shows so bad that paper houses were required. The A.A. sent a deputation to the Prime Minister. It consisted of Ellen Terry, H. B. Irving and Sidney Valentine. Wisely the other two left the talking to Ellen Terry.

Now almost every man in the country, including Bernard Shaw and Mr Gladstone, had at one time or another been hopelessly in love with this remarkable and wonderful person. It was hardly to be expected that the Prime Minister would resist her pleading; the deputation left Downing Street with the tax removed forthwith from complimentary tickets.[10]

Again, the aspect of the countryside was changing. In London by the end of 1915, twenty-eight out of thirty-one theatre buildings were open at once, a number not exceeded in peacetime. Outside London resident theatres were starting: the repertories of Manchester, Birmingham and Liverpool consolidated themselves. Elsewhere touring companies which had been carrying two or more plays at a time now turned into resident stock companies on a new model: J. H. Savile's at Paisley and Perth, Peter Davey's at Portsmouth, Jones and Douglas at New Brighton, and many more. Behind the backs of the actors fighting in Flanders and France, the stage was being set for the post-war repertory scene, which would prove a partial answer to demobilisation problems when they came. Only at present the stock company actor was in no very happy plight. His pay was still at the reduced 'war calamity' level; and instead of being engaged permanently, like the old stock actor, or for a whole season as in years to come, he was too often bound only by his old touring contract for the run, which might be ended at any time, and he would count himself lucky if he had a fortnight's notice.[11] Actresses too were playing their part in war. The Actresses' Franchise League got up a Woman's Theatre to give entertainments to the troops. Special matinees raised large sums for war charities and relief. The stage gave an emotional lead to the whole country.

The A.A. too had its share of good fortune. Though still in numbers small, it had balanced its budget, primarily thanks to Tree, Alexander and H. B. Irving who addressed public meetings in aid of it. Under Willie Fay's chairmanship it grew stronger. Little W. G. Fay was the Irish actor and producer who had been the central stage figure in the founding of the Abbey Theatre, Dublin. He had gone to England in 1908, when he felt the original Abbey spirit was tarnishing. A lively little figure, very indignant against the British actors who had run away to America or were remaining there in what seemed to be safety, he used to urge that they be deprived of Association membership. His services to the A.A. cannot be over-estimated;[12] he kept it together at a very trying time; he increased its prestige.

Its prestige had become such that Government departments looked to it as a means of negotiating with the stage profession, for example in questions of exemption from military service, jointly with the N.A.T.E. This was tantamount to recognising it as a trade union of blackcoated stage workers, so to speak. It was also getting minor results out of mean managements. Cases are reported such as: 'a star refused to play because of the rowdy audience, and the company were out the week, for which the manager refused to pay. Upon our application, however, he paid our member.'[13] By the end of the war, it was prospering. Its credit balance stood at £700.

The landscape outside went on changing. Between 1915 and the end of the war, membership of trade unions and of the Labour Party rose by 50 per cent.[14] This was not altogether limited to the working classes; the middle classes too were coming to view things differently. The bogey of 'State Control' which had caused wailing and terror in many places was seen to be in many ways a benefit. Class distinctions which had been much more fixed and forbidding than we are apt to remember, had vanished in so many wartime crises, and the war itself had lasted so long, that many respectable folk began to wonder whether the old slogan 'Jack's as good as his master' were not in fact quite true. At least the idea of Britain as a democratic state began to look less alarming. The Representation of the People Act of 1918 was to carry this process toward democracy one step further. Such ideas penetrated also the theatre. No longer could *The Era* sneer, as it had done in 1910, that organisation would 'turn acting into an industry', with 'exact payment' for 'definite, mechanical, concrete work'. On the contrary, ordinary people had had experience both at the front and at home of the effectiveness of good organisation, where individuals could do nothing.

Again, you cannot give an account of a theatre without giving an account of the audience; and the old aristocratic Edwardian audience had gone for ever. Mixed was the audience now on whom actor and management depended, of all three classes, but mainly the middle one. The middle class had discovered that in a democracy, even in one that was only just forming, if you want your voice to be heard, it is no use shouting; you must get others who think like you to talk like you in a normal voice. That is all a trade union is. The duchess's smile no longer counted. No sooner was the war ended, than the word 'reconstruction' was on every lip and every page. This did not mean the replacement of everything exactly as it had been before, as was made abundantly clear. Common talk in the street admitted that something had gone from the world, which would never return, good or bad. For the first time in British history since Queen Elizabeth or James IV, the future was more interesting than the past.

In such circumstances, one would expect a body like the A.A. to show a new impulse, as other bodies were doing; and if it found a suitably gifted leader, to get results at last. A new impulse it certainly showed; and fortunately it found such a leader, too, in Sidney Valentine.

At this time Sidney Valentine was a well-liked actor in his early fifties. He had been born in Moseley, Birmingham, with the family name of Nossiter and christened Valentine because he was born on that Saint's day in 1865. The theatre was the be-all of his life, and a theatre dressing-room was nearly the end-all of it in his twenties. For insanitary conditions at the Strand Theatre struck him down with an illness which laid him on his back for two years and left him not only with one leg shorter than the other, but also with an internal trouble that made the rest of his life one continual ordeal of pain and distaste. When he was able to be moved, a travelling bed took him to Margate, where he knew the Thornes; and his first return to the stage was as Shylock in Sarah Thorne's theatre there. His Tony Lumpkin and Joseph Surface with the Compton Comedy Company had been the talk of London; but the brilliant career that had seemed his was now, with a permanent limp, out of the question. However, so strong was the call of the theatre, that he went on with it. Because he developed a superb range of character parts, especially dialect and foreigners – he was a Vice-President of a French cultural society in London – he was seldom out of an engagement. His subtle, dignified old men, too, were unrivalled. Barrie thought him the finest actor of his time. So did Martin Harvey, Wyndham, Irving, and Cyril Maude for whom at various times he worked, all of whom had a high regard for his talent; and his entrancing smile was familiar to most London playgoers.[15]

Like many who have spent long periods on beds of sickness, he was gentle and sensitive; but he was no fool, and his ability to see an opponent's point of view in no way weakened his own. On the contrary, it strengthened his attack with foresight. Again like many invalids who have learned to steel themselves to activity hour after weary hour and daunting day by day, he had a will of iron, which allowed him plenty of margin to be polite, and therefore more persuasive, with his deadly reasoning.[16] Nor did all this prevent his listening to argument and changing his course if his previous one could be demonstrated wrong, as we will be seeing. Even allowing in obituary notices for the affectionate exaggeration of friends, there is no mistaking Valentine's effect on all who knew him; and his own deeds, which we must now pleasantly chronicle, show him to have had all the qualities of a most exceptional man, if indeed he may not be counted a great one.

His comparatively brief but blazing public life justifies, for once the epithet 'meteoric'. The A.A. needed him, but never expected him; nobody guessed from his quiet past what his future would be. But the night into which he vanished so soon, and so tragically, could never again be as it was before he shot through it. He had put up for the Council in April 1916, nominated by A. H. Steerman and seconded by Laura Leycester, but was unsuccessful; from which it may reasonably be inferred that his personality and ability in public affairs were little known. Yet exactly a year later, a scene occurred so extraordinary as to be beyond most people's experience in committee matters. At a Council meeting the Chairman, W. G. Fay, proposed that Mr Sidney Valentine be co-opted on the Council in place of Mr W. R. Staveley, who would resign for that purpose; and that if this motion were carried he, the Chairman, himself would resign the Chair and nominate Sidney Valentine into it.[17] This remarkable proposition was at once seconded by A. Harding Steerman, and carried *nem. con.* by the thirteen Councillors present, an attendance unusually large at that time.

After this Napoleon-like appointment, for Valentine's first year of office there was not much to show. 1917 was not a year marked by spectacular moves in any industry; large strikes had in the main given way to small spasmodic ones and demonstrations. It was the year of the intensified German submarine campaign, threatening our islands with something near starvation. It was a year of Whitley Councils, of state control almost nation-wide. A year of an all-out effort to smash the Hindenberg Line and finish the war. But in 1918 things began to happen in the A.A., and to happen fast. It is not difficult to connect their speed with the appearance of another unusual figure on the Council; Alfred Lugg.

Lugg was the direct opposite of Valentine. Where Valentine was rational and firm, Lugg was fiery and romantic. Where Valentine spoke slowly, if fluently, giving his hearers time to think over the truth of what he was saying, Lugg was an orator of outstanding gifts, who swept people off their feet into compliance. If Valentine could argue the hind leg off a donkey, Lugg could make it walk. But what was of more consequence, in intellectual make-up they were opposites: Valentine was a staunch Conservative, by no means convinced of the value of trade unionism, while Lugg was a left-wing Socialist, an innate rebel, consistently pleading that trade unionism, and nothing but trade unionism, and out-and-out and instant trade unionism, could save the Association. But they were both devoted to the cause of the ordinary actor and actress; and it is difficult to conceive any more useful pair than these two opposites, so united. The Association was lucky to have them in office at the very time when two such men were required. It may not have seemed so at the time, however. Valentine bitterly opposed Lugg, and other members of Council talked of removing Lugg from his position as Chairman of the Propaganda Committee because of his earnestness. Finally, Lugg challenged Valentine to come with him and hear about trade unionism from some notable trade union leader, promising that if Valentine were not convinced, Lugg would drop his own line and adopt Valentine's for a year.

The reasonable mind of Valentine could not overlook this challenge; and he consented. Lugg fixed an appointment with James O'Grady, the Secretary of the National Federation of General Workers, the largest and most powerful union in existence. At that time O'Grady, a Bristol man, was one of the firmest trade union leaders, though later on, in fact quite soon after, he was to be appointed Governor of Tasmania and knighted.

It was a pouring wet day in April when they arrived at the House of Commons, O'Grady being also an M.P.: Valentine, who was under permanent treatment for his trouble, was in great pain and a very bad temper; symptoms that did not augur sympathetic listening. Indeed, he was no passive listener. I can best quote Lugg's own account of the interview: 'For two hours Valentine fired questions at him. Finally Valentine left the meeting without a word except to thank O'Grady; but on the doorstep he stopped and with a mouth like a rat trap he said: "It's the only way." And from then on he went all out. He made me General Secretary, and the rest I think is known.'[18] The rest is perhaps not so well known to the general reader as it deserves to be.

The first step was to make the Association powerful enough to act. Valentine began by getting himself a right of access as official A.A. delegate to the companies of all the West End London theatres except the Queen's, the Alhambra and the Savoy. The licensees and managers were respectively: Sir Alfred Butt and Percy Hutchison; Oswald Stoll; and H. B. Irving and Gilbert Miller.

The second step was to get trade union status. This meant obtaining a mandate from the Association at a general meeting summoned specially for that purpose. It is typical of Valentine that he lost no time in broaching the matter. It was in April that he had been 'converted'; it was in May that he asked for such a general meeting. A discussion had been called on the subject of early closing, which had been fixed at 10.30 p.m. to conserve fuel. At this he introduced the burning question. 'The days are critical', he said, 'and we cannot go on in the old lazy-going manner.' Sounding their reactions he saw that there would be nothing like the necessary majority. Stage folk were no more awake to the need for trade union status than he had been himself and for the same reasons. For weeks thereafter he met and talked over with Lugg and Stephen Wentworth and others how best the membership could be educated and informed; for like an honest man, he was sure that they would only need to hear the truth well explained and they would agree. But it was not easy; for an article by Lugg in *A.A.*, the official organ of the Association, had given offence by its attack on the Conservative Party, and had required – or at least acquired – an editorial and Council disclaimer as recently as the previous November. The ghosts of the old style actor-managers still haunted them, though the bodies of the most prominent had died during the war.

Fifteen times the Council met between May and August. All the implications and aspects of becoming a full trade union had to be examined and explained to doubters and opposers. But the very prospect was enough to influence the managers. In June a draft standard contract was under discussion with the Touring Managers' Association. It was probably the notion of a full Actors' trade union that had got them as far as even discussing such a thing; but it is also probable that they did not believe the Council could put it through; and so they temporised, to see what would happen. This gave to the question which way the membership would vote a double importance; for if the actors rejected trade unionism, there was little doubt the managers would reject a standard contract.

The day came: 23 August 1918: the Rehearsal Theatre in Maiden Lane was well filled; Sidney Valentine took the chair. What most members wished to hear was exactly what use trade unionism had been to any comparable group of artists; and Valentine had provided just the man to tell them. Monte Bayly, the National Organiser of the Variety Artists' Federation, which had not only benefited by the support of the General Federation of Trade Unions in its fight against music-hall proprietors, but had also in 1917 managed to secure for choristers a standard contract containing payment for performance, payment for rehearsal, and, where possible, engagement for the entire run. In fact, it had done what the A.A. had been unable even to try, although there were choristers too in the A.A. In other words, he demonstrated to his spell-bound audience that what they were hoping one day to get was not only obtainable, and not only obtained by others; it was their *right*. After that it was not difficult to prove that only trade union action, or trade union sanction, would ever make the other side recognise it as a right.

The motion was then put to the meeting: 'That this meeting, having heard Mr Bayley of the V.A.F., thoroughly supports this proposal to form this Association into a trade union.' The motion was carried 'with enthusiasm' – and with only one dissentient vote! I imagine the voting surprised even those Councillors who thought they were in touch with the general feeling of members; though Valentine possibly expected it, and Lugg certainly must have. But expected or not, it was sensational.[19]

At once the Council set to work on a new constitution. The name, Actors' Association, was retained; and the following aims declared for what was in effect a new body:

1. To promote and protect the art of acting.
2. To regulate the relations between actors and proprietors, managers, agents and others; and between member and member.

These should be compared with the first aim of the original constitution: 'to further in every way possible the best interests of actors and managers'.

3. To secure unity of action by organisation and otherwise in order to improve the position and status of all artists admitted to the Association.

Other objects were to secure a minimum rate of pay, to provide benefits of various kinds; and a proviso was made that if any manager became a member of Council he was not to be entitled to vote or to hold office.

Membership was opened to all actors performing to theatrical, music-hall or kindred audiences, and to producers and dramatists, and also to authors and performers in the new film industry. They could contract out of the separate political fund, which was authorised, if they so desired. This was a necessary proviso under the Trades Unions Act of 1913. To make quite certain that members knew what they were doing, or rather why they were doing it, another preliminary meeting was held at the Savoy early in October, at which J. A. Seddon, the Chairman of the British Workmen's League told again how unionism would help them; and then at a final meeting on 1 November 1918, the constitution was put and adopted by a vote of 1,191 to 15.[20]

So at last, and suddenly, the A.A. took the only step that could free it from its pathetic ineffectuality. That step itself was enough to trouble the managers. For now in any dispute stage staff and musicians and company would all be in touch with each other and with their like all over the country. This was truly meeting power with power; and a dramatic year was ahead. A dramatic year indeed: a little over a week and the war ended; a little over twelve months and Sidney Valentine was dead.

Notes and References

1. Harold Scott, in personal conversation with the author.
2. *The Stage*, 3 December 1914.
3. Ibid., 22 October 1914.
4. Ibid., 28 October 1914.
5. Letter to *The Stage*, 17 December 1914.
6. Letter from a touring manager to *The Stage*, 3 December 1914.
7. *The Stage*, 3 September 1914.
8. Ibid., 7 January, 28 January, 8 July 1915.
9. Ibid., 13 January 1916 and Alfred Lugg in a letter to the Author.
10. W. G. Fay and Catharine Carswell, *The Fays of the Abbey Theatre*. London, 1935, pp. 270–1. And *The Stage*, 9 March 1916.
11. *The Stage*, 6 January, 27 January 1916.

12. Fay and Carswell, op. cit. And Alfred Lugg in a letter to the author.
13. *The A.A.*, Vol. I, No. 12, December 1917, p. 101. 'Legal Notes', case 56.
14. G. D. H. Cole, op. cit., p. 230.
15. This quite inadequate account of Sidney Valentine is derived from the following sources:
    The Stage, 25 December 1919.
    Obituaries in the daily press, 23 and 24 December 1919, especially Hannen Swaffer in the *Daily Express*.
    The Pelican, 11 April 1891.
    Sidney Paxton in *The Stage*, 20 December 1919.
    Miles Malleson in personal conversation.
    Hannen Swaffer in the *Sunday Express* 'The Tragedy of a Great Actor', 8 December 1919.
    Bernard Shaw wrote appreciatively of his 'sincere and kindly smile' in *Our Theatres in the 90s*, Vol. I, p. 119.
16. Sir Lewis Casson in personal conversation.
17. *The Stage*, 6, 10 and 20 April 1917. 'Anything that Fay proposed could be passed; he had the gift of the Blarney and was very capable and devoted. The whole thing was of course irregular, but effective.' Alfred Lugg in a letter to the author.
18. Sidney Paxton in *The Stage*, 25 December 1919; and Alfred Lugg in a letter to the author replying to his inquiries.
19. *The Times*, London, 24 August 1918.
20. *The Times*, London, 2 November 1918, gives the figures as 1,100 to 15.

CHAPTER TEN

Exercise Develops
the Muscles

> As soon as the sun shines, it ever melts
> Both form and matter. I have ever thought
> Nature doth nothing so great for great men
> As when she's pleased to make them Lords of
> truth.
>
> John Webster

In the last chapter or two we have been so busy watching the growths of militancy or supineness in the Actors' Association that we have tended to neglect the changes outside it during the war in the actual conditions it was formed to improve.

There were few; and what there were, were sinister: 'Half a dozen or so large managements now control the majority of the West End theatres,' said *The Stage* on 23 January 1919. Inside the entertainment industry, owners and managers of theatres were only following the example of music-hall proprietors; but outside it – another example of the freemasonry of employers in all trades – there were many other far more powerful examples of amalgamations. Three years previously the Federation of British Industries had been formed: if this dealt mainly with commercial and economic questions, that was only because in 1919 another federation was to be formed: 'for the main purposes of representing to the Government the general views of organised employers upon labour matters, of taking appropriate action with the object of ensuring that labour and social legislation should not harmfully affect the interests of employers, and of arranging for the proper representation of British employers in the work of the International Labour Organisation'.[1] This was the National Confederation of Employers' Organisations, an immensely powerful body uniting representatives of employers organised in separate trade bodies, each of power great enough in its own sphere. The natural enemy of this multi-ventral leviathan was a trade union – any trade union and all trade unions. The monster was flexing its muscles in training for the General Strike of 1926. Against it, by implication in both senses of that word, the little weakling lamb of the A.A. ventured out into a very wide field, bleating half believed complaints about the neglect of its rights.

But apart from the unionisation of big employers, there was little other change. The A.A. might never have existed: the abuses and grievances were as they had been since 1909; indeed since 1889. Dressing-rooms could still have, and did have, open drains, if any at all, choked with cigarette cartons under cracked and unclean basins; public lavatories could and did still overpower the odour of powder and greasepaint; five ladies could and did still share one small room, and an entire company one watercloset, which was on the stage itself and could seldom be used.[2] A doctor could still report that when he asked a chorus girl how she managed to live on thirty shillings a week, she replied shortly 'I don't'.[3] By now the cost of living had gone up 225 per cent since 1914 and was still rising; while, as we have seen, actual theatre wages were below the 1914 level by a third and perhaps a half. It is not to be wondered at, if elderly actors who had known the worst of the old times sadly informed the younger generation that in the old days life was easier, times were better.

Realising how things were, Valentine drew up standard contracts, one for London, one for outside; at once gained the association's approval for the former; and tried to negotiate it through the managers. Now it was clear how sensible had been the decision to take trade union status. The managers were impressed by the unanimity shown in the adoption of that; they were even more impressed by the immediate consequent increase in membership. New names were being registered at the rate of five or six score every week; since the decision, the total membership had already doubled itself. But the managers were business men, almost entirely now, Tree had died in 1917. The man who stepped into that gap in the managers' fighting front was C. B. Cochran. When people complained about the one sided contracts he had issued in presenting Robert Loraine as *Cyrano de Bergerac*, he wrote to the *Evening News*: 'I consider the so-called one sided contract is absolutely necessary for the protection of the manager . . . . I should be the first to agree that the actors should be paid for rehearsals, but in that case I could not pay the salaries I am now paying to perfectly incompetent and inexperienced people'.[4]

Apart from the implied confession that either Cochran or his casting manager had poor judgment when engaging new talent – which if it had been true would have rather raised the question why they were in the business at all – and apart from any question of gratuitous insults, this tactful letter was not greeted with any very great enthusiasm by the hundreds, possibly thousands, of competent and experienced players who after being demobilised from the armed forces had been unable to get an engagement from Cochran or anyone else. Nor indeed by his own company who, competent or not, had been rehearsing for eight weeks without a shilling, and had been forced into further and unnecessary expenditure by being kept beyond the hour of the last transport home two Sundays running, at Cochran Dress Rehearsals, which were notoriously long and muddled.[5]

There were, however, other grounds both in contract and in treatment, for the A.A.'s official complaint about *Cyrano*. This enraged Cochran; he announced that he would never employ anyone who was a member of the A.A. I find it rather hard to believe that the timing of this announcement was not deliberate. It was made in March, at the very moment when Valentine was trying to negotiate the standard contract with the managers as a whole. The issue was still in doubt; and outspoken declarations of such a kind from a by no means unsuccessful impresario, even one who was as much interested in the money to be made out of boxing matches as out of Rostand, might still influence their decision.

If so, Cochran was judging the A.A. by old standards, as if Valentine had not appeared. Valentine knew what to do. He summoned a general meeting to approve a resolution that no A.A. member should appear in any cast not entirely composed of members or probationary members. This uncompromising decision, which was approved at once, showed what loyalty the Council could now expect from its 5,000 members.

Cochran may have been disconcerted; but he prepared to fight. His production was in the North of England prior to the London *premiere*. Loraine at Newcastle called the company together before the curtain rose and advised Cochran later that he had asked for complaints, but nobody had any. Cochran issued a press statement to this effect, complaining pettishly that he was paying £5 to non-speaking men and £4 to ladies who had never been on the stage before, and adding that if any rehearsals had been long, that was because members of the A.A. had arrived late.

Cyrano de Bergerac had opened in Edinburgh on 3 March with a three week tour ahead of it, after which there was a gap of five days, without pay, till the opening night in London. The company by then had worked for twelve weeks, and received pay for three. The day after the play opened in London, on 1 April, Valentine had a meeting about the standard contract with the managers. But they were waiting to see who won over *Cyrano*. No progress was made.[6] Cochran wrote to the *Morning Post* that the A.A. was dangerous; its leaders had Bolshevik tendencies. 'The young actor of today', he added, 'is neglecting his art for the study of Bolshevism.' He might have been seventy-seven years old, not forty-seven.

More than the entertainment industry found the struggle interesting, not so much for itself as for what it might at any moment develop into. The Government was asked in the House of Commons whether it would intervene in the *Cyrano* case. Sir Robert Horne replied that since he had had no complaint from either side, he could not.[7] The combatants were thus left to settle it by themselves. It was a cold war, both sides dead quiet, watching each other.

Not so the entertainment world. It was loud with shouting all round. The V.A.F. stated that Cochran's attitude, if it were not just a piece of his usual publicity, struck at the root of all trade unionism and that strike action in this case was justifiable. All trade unionists should be withdrawn from *Cyrano*, especially since it was the success of the season. (It was indeed: I remember well how wonderful it was). But Valentine did not budge. The Joint Committee of the V.A.F. and other entertainment unions offered to send a deputation to Cochran; but Cochran said he was just leaving for Paris. Valentine did not move.[8] The Theatre Alliance at its Annual General Meeting deprecated any attempt by the A.A. to restrict the liberty of the subject by interfering with either artists' or managers' freedom of choice. But this did not draw Valentine out, either; he bided his time, watching.

That week 184 new members joined the A.A. – another record – and by now ten of the London theatres had 100 per cent membership. Valentine's position was strong, as strong as his purpose; but neither did that draw him aside. He went on waiting and watching, till he had achieved the latter by remaining in the former. On the afternoon of Sunday 27 April 1919 the snow was whirling thickly and violently down the Haymarket, as quantities of actors and actresses converged from Piccadilly Circus, Trafalgar Square, Leicester Square and several side streets upon the imposing entrance to His Majesty's Theatre. It was the largest attendance at any meeting of actors. The whole profession was agog. To this gathering, tense with that nervous excitement which is more noticeable in a gathering of stage folk than of any others, Valentine put a motion that was revolutionary: nothing less than the empowering of the Council to take action for 100 per cent A.A. membership in Cochran's companies, now and at all future times.

But now there was no doubt about the feeling of the members. At last the profession was awake. It knew what was before it, and what it had to do. It greeted the resolution with terrific enthusiasm, passing it at once with only two dissenting voices. That must have been a great moment, for Valentine, for Lugg, and for all the progressive minded people there. Nor did it end at that; a fund must be got up to compensate any member who suffered as a result of the A.A.'s action. Within an hour of that suggestion, £700 had been contributed. The gauge of the general attitude was a gift of £50 from old Madge Kendal, who was there; she had always disliked trade unionism.[9] Valentine stood surveying his flock with affection and pride. He was not tall, but very striking to look at, with rugged features, a heavy nose, iron grey splendidly wavy hair, and eyes that danced in his head when he was amused. Very likely they were dancing now; for he had more to say, he had another surprise up his sleeve.

American Equity had forbidden its members to work for Cochran after 1 June; the V.A.F., and A.M.U. and N.A.T.E. were solidly with them. Sir Robert Horne, Minister of Labour, had seen both Lugg and Valentine in the presence of a Ministry official, and had agreed that they had good grounds for resisting Cochran; but he had asked Valentine, if he could, to smoothe matters over.[10] And this, said Valentine now with the famous smile playing over his face, he had agreed to do so. For he had yet one last and biggest surprise; this was one of the greatest moments of his life. Very adroitly he had turned Cochran's own recalcitrance and timing against him. The West End managers had thought that the A.A.s decision was aimed against them; and when they heard that it was against Cochran only, the ground of their delaying tactics was drawn from under them, and they had consented to accept Valentine's Standard Contract.

From now on in London, no honourable member of the W.E.M.A. would pay any speaking actor or actress less than £3 a week, nor less than ten shillings for any rehearsal, nor would hold a rehearsal longer than six hours, nor would call one more often than six times a week and never on Sunday. The scene when this was announced may be imagined. The first fruits of firmness and courage, and of wisdom, too, in their leader, were now plain to everybody. It seemed as if the A.A. was on top of the world. Cochran announced, that same week, that he was going out of management. He was proposing to retire.

So far, so very good. The new trade union had only been in existence for three months, as Valentine said, but already it had won a first very telling round, not so much in routing Cochran, as in impressing the other managers that it meant what it said. But this was only half the battle, and only half the first battle at that. A more difficult task lay ahead with the Touring Managers. Many of the London managers had proved decent fellows, artists; some of the touring managers were the same, but not nearly in so big a proportion. They were mainly commercial speculators; they controlled the fate of the majority of actors; and they were much more thrawn in their attitude to standard contracts. All that summer Valentine wrestled with them. Sometimes they were more amenable; at other times they stiffened and turned and twisted like salmon. In the latter mood they would get behind any minor rock that happened to be handy. When the public press printed unfortunate captions like 'More Managers Approach the A.A.', they claimed that this was intimidation, as if the A.A. had inspired it.[11]

Cochran made another *démarche*. He changed his mind about retiring, so far as to prepare no fewer than three shows simultaneously. Some of the artists he engaged were A.A. members; but he refused to see a deputation when the A.A. sought an amicable settlement of their differences of opinion. A few weeks after this refusal, he sacked an actor whom he had just found to be a member of the A.A.[12] This was in July, when Valentine's negotiations with the touring managers were at their most difficult. It was part of Valentine's principle that the members must be kept fully cognisant with the way things were going. From time to time he called general meetings, to explain. Attendance at these was very different from attendances in the pre-union days: now there were generally about a thousand present.

Valentine called such a meeting at the Queen's Theatre on the afternoon of Sunday, 27 July. He had to report that a deadlock had been reached with the Touring Managers. They were saying that to pay for rehearsals would wipe out their profits. But this could hardly be true; few tours got more than a fortnight of rehearsals. The manager Dance had agreed to pay a £3 minimum for a seven house week with one seventh extra for any extra house; and even with that, he could afford £1 a week for rehearsal pay. If Dance could do that, so could others. Valentine was right to stand firm. But, he warned them, they might have to compromise a bit for the time. This is important, in view of what followed.

Now for a negotiator to feel he must defend, in the presence of those whom he represents, his line of negotiation before it is complete, is very hard. It is doubly hard when he is arguing with the other side over terms which rising costs have turned into rock bottom, starvation line terms. A negotiator must always have something in hand to give way on, in order to win something bigger. That has been the law of bargaining since the Patriarchs' day. But if he has to plead with his principals during negotiations, and no society is without its secret traitors and snoopers, he must sound apologetic; and if apologetic, then defensive; and defence in attack is always weakness. Valentine was not weakening in himself, although he certainly was a sick man physically and had been due for a long and complete rest for many months past. But with every word of explanation to his audience, he was losing power with the absent managers. Maybe the meeting felt that; at all events, when a member called F. B. J. Sharpe moved that it stand adjourned until the Council saw fit to re-summon it, this was passed *nem. con.* with relief.

The First Act of this dramatic twelvemonth had been the unionisation of the A.A.; the Second Act had ended with the managers' acceptance of the London Standard Contract: both happy scenes. Valentine was determined that, if it was in his power, the Standard Touring Contract also should have a happy curtain line. But alas! the play was written to be a tragedy and already the lights were darkening for the hero's death.

The next month Clifford Rean, an actor with much knowledge

and experience of touring, and who had been largely responsible for crystallising the feeling of the meeting against Valentine's hint of compromise, wrote an eloquent letter to *The Stage*[13] showing that a touring actor needed rehearsal pay far more than did a London actor. Often he would have to face the financial strain, after two weeks unpaid, of fare to destination (£1), porterage of clothes basket (four shillings), extra clothes for play (£3), one week's rent in advance (at least sixteen shillings) making £5 in all; and no money coming in till the end of the first week of playing, and no credit for a touring theatrical in any provincial city.

His opinion that if rehearsal pay were sacrificed, touring players would be bitterly dismayed and angered, was shared by many, especially the touring players themselves. The entire profession had taken heart from the news across the Atlantic, where American actors against even more strongly organised foes were winning their rights by militant action; with famous stars parading the streets, audiences evicted from theatres, strikes, boycotts, and an all-Star Equity propaganda show crowded out night after night. They had learnt all too well the lesson of militancy that Valentine and Lugg taught.[14]

Next month a group of nine players broke into open revolt, Cicely Courtneidge among them. They expressed in *The Stage*[15] their fear of lassitude and lack of organised purpose on the Council. Not that they accused Valentine himself of this, 'no member of the profession', wrote *The Stage* some time later, 'is more respected or better loved than Sidney Valentine'.[16] But they had seen this happen before. The best of intentions can so easily sink in the well meant deliberations of committee government.

Uneasiness grew: there were rumours that a compromise agreement, excluding rehearsal pay, had actually been reached by the Council and the Touring Managers. This was not inaccurate; a compromise had been agreed; and when the terms were published, there was an outcry. For £5 a week minimum meant £2 a week actual, at the best of times, throughout the year. It was not enough; lodgings might cost anything up to forty-five shillings, for a single person, with firing extra. Twenty per cent extra for Twice Nightly was not enough. Even those receiving £6 a week said that this was equivalent to £3 before the war; and not to have rehearsal pay at that rate was pure penalisation. A term that gave particular offence was one that allowed a week 'out' in ten: with unpaid rehearsals this meant that the actor might get not his £3 minimum, but only seven tenths of that.[17]

Besides this some London managers were now disputing the agreed Standard London Contract. In these circumstances it was small comfort – it was irrelevant – that Cochran withdrew his ban on A.A. membership. Disaffection and doubt were widespread: the Council rightly called a special general meeting at the Globe Theatre on the afternoon of Sunday, 30 November.

Well over 1,000 members attended, some travelling long distances to do so, and facing maybe longer ones when it was over. Speaker after speaker rose to reproach the Council for their betrayal. It was not Valentine they blamed; this they made clear, one after another, in that warm generosity of affection that the actor speaker best can express. It was the system itself, to alter which they were one and all prepared to fight. Moreover the Council had exceeded its remit. The motion proposed by Sharpe at the Queen's Theatre in July had not given the Council power to agree to any standard contract; that had been a meeting called to decide what was to be done; the motion to adjourn was tantamount to dropping the Council's proposals; and no alternative proposals had been made. Nor was this meeting now at the Globe being influenced by any sudden hysteria. Members present had had plenty of time to study and discuss the terms announced by the Council in *The Stage*.

Facing them Valentine must have known that they were right. If he had been better in health, he might indeed have congratulated them on their attitude in all sincerity; for this was the very spirit of conscious and determined decisiveness that he had sought to kindle in these very people. But he was not in good health; he was deadly ill; and he had a difficult task before him that afternoon. He could have submitted to them: he could have resigned. Either would have been easy; and cowardly; and wrong. He stuck to the task the Council had laid on him; and even paler than usual, talking, indeed even being there by a pure effort of sustained will, sought to convince them that the prudent way, disappointing though it was, was the best way at present.

He spoke without notes in a clear, carrying voice, with his usual ease and fluency, but with no humour. Neither the time nor the state of his health were right for humour. The Touring Managers, he said, had turned down the first draft flat, and if it came to a fight, they would win this time; for the A.A. though it had made great progress, was not yet strong enough to beat them. On this even the uncompromising Alfred Lugg agreed. Delegates from the A.A. were not masters of their own time, as managers were. The deputations had been thinly attended; once by himself alone. At present an ideal contract, even a satisfactory one, was out of the question. They must aim first at stopping abuses, and limit themselves to that for the time. 'Patience', he said, 'perseverance and courage are the things we need most at the present time. We are doing so well that nobody need have a faint heart.' These were words that he might have been saying about his own physical condition, to hide the truth about that from himself.

By now Valentine was looking so ill, that F. J. Austin jumped to his feet and appealed against the interruptions that had punctuated this speech. Everybody saw how ill their beloved, if on this occasion chided, leader was. Clifford Rean, to end the strain on Valentine and the deadlock of counsels and the obstacles to his own party's aims all at the same time, moved in a most praiseworthy manner that a ballot be taken of the views of the whole membership; which was willingly accepted by the chair. Put as an amendment to Valentine's motion that the contract be accepted, this was carried by the whole meeting except for two dissentient votes, so that Valentine's motion was counted lost. In a very quiet voice Valentine closed the meeting, and the curtains closed on the platform party.

In the queer twilight of the stage working light, as beyond the curtain the members filed up the gangways and through it their voices could be heard discussing the meeting and the sick looks of their chairman, Valentine turned to Alfred Lugg at his side, saying: 'Lugg, I think I've had a stroke. I don't know what's happened, old man; but I can't get out of my chair.' He was helped to a little room at the back of the stage; and Mrs Valentine was sent for, from their house at Clarence Gate, Regent's Park. She was a quiet, capable person, and made no fuss; but when she found him lying on a camp bed in terrible pain, she knew that he was even more seriously ill than he had admitted. With the help of Lugg and Theodore Goddard the Association's solicitor, she got her husband to a taxi, and called on their way home at a specialist's in Harley Street who was available that Sunday. He made an examination, and pronounced cerebral haemorrhage indeed. Valentine sank almost at once into a coma, and after lying unconscious for about three weeks, died on 22 December. He was only fifty-four, and had not been in office two years.[18]

Some measure of what the Association and indeed the whole profession had lost was felt when at the A.G.M. next January all the members stood in silence to his memory. Now the total membership was 5,685; now the credit balance at the Bank reached £3,568. Norman McKinnel, his successor in the chair, proposed that as a tribute, the Association should bestow on some person who had deserved well of the profession, a permanent pension to be called by Valentine's name; and that, again as a tribute and not as a charity, for he had left his widow provided for, the first recipient of this should be Mrs Edith Valentine, herself an actress whose maiden name was Penrose, whom he had married in May 1890. The sum of the pension should be £3, the amount of the minimum pay he had quite literally given his life to secure. It was a tribute which Valentine would have liked best, as everybody who knew him agreed.

Apart from a portrait there is no other memorial of this good, wise and heroic man. There should be; for without him, things would be very much harder for us all today. It was not only that he achieved trade union status vital though that was; it was not only that he compelled the London managers to accept a standard contract. Trade union status would have come without him, for it had to come; and the terms and scope of his model agreement, though it is the basis of the Equity contract to this day, have had to be reshaped and extended by others, as conditions altered. Nor was it only that so many of the rights he formulated continued to inspire and be fought for by those who succeeded him, long after his death. It was rather his spiritual force, his mental clarity, his integral personality and firm example and that these were ready at the right time. 'He knew he was a sick man,' wrote Norman McKinnel, 'months before the end came: he knew he ought to stop, but he chose to go on, because he felt it to be his duty.' It was his duty, because the time and himself coincided. There have been men with his qualities who yet failed to see the way the world was going. There have been others who have seen what was needed, but lacked the qualities to lead their fellows toward it. Yet others saw and did lead, but failed in generalship when the battles came. Valentine did not do so: the reverse over the touring contract was only a tactical reverse; he would have led them beyond it to ultimate victory; of that there is little question. He had the qualities; he saw the times; and he had already accomplished in less than a year what others had failed to start in thirty years. If that is not a proof of greatness in a man's character and life story, I do not know what is. His features, character and outlook should be made familiar to all young beginners in our profession, and be remembered by them later on, when they become rich and famous and leaders themselves.

Notes and References

1. Professor J. Henry Richardson, op. cit., p. 147.
2. *The Stage*, 6 February and 22 May 1919.
3. Ibid., 13 February 1919.
4. Quoted in *The Stage*, 20 March 1919.
5. *The Stage*, 3 April 1919.
6. Ibid.
7. Ibid., 10 April 1919.
8. Ibid., 17 April 1919.
9. Ibid., 1 May, 8 May 1919.
10. Ibid., 10 July 1919.
11. Ibid., 19 June 1919.
12. Ibid., 10 July 1919.
13. Ibid., 14 August 1919.
14. Alfred Harding, *The Revolt of the Actors*. New York, 1929. Chaps VII to XIII. An exciting book.
15. *The Stage*, 18 September 1919.
16. Ibid., 4 December 1919.
17. Ibid, 6 November, 20 November 1919.
18. *Evening Standard, London*, 23 December 1919. *The Stage*, 4 December, 11 December 1919, 25 December 1919, 8 January, 5 February 1920.

CHAPTER ELEVEN

The Managers Dig
Themselves In

*The existing state of affairs will continue in
England for actors until the A.A., working as
one individual, insists on its being altered.
That is to say, until the highest and the
lowest members of the Association are ready
to back their opinions by going on strike
for bare justice.*

Arnold Bennett, in a letter to
Sidney Valentine

After Valentine's collapse and before his actual death his personality was given what then seemed permanent memorial by J. M.
Gatti, President of the West End Managers, who asked that the
agreed London Standard Contract should be called by his name.[1]
A month after an impressive solo voice had sung *Crossing the Bar*
from the organ loft during the private funeral at Golders Green,
his other chief adversaries, the Touring managers, holding their
first annual dinner at the First Avenue Hotel, Holborn, drank to
his memory a solemn toast proposed by their Chairman, Bernard
Hishin.[2]

These expressions of regret by the managers were sincere; but
the A.A. Councillors would have been foolish if they had thought
them anything more. These were but salutes of honour to a fine

enemy general killed in battle. Preparations for a prolongation of the war, indeed of a final offensive to end it in victory for their side went on.

The Association flock was not shepherdless. If trade unions cannot fight without leaders, neither does one leader make a trade union. Valentine had educated or released, but not created. It is no detraction to him to say that the witty Norman McKinnel took his place. McKinnel was another sympathetic character, liked and respected by the managers,[3] and well fired by Alfred Lugg as Secretary, even if he lacked Valentine's warmth and patience, and was indeed once heard to say in a moment of exasperation, that he was not going to kill himself for a lot of unemployables.[4] So led the A.A. marched forward on the Valentine line.

The ballot that had been demanded by Clifford Rean, taken in December, showed an enormous support for the agreed contract, however inadequate it was: 1,072 to 424 votes. Possibly Valentine's seizure had something to do with this; but it shows what he might have been able to do as a leader if he had lived. It had been made clear to the voters that this was only a temporary expedient as Valentine himself had tried to make clear; it was repudiable by either side after being tried out for fifty-two weeks, and then at one year's notice. Valentine was lying unconscious when the Touring Managers agreed to reduce the notice to three months. The bargain must hold till the Spring of 1921; and the Council turned to other matters. First, the licensing of managers, which seemed the only cure for bogus managements.[5]

The drive for this had been started by Valentine, McKinnel and Lugg the previous year. They called on the L.C.C.'s Public Control Committee, who laid the idea before the L.C.C. itself, which agreed and sent it on to the Home Office. But by now the A.A. was too wise in its methods to leave it there to cook. At a meeting of 'all people interested in the theatre' convened in St Martin's vestry by the Bishop of London, Sir A. F. Winnington Ingram, Valentine explained the scheme; the Bishop promised, if necessary, to introduce a Bill into the House of Lords. The Lord Chamberlain was also interviewed, and promised his serious consideration. It was rumoured that a Private Member's Bill might be laid before the Commons to stimulate government action. Thus there was the possibility of a threefold encircling movement.[6]

The Managers opened fire at once. A body called the Provincial Entertainment Proprietors' and Managers' Association protested to the Home Secretary that all proprietors and managers were already licensed locally, and that they viewed this threat of bureaucratisation with grave concern. This was a clever decoy; and the Touring Managers, the real quarry, escaped into the bushes. A week later the Home Secretary, Edward Shortt, announced in the House that he did not see his way to introducing legislation on the lines suggested.[7] McKinnel and Lugg therefore approached the Touring Managers' camp for a direct parley. They met Herbert Ralland, Arthur Gibbons, Frank Weathersby, Carlton Wallace, and their Secretary Louis Casson[8]; but the Touring Managers would not give way an inch. Indeed they snubbed the envoys. To a gathering of managing societies at the Empire, Leicester Square, the following week, no invitations were issued to the Association or any stage trade union. Indeed, a counter-suggestion was made that in the interests of managements, artists should be licensed.[9]

Battle was joined. Their first two reverses showed the A.A. Council the hidden power-lines behind the enemy. They referred the question to the Joint Industrial Council of the Entertainments Industry, and tried other avenues of attack. In these new avenues they made some mistakes. Complaints of insanitary theatres were sent straight to the Ministry of Health, before approaching local councils. This enabled the Minister, Dr Addison, when the 'actors' MP' Charles Palmer asked a question in the House, to reply that out of nineteen cases brought to his notice, four were being already dealt with locally, and twelve should have been so dealt with before applying to him.[10] However, the Council persisted, and published lists of 'good' theatres in *The Stage*. The Minister had to investigate, and as a result of what he found, two years later a circular was issued advising all local authorities that in future inspectors of nuisances would periodically visit all theatres and report any un-satisfactory sanitation. From now on complaints to the Council became fewer and fewer, until they were quite unusual.[11]

The Association grew in size and in prestige. There had been, by the A.G.M. of 1920, only fifty-seven resignations and new members were joining at the rate of eighty-six a week. Lugg claimed a total membership of 6,700; but this was still a small proportion of all actors and actresses, compared with 13,000 stage hands organised in the N.A.T.E. and 16,000 stage musicians in the M.U. A new drive for membership was begun; Councillors under-took a personal canvass of suburban companies. Lugg visited the Carl Rosa Company at the King's, Hammersmith, and came back with 143 new applications for membership! Public meetings were held outside London, the first at Manchester with Lugg in the chair and splendid services rendered by Jessica Black and Clifford Rean. As a result of this, five companies became 100 per cent A.A. James Stilwell even began to publicise his company as a trade union one, deserving the support of all trade unionists. It was decided to hold such meetings monthly in the provinces and Scotland.[12]

The managers were now attacking back in earnest. Already in January 1920 one provincial management which had been displeased by the quite imprudent behaviour of an A.A. representative in his company threatening all kinds of offensive action and triumphs when the original standard contract should be agreed, noted how quickly, when its actual terms were published, this member resigned from the A.A. saying haughtily that it would do him no good.[13] The management then victimised the small part A.A. members in the company.[14] Such cases were hard to prevent happening and equally hard to deal with when they had happened. It was impossible to tell on which managers even the temporary and unsatisfactory standard contract could be enforced; for the Secretary of the Touring Managers, Louis Casson, refused to reveal the names of managements belonging to that body, on whom it would be binding. 'They have very good reason for not doing so', muttered McKinnel fiercely.[15]

Some managers were members, but not the managements for whom they worked. A Mrs Kimberley, for example, among the biggest of touring managers, owned a company playing *Little Old Mother of Mine* twice nightly. The manager in charge, Carlyle, though a member of the T.M.A. in his own right, and therefore individually bound by its agreement, refused to pay the agreed one-twelfth extra for extra matinees. When the A.A. challenged him as bound by the bond, he changed his mind, and said he would pay; until Mrs Kimberley herself appeared on the scene, a powerful-minded business-woman, denying that he had authority from her to do such a thing, nor would ever have, because she was not a member of the T.M.A. The A.A. called on its members to make a stand on this issue, with a backing if they were discharged of £3 a month, till they got other engagements. It would have been happy if the first actors' strike had taken place on such a principle, which was a good, clear and important one. But Mrs Kimberley was shrewd enough to avoid this. She announced that she would adopt the standard contract.[16]

One had to be very careful with one's words. Managers were on the alert, and the use of the laws of defamation was and still can be a favourite method for a person of position to silence an attack, sometimes for ever. For a small but significant example; Lugg happened to remark at a meeting with the Bishop of London that in the 'smalls' of Scotland, Wales and England, the bogus manager outnumbered the legitimate. This was reported to the Joint Council of the Entertainment Industry as if he had made the charge against all the managers in the country; and the A.A. had some trouble in clearing this up.[17]

Indeed it is hard to see how else the Touring Managers could have behaved. Their plight was becoming desperate. Just as the London syndicates had squeezed out the actor-managers, so now the provincial proprietors and managers were squeezing out the touring ones. There was a financial slump in the theatre due to many causes. Many a sound touring manager began with adequate capital and anticipated adequate returns; but by misrepresentations of what may best be called 'bogus resident managers' they sometimes lost most of what they had, and were faced with either going out of business or forcing harsher terms on their employees. This happened, at any rate, to some of the smaller independent firms; the larger ones and the combines, some of which were mere subsidiaries of multiple managements and amalgamated owners, kept the best dates to themselves; or, if they did not themselves require the dates they had bespoken, they would sell them to other large firms who could afford the extra prices. On this tendency the agencies 'cashed in', thereby further increasing the price of a good date in the provinces; until at last it became impossible to get one that would be worth taking without doing so through an agency, which might well be another subsidiary of a multiple firm. One independent touring manager did in fact receive only five available dates out of 300 applications that he made.[18]

Agencies charged at least ten per cent of the small manager's takings. If the play had any reputation another ten per cent went to its author. But the resident manager did not contribute to these charges; his 55 per cent or 60 per cent was taken from the gross, before division. Printing bills, which were payable by the touring manager – and some resident managers insisted on large pictorial posters – might consume £50 a week. Railway rates were up; travelling might consume a further £25. That is to say nothing of extra charges for supplementary furniture and so on for actual performance.[19] In many ways it would have been to the interest of the small independent touring manager to have thrown in his lot with the actor; for multiple firms have very big mouths, and are apt to swallow a gowpen of small employers when they gulp at a shoal of small employees. But this the T.M.A. took good care they should not do.

So the actors had to defend themselves by themselves. This they did, drastically, in the autumn of 1920. It was the first actors' strike in history called by an organised trade union on an industrial dispute. It caused a sensation, even though it lasted less than half an hour. Bromley Challenor, touring his capital farce *When Knights were Bold*, was reported to have issued no contracts at all. The A.A. representative in his company was instructed to ask for standard contracts, and did so in August when they were playing King's Lynn. About the same time Challenor put up a notice saying that the tour could be ended at one week's notice. The A.A.'s solicitor, Goddard, wrote to him, pointing out that this was a breach of agreement, since he was a member of the T.M.A. Challenor made no move. At Shrewsbury the show was given twice nightly. The A.A. representative was instructed to ask for twenty per cent extra. This was granted.

When the company reached St. Alban's in September, Lugg went out to see Challenor, who said he might consider granting the terms of the standard contract, but would first have to consult Rowland, the secretary of the Theatrical Managers, on his way through London to Chatham where they were playing the following week. He made no such call. Lugg wrote to him at Chatham, warning him that the A.A. would boycott his show if he did not soon make up his mind. Challoner did not reply. At Chatham also the show was given twice nightly with a Saturday matinee; and Lugg instructed the artists not to appear at the Friday second house unless they were guaranteed one twelfth pay for the matinee next day. Challenor refused. The artists accordingly remained in their dressing-rooms. The audience were in; but the curtain remained firmly down.

Challenor would not give in. Neither would the company. After twenty-five minutes the audience was getting restive and something would have to be done; either Challenor must give in, or he must go in front and tell the audience to go and get their money back from the Box Office. Then a certain Lionel Barnard stepped in, saying he would guarantee payment. So the show went on, after all. But in Plymouth again Challenor refused matinee payment, and only a telegram from Lugg instructing similar action by the company exacted the required additional payment. Later the position was remedied by 'amicable agreement'.[20]

A small affair, this Chatham strike; but it showed one thing clearly, and that was not small. It showed the actor what he was up against, that even this hard-won disappointing standard contract was useless as protection, unless, as Lugg had long foreseen, actors were bonded together in a closed shop powerful enough to resist such twistings of managements without having continually to be in threatening attitudes. For thirty years the Association had been remedying abuses by threats of legal action; now it must prevent abuses by threats of industrial action. This lesson was clear if Challenor was a representative manager; everyone knew he was.

On the other side the strike showed the Managers that the Actors' Association, despite the loss of Sidney Valentine, was as determined as ever. It also inspired the managers to as great a stubbornness as ever. They saw to it that the Joint Industrial Council got nowhere in discussing the licensing of managers. In October, feeling strong enough to do so, the A.A. withdrew from the Joint Council on the grounds that it could serve its members better from outside. Nor did the Bishop of London get very much farther; he took the Council's delegates officially to the Lord Chamberlain together with other delegates from the V.A.F. But Lord Sandhurst observed unhelpfully that he had not in his department the necessary machinery, and suggested setting up a Grand Council of managers and performers, not unlike the General Medical Council, to license touring managers.[21]

Then the Bishop grew more cautious, saying that until he had received the Bill 'from the other side' he could not go through with his offer to sponsor such a thing through the Lords, but promised that if he did receive anything in that way, the A.A. would be given an opportunity to approve it before he acted.[22] Impatient at such common bureaucratic evasions, the A.A. now turned to the other trade unions, and made full use of its trade union status by bringing the question before the Annual Conference of the T.U.C. at Portsmouth in September 1920. Their resolution, spoken to with great eloquence and effect by Alfred Lugg and Sydney Paxton whose speeches were the talk of the conference, was carried unanimously by that body; as was a similar resolution concerning theatrical agencies moved by the V.A.F.[23] As an ultimate but direct result of this, in 1922, C. W. Bowerman, MP for Deptford, introduced a bill for the minority Labour Party, under the title The Theatrical Employers' Registration Bill, on terms agreed by the A.A., V.A.F., N.A.T.E, and M.U. The Theatrical Managers' Association went at once into action; they circularised M.P.s asking them to vote against it. Bogus managers, they said, were so few, that 'the inquisition into the whole management of theatrical affairs' which this would give rise to, was unnecessary. The cry of 'freedom' in the gentlemanly short-hand quoted above was immediately effective, as it generally is among property-owners, and the Bill was duly blocked by Sir Walter de Freece.[24]

On the other hand, there were small but pleasant indications that the doings of the Association were of agreeable interest to the general public. When it opened a Manchester branch in 1923, the enterprising manager of the big Clarendon Hotel offered it accommodation free of charge, because he would like it to be known that the A.A. met there. He would hardly have made such an offer, unless he had expected it to bring in business.[25] There were some other indications that it was thinking along the right lines. The case of *Clayton-Greene* v. *De Courville*,[26] concerning *The Very Idea* at the St Martin's Theatre and subsequently on tour in the spring and summer of 1919, in which the A.A. was supporting the plaintiff, was heard by Mr Justice McCardie in July 1920. That learned and admirable judge, who spent so much of his free bachelor hours in poring over the principles and practice of any technical case that came before him, and who had also gained much first-hand knowledge of stage law when himself a barrister, gave judgement on two matters over which the A.A. had hoped for just such a progressive ruling. First, Mr Justice McCardie found that a 'London engagement' meant, by theatrical custom of which judicial notice was taken, an 'engagement for the duration of the run' if nothing were said specifically to the contrary. Secondly, he found that a producer working for a management engaged artists as the agent of that management, and it was accordingly bound by his actions in the relation of principal and agent. Both these rulings, of which the former was evidence that the law had developed since 1911, were of great importance in reducing the advantage that a management could take of an innocent player: and players could and can be innocent to a degree almost of imbecility in legal matters. In 1896 Kitty Loftus, wishing to correct a wrong impression that had been given of her in a report of a lawsuit, wrote to a society magazine: 'I signed my contract without reading all the rules and regulations on the fly-leaf, as they always seem to contain so many unnecessary things.'[27] Nor was that unknown in 1920; nor is it quite impossible today.

For the next two or three years the Association fought to clear away the evils that still clung round the lives of actors and actresses, still almost as deplorable as those described in our first chapter. The particularly nasty scandal known as the 'Arnold Case' focused attention on one of these. A manager paying his company by shares in the net profits with £1 a week guaranteed to three of the girls, when one of these girls was taken to hospital with scarlet fever, had compelled another to wear her costume not disinfected or even cleaned. Subsequent investigation revealed that the low pay actually given to the company had compelled a girl of eighteen to become the paid mistress of a creature mentally and physically deformed.[28] Other cases that offended the profession deeply were a swindler who in his period out of jail described himself as an actor; and also the number of prostitutes claiming stage careers when arrested, which caused a policeman once to observe that the streets were cleaner during pantomime seasons. Stranded companies were as frequent as ever, certain theatres like the Empire at Maidstone and the Theatre Royal at Stratford being notorious for this. Chorus girls who earned only thirty shillings a week were frequent. Manager after manager was proceeded against on one count or another; but fines seemed to make little difference.[29]

Negotiations with the Touring Managers for a more equitable contract to replace the one agreed by Valentine as a temporary measure broke down altogether in 1922, the Secretary, Louis Casson treating a further application by the A.A. with a rudeness and brusquerie that indicated utter contempt.[30] Even the Valentine London Contract was often disregarded in the West End, and sometimes A.A. members in such companies, afraid of victimisation, would accept whatever terms they were offered.[31] Managers like Fred Karno granted verbal concessions to Lugg and his helpers in interviews, and then twisted out of them when the visitors had gone. Comedians like Jackson Owen pressed junior artists not to join the A.A. at all. The root causes of all these things could be analysed down to three: recalcitrance on the managers' part; bogus managers; and unregulated entry to the profession.

There was only one form of counteraction possible: the Closed Shop. Hitherto this had seemed to be a remote dream; now it was considered to be practicable. For this purpose a series of explanatory special meetings took place throughout 1923, addressed by such believers in the principle as Miss Horniman, Patrick Hastings, K.C., Donald Calthrop, J. B. Williams, the founder of the Musicians' Union. In a ballot taken thereafter a majority of 596 approved of making an attempt at a Closed Shop. But nothing could be done without close ties binding the A.A. to the other stage trade unions; and a further ballot, taken after a meeting had been addressed by John Emerson, the President of American Equity, who recommended one grand Federation of them all, approved of the idea of federation in the following figures: with V.A.F., 1,106, with A.M.U., 830; with N.A.T.E., 660.[32]

It seemed, therefore, as if the feeling of members favoured, and therefore justified, the drive for a Closed Shop; but the Association was still a sad minority of the profession as a whole. It was therefore prudent, as a final alternative to force, to consult those still outside, and the managers as well, in the hope that some means might be found by joint action to put an end for ever to undesirables in the profession, whether bogus managers or bogus players. A public meeting was accordingly held in April 1924 at the Haymarket Theatre with Arthur Bourchier in the chair, over which Time played a curious trick on the Council. Even while peaceful methods were being discussed, that very Sunday afternoon, war had broken out at Barrow-in-Furness.

I do not know of any instance when the Closed Shop policy has just happened by rational discussion between both sides. If all employees and all employables are to be members of a trade union, whose aims and rights are bound sooner or later to conflict, then no employer in his senses would do anything but resist its growth and fight while it is still small. Strike or be struck is the jungle law for both sides of every trade at early stages. Later when both sides are equally strong, discussion and concession are possible. Later the theatrical trade could learn, as Lord Esher was to put it, 'that compromise in conflict is the civilised way'.[33] But that would only come from a balance of power. That depended, as Alfred Lugg foresaw in November 1920, when he wrote to *The Stage* to that effect, on 'real co-operation between managers and actors by all of each being in the Theatrical Managers Association and the A.A.' At present not all were in either; might ruled in the jungle.

At Barrow-in-Furness a company touring in *Anna Christie* were due to play a week in the Tivoli Theatre. Three weeks before, they had been at Penge where George Fry, an A.A. organiser, had visited them, warning that the Closed Shop policy was to be put in action by the time they reached Barrow-in-Furness, and that they must all join a Union. Two of the company filled in forms of application to join the A.A.; and two others said they had already done so. According to Fry no one else was at that time a member of any Union. However, a week before they got to Barrow, the A.A. learned that the whole company had joined the V.A.F., and received a letter from the V.A.F.'s secretary, Fred Herbert, hoping that they would not be molested. Lugg replied with a moderate-toned desire that for trade union purposes some satisfactory line could be drawn between variety and legitimate stage performers.

Later still it was reported that the V.A.F. and the Touring Managers had come to an agreement against the Federal Council which had been set up by the A.A., N.A.T.E. and A.M.U.[34] Lugg took what he considered correct action, and informed the General Secretary of the T.U.C. Meanwhile the V.A.F. had applied to the lawcourts for an injunction restraining the A.A. from boycotting *Anna Christie*.

Keith Kenneth, the manager of the *Anna Christie* company now had a chance to discredit in public the A.A., which, he said quite truthfully, had told his company at Penge that they must join *a* Union and now told them that they ought to have joined the A.A. His company, he said, did not wish to join the A.A., as was obvious from their unanimous act in joining the V.A.F.; and he, as manager, was in peril of being victimised by a squabble between rival trade unions. A not unreasonable complaint, in the circumstances. Once committed to action, the A.A. picketed the railway station, so that no scenery, costumes or properties could be removed. No musicians presented themselves at the Tivoli; but the stage staff did, having apparently received no instructions from London to the contrary. The house filled, and the curtain went up on a play without scenery or costumes, but was shortly lowered again, having commenced a formal performance. Notices were posted that the theatre was indefinitely closed; and the unfortunate Tivoli manager had to refund £50 for booked seats.

Monte Bayly, national organiser of the V.A.F., and Hugh Roberts, general secretary of N.A.T.E., both of whom had just arrived post-haste in the town, went into conference till 11 o'clock that night; but could reach no agreement. Monte Bayly's comment later was: 'The closed shop is the gospel of the incompetent to bolster up the unemployable.' Alfred Lugg arrived, straight from the Haymarket Theatre meeting, but too late to change the situation in any degree. Bayly, with Keith Kenneth and all the company, had just left for London. Bayly, curiously enough, was in the awkward position of being also a member of the A.A., which now formally suspended him.

That week the Incorporated Association of Touring Managers,[35] in the American phrase, here aptly descriptive, 'went to town'. It put a half-page advertisement in *The Stage*, printed in 30-point type with banner headlines, which stated that the I.A.T.M. recognised the right of any artist to become a member of a trade union, but protested against intimidation, victimisation, or coercion to '*enforce* joining in those many cases where persuasion and argument have not availed.' This was signed by Percy Hutchison, Chairman, and Louis Casson, Secretary. Every manager in Britain was delighted.[36]

The incident was unfortunate in becoming so celebrated. It had none of the features of a good test case. Nothing would have arisen if Mr Fry had been a little more adroit and persuasive at Penge, if he had refrained from tempting the V.A.F. to do a little extra recruiting. At the same time it is not easy to see what possible future in the music-hall world, which was the province of the V.A.F., there could be for artists appearing in a play like *Anna Christie*. Even if their act were helping trade unionism in general, the V.A.F. was, to put it vulgarly, poaching. Once poaching had started, the A.A. could not have drawn back its hand or stopped the boycott without admitting itself to be in the wrong and weakening its future bargaining power.

The theatre world rang with the quarrel, while it was still in the distance. Bourchier ruled it out as a theme at the Haymarket meeting, but Bronson Albury for the managers nonetheless brought it in. He made the case his text in moving an amendment to J. Fisher White's motion endorsing the action of the A.A. in trying to regulate entry to the profession. Endorsing the A.A., he said, meant endorsing Barrow; and endorsing Barrow meant endorsing war to the knife and ruin to the industry.[36]

In a sense, these were prophetic words. War to the knife certainly ensued, but the armoury belonged mostly to the managers. Even at the Haymarket, there was an abrupt and decided cleavage. Actor-managers like J. M. Glover, Lady Wyndham, Lena Ashwell, ranged themselves on one side; players, like Gladys ffolliott (Valentine's mother-in-law), and Robert Young, on the other; with Miss Lilian Bayliss characteristically, caustically and concisely announcing that if they didn't place the matter in the hands of the A.A., there was nowhere else to place it.[37]

If it had been a mere cleavage on a matter of future policy, the fire of Alfred Lugg, the sage counsels of Fisher White, and the devoted service of the organisers and staff might yet have prevailed. No one side ever really declares a war; but the managers were doing well enough to have avoided one if they wished, whereas the A.A. had to fight. Ruin indeed did now face the industry; but it was not due to Barrow. It was due to the rot that had long set in within the Association itself.

Despite the growing prestige and energy of the A.A. since 1919, a crisis was occurring; a crisis imperceptible, perhaps, except to the unsuspecting clerical heads which number membership cards or total up figures. But the truth lay there, all the same. By November 1920, the membership of the A.A. had dropped to about 5,500. By February 1923, although in the previous year new members had over-topped one thousand, the total had fallen seriously; to 3,766.[38] Only one conclusion can be drawn from these figures. New and presumably younger members were attracted by something in the A.A.'s policy; older members were repelled by something that made them distrustful.

What else could this be, but the trade union policy itself? The very vigour; the fire and wisdom; the new turn to the old debate: Managers, For, or Against? Mistake though it was, Barrow had this one usefulness and value: it showed everybody where they belonged. It tore aside uncomfortably the beautiful curtain that had concealed the gulf; it compelled the whole profession to take a stand definitely on the one side of it or the other. The pity lay not in Barrow; but in the result. So many actors and actresses, perfectly sincere in their wish to do the best for the profession they loved, went and stood on the wrong side – As the managers counted on their doing, while they prepared their own next advance.

Notes and References

1. *The Stage*, 11 December 1919.
2. Ibid., 29 January 1920.
3. Sir Lewis Casson in personal conversation.
4. Letter from Alfred Lugg to the author. *The Stage*, 25 December 1919.

5. *The Stage*, 11 December 1919.
6. Ibid., 5 February, 19 February 1920.
7. *Hansard*, 24 February 1920, 1474, 34, quoted in *The Stage*, 26 February 1920.
8. A word of warning in this confusion. This R. Louis Casson, who had been in business and later owned some light musical companies of his own, should not be identified in any way with our own staunch and eminent Lewis S. Casson. Such confusion did at one time exist, and was not helped by *Louis* Casson dropping his distinguishing first initial. I do not think I am breaking any confidence if I quote Sir Lewis for saying that matters became still worse when it was found that both had married ladies called Sybil, and both had children called Christopher and Mary. Neither Louis nor Lewis is a common Casson name.
9. *The Stage*, 4 March, 11 March, 18 March 1920.
10. *Hansard*, 19 May 1920, 1401, 35. *The Stage*, 27 May, 24 June 1920.
11. *The Stage*, 2 September 1922.
12. *The Stage*, 5 February, 22 April, 24 June, 1920. I think Lugg was misreported, and that the total of membership was 5,700, not 6,700.
13. Alfred Lugg at the A.G.M., 4 February, 1923.
14. Letter from 'A.A. 3402' in *The Stage*, 8 January 1920.
15. *The Stage*, 5 February 1920.
16. *The Stage*, 29 January, 5 February 1920.
17. *Minutes of the A.A. Chairman's Committee*, 29 March 1921. Also Archibald Haddon, *Green Room Gossip*, London, 1922, pp. 29–30.
18. *The Stage*, 22 January, 29 January 1920.
19. Editorial article in *The Stage*, 18 November 1920.
20. *The Stage*, 14 October 1920; but see also a letter to *The Stage*, 30 December 1920.
A good deal of threatening and manoeuvring went on behind the scenes. Thus the Council was preparing to deal a hard blow at Percy Broadhead in Manchester by following up with boycott action each of his four companies wherever they toured after leaving that city. But happily Broadhead proved amenable. It was really the touring managers using his theatres who were to blame, not he himself. *A.A. Chairman's Committee*, p. 12, undated, but about November 1920.
21. *The Stage*, 1 July, 8 July 1920.
22. *Minutes of the A.A. Chairman's Committee*, 29 March 1921.
23. *The Stage*, 9 September 1920.
24. Alfred Lugg at A.G.M., 4 February 1923. And *The Stage*, 11 November 1920.
25. *A.A. Council Minutes*, 7 May 1923.
26. *Clayton-Greene* v. *De Courville*. K.B.D. 36 T.L.R., 790–1. Sometimes referred to erroneously, as *Greene* v. *de Courville*.
27. *The Pelican*, 1 February 1896.
28. This case is well known to law students as *Brimelow* v. *Casson and others* (1924), 1 Ch. 302. The plaintiff, professionally known as Jack Arnold, applied for an injunction against Messrs. Casson, Voyce, and Fry, as officials of the Joint Protection Committee set up by the Association of Touring Managers, the V.A.F., A.A., M.U. and N.A.T.E. which had persuaded a theatre proprietor at Dudley to cancel his date for accepting Arnold's revue, which constituted an interference with contractual rights. Russel J. in an enlightened and

courageous judgement held that 'if such interference might not exist here, he could hardly conceive a case in which it would be present'; he found that there was in fact here a trade dispute, and the presence of the Touring Managers on the Committee did not alter this. 'It was a dispute which concerned the general body of actors on the one hand, and an employer of actors on the other'; and he dismissed the application with costs.

A notable triumph for the actors' cause.

29. See the *A.A. COUNCIL Minutes* for the winter of 1923–4.

30. A. Harding Steerman in the chair at the A.G.M., 4 February 1923. Alfred Lugg at the same meeting. The correspondence was published in *The Stage*, in January 1923.

31. *A.A. Council Minutes*, 3 April 1920.

32. Alfred Lugg at the A.G.M., Aldwych Theatre, 4 February 1923.

33. Quoted by Hannen Swaffer, 'The Theatre's Future', *Daily Herald*, 22 April 1942.

34. The Federal Council (A.A. + N.A.T.E. + A.M.U.) should not be confused with the Joint Protection Committee set up by the V.A.F. + Touring Managers to eliminate bogus managers. This latter failed, because it eliminated the right to strike. See H. R. Barbor, *The Theatre: an Art and an Industry* (London, 1924), p. 15. A joint Committee of all four was established in March 1919 and dissolved in June 1924 for lack of cooperation.

35. This was the new title of the old A.T.M. I should point out for the benefit of any scholars that even stage papers and semi-official documents refer throughout to managers' associations somewhat ambiguously, sometimes calling this body, for instance, the Touring Managers' Association, and sometimes even using the initials T.M.A., which only the context can differentiate from the Theatrical Managers' Association; and not always that.

36. This account of the *Anna Christie* case is drawn mainly from the A.A. Council Minutes during April, May, June and September 1924. Also the theatrical and general press of the time.

37. According to a special entry in the A.A. Council Minutes for 1 May 1924, Alfred Lugg had, at the Haymarket meeting on Monday, 28 April, made another 'brilliant speech'. My account is taken from the press of the time.

38. These figures were given by Lugg at the A.G.M., 4 February 1923.

CHAPTER TWELVE

The Stage Guild

The profession will have to make up its mind
whether it is practising an art, or smelting.
Bronson Albery on
The Closed Shop Principle

Within six weeks of the Barrow case and the Haymarket meeting,
the Touring Managers founded the Stage Guild. It had nominally
equal divisions of actors and managements; and one of its two
joint secretaries was the Touring Managers' secretary, Louis
Casson.

Some such action had been preparing for a long while; but at a
Committee Meeting of the Touring Managers, G. Carlton Wallace,
who had been a member since 1903, happened to observe that
judging from his own twenty-one years' experience in management, all difficulties arising in the course of theatrical business
could be easily settled by goodwill and discussion round a table.
The hint was taken at once: heads of all sections of theatre
business, actors, managers, dramatists and orchestra conductors,
were brought together; the Stage Guild was the inevitable result.[1]
'I think Mr Barbor is right', wrote Sybil Thorndike in 1924, 'in his
view that the Stage Guild was originally founded by managers to
counteract the menace of a strong union, and has been greatly
assisted by a number of actors who live in a dreamland where the
theatre is still run by artists.'[2]

The Guild was a 'company limited by guarantee'; and the subscribers to the Memorandum and Articles of Association were: Athole Stewart, actor; Sir Johnston Forbes-Robertson, retired actor-manager; F. Leslie Moreton, manager; G. Carlton Wallace, manager and author; Arthur Gibbons, Manager of the Royalty Theatre; C. Aubrey Smith, actor; Lyn Harding, actor; Sir Frank Benson, actor-manager; Eva Moore, actress shortly going into management; and Fred Terry, actor-manager. There were three sections: actors', managers' and authors'; with equal one third representation on the Grand Council.

The Council became very grand. Sir Johnston Forbes-Robertson was President, and the twelve vice-presidents included Benson, Pinero, Du Maurier, Martin Harvey, Godfrey Tearle and Henry Arthur Jones; while among the eighteen members of Grand Council were Harold Brighouse, Aubrey Smith, Sir Barry Jackson, Ian Hay, Franklyn Dyall and Carlton Wallace. Louis Casson was secretary of the managers' section, and A. Dixon Taylor of the artists'. Before long F. J. Nettlefold, the big industrialist (screws, etc.) was Chairman of Council, and a Major McGowan was engaged as General Secretary.

Within one year its total membership reached 2,000, which included a large number of actors and actresses. The individual managers numbered only some 400; but these were mostly of the commercial type, potentially influencing any number from twenty to 200 employees; and the power of the managers' section, if not on paper, was in fact very great.[3] Many of the players who joined were prominent West-End stars on the road to success, and suspicious and scared of trade unionism, which they did not understand, and about which they had been misinformed. It is curious that few, if any, of them seem to have seen anything suspicious about the Stage Guild, although its first 'object' mentioned in Clause 3 of the Memorandum, empowers the Guild to take over the Association of Touring Managers if it so wishes; and within two and a half months of formation it had drafted and gained the agreement of both Managers' and Artists' sections to a Standard Touring Contract which was anything but an improvement for actors on even Valentine's unsatisfactory project. But the reason lies in the inability of enough people to appreciate the difference between conditions in London and conditions outside it, which were harsh and intolerable. Too many indeed believed sincerely that protection against exploitation was unnecessary. In their own cases the good actor was the successful one, who

THE ACTOR'S RIGHT TO ACT

It abolished a minimum period of employment: two weeks' notice, at any time, ended an engagement. It retained a minimum salary, but any manager could now engage a proportion of his company at less than that: one quarter of the cast in musical, repertory, and Shakespearian shows, one fifth in all others. Now an actor had to give two weeks or one week of rehearsal unpaid, according to the length of the proposed tour; this in itself was, of course, a purely nominal period if two weeks' notice could at any time terminate it. The managers smuggled through a brute of a 'safe-guarding' clause: if after the third rehearsal an artist were not perfect in his part, words and business, he could be dismissed without pay. This proviso could be used to shorten the rehearsal period, and so reduce rehearsal pay. In costume, too, there were now strictures. Ladies must no longer expect to be provided with any dresses or hats, or any allowance toward these, except in specifically 'costume' parts. Every ten weeks there could be a week 'out', without pay of any kind; a week was to consist of seven performances, and any extra performance beyond that would entitle the artist to an extra one-seventh of the salary. In all these, and other, respects the advantage was given back to the managements.

But, grand though it sounded, this Stage Guild was no more exempt from financial difficulties than was the most modest group of university poets seeking publication. Various schemes were advanced, as had been in the Actors' Association, for raising funds. Perhaps the most ingenious was that proposed by Carlton Wallace. Percy Hutchison had suggested that provincial managers, considering the advantages that the Guild might bring to them financially, should provide special benefit matinees. Now not every manager could afford so expensive a subsidy. Carlton Wallace therefore submitted that the Guild should buy one stated house for a lump sum in each theatre chosen, publicise the performance as a Stage Guild Benefit Night, and pocket the difference between the gross takings and the sum paid to the theatre. Nobody would lose; and the Guild would gain.

The covering letter that was sent with this proposal, apart from one rather specious sentence about the Guild's ability to smooth over any difficulties that might arise in relation to employment, describes the Guild as working without fear or favour entirely in the best interests of both sides; as, I am certain, many members truly believed it would. Godfrey Tearle, an active Councillor, most decidedly did so at the outset of his membership. Most of them, I am convinced, truly believed also that this anomalous herding of employers and employed, of sheep and goats, into the one pasture would result in the elimination of rival interests, not in their suppression by greater force.

No provision was made in the constitution for arbitration between actors and managers within the Guild. Such matters were to be settled by amicable discussion. This was indeed to be the chief rock of foundation.

Just how well it worked cannot at present be told, for there are very few Minutes of meetings that are available. The Association of Touring and Producing Managers in whose possession, if they still existed, such documents might have been expected to lie, has in fact only six leaves, dated November 1925 to March 1926, torn from a quarto ruled minute-book and signed by Percy Hutchison or Alfred Denville. These appear to be of a series of meetings of provincial members of the Managers' Section held at Manchester, but they are too vague to be of much use without more knowledge of the background thereto.

Carbon copies must have been circulated to all Council members; but the only specimen to which I have had access is a single one in the possession of Mr Carlton Wallace. This contains a somewhat mysterious entry, which I print in full because of its ambiguous phrasing.

Arising out of correspondence from two parties to separate Arbitrations pending which, in both cases, objection was raised to signing a submission in view of the disputants having already signed the Guild Contract, and further objection being taken to the ruling out of the right of legal representation. Mr Sarton Pearman, the Guild's solicitor, attended and advised Grand Council that he agreed that the objections were valid, but that the difficulty could be overcome by making an alteration in the Guild contract clearly stating that legal representation be dispensed with. In the meantime he would advise the General Secretary of the lines on which to reply to the parties in question.[5]

In the absence of further information, there is only one conclusion to be drawn from this entry as it stands: actors and actresses who signed the Guild contract, as all Guild members had to do, signed away thereby the elementary legal right of all citizens to get a legal arbitrator to any dispute over interpretation. It should be remembered that these surviving Minute pages, in both cases, are those of the *Managers'* Section of the Guild. Evidently the managers intended to keep strict control over the other section.

This view is confirmed by another curious entry in the pages possessed by the A.T.P.M., which refers to a telegram from provincial managers in the following terms:[6]

A telegram was read from Harry Russell apologising for his absence and desiring that a resolution submitted by him should be submitted to the Meeting. This Resolution had reference to the General Secretary being allowed to attend meetings of the Managers' Section and read as follows:

'That this Meeting of Provincial Members strongly protests against the attendance except by special invitation in writing at any Managerial Meeting of any official not directly connected with the Managers' Section, feeling that such attendance will tend to destroy the confidence of provincial members in the independence of the Managers' Section. It further urges the Managers' Council to give effect to this Resolution at an early date.'

After some discussion this resolution was seconded by Edwin T. Heys and upon being put to the meeting was carried unanimously.

Uneasy is the firm in which one partner protests if a joint-clerk, paid to do so, enters his office! The Stage Guild was no partnership; indeed it was a poor sort of 'company limited by guarantee' if one section was secretive about its safeguards of independence. Dissensions must have been frequent; lobbying and intrigue the rule; agreement hard to win; and action, therefore limited.

It was otherwise with the Actors' Association, dwindle though it might – and did. The A.A. was vigorous, even if on some occasions it was not so tactful or prudent as it should have been.

Its Council met weekly, with good attendances. It dealt with many critical conditions for A.A. members. It kept them on relief from the Protection Fund if need be, till their cases were settled. In the case of Fred Karno, for instance, sometimes minimum demands led to his capitulation; but sometimes this was followed by his victimising A.A. members, and this led to further action by the Council against him.[7]

There were more tiresome cases, like that of Sir John Martin Harvey. During his tenancy of the Garrick Theatre in the winter of 1922–3, Martin Harvey altered the terms of his contracts in the manner known to diplomats and journalists as 'unilaterally'. He suddenly refused to give any rehearsal pay. He 'looked upon the Association's interference as unnecessary, and in the highest degree offensive'; for that great little man was still mentally living in the days of the old stock company and really thought his employees had only to come to him for fatherly affection if there was anything which troubled them. Bitterly he refused permission for any A.A. representative even to enter his theatre, and promptly added an eighth weekly performance without pay.

On tour with *Via Crucis*, he kept up this attitude, and it raised the Glasgow Trades and Labour Council against him. At Dundee, challenged by Alfred Lugg, he at last agreed to arbitration, as a result of which his company were awarded the sums he had refused them. But next year he was again offending. This time he was brought to bay at Liverpool, where the hunt was up with the help of N.A.T.E. and the carters. A public boycott was declared at Manchester. Sir John called out the police against the sandwich-men distributing leaflets about it. This was an error on his part; for the matter was a trades dispute, and the police had no authority. They had to be called off. The sandwich-men did their work well. Sir John had very small houses.

As ill luck of the A.A. would have it, however, one of these houses was a charity performance for the Actors' Benevolent Fund, which the Council did not know till it was too late. It was a doubly unfortunate twist: for it gave a fine chance to the other side for adverse propaganda, which they took.[8]

Eva Moore, the actress, had had to resign her A.A. connection when she went into management. She followed Martin Harvey's example, but in a manner much more suited to the modern world of business. She brought an action for defamation against her late comrades. It was justified by some remarks made in a leaflet issued by the A.A. organisers in trying to boycott her show at Huddersfield for certain irregularities. Robert Young the chief organiser tried to reply with an official disclaimer of these remarks; but Miss Moore was too quick for him. She won her case before he could apologise. The Association's legal adviser recommended leaving this agile person alone; but a principle was at stake. Boycotts followed her tour, at Woolwich, at Cardiff. She applied for an injunction, and this would certainly have been granted; but the A.A. issued an undertaking which satisfied her and that case was dismissed. The Cardiff affair did the Association little good. Stink bombs had been thrown, a most unprofessional proceeding, and one indignantly repudiated by the Council; but unhappily too late to correct the false impression given by the London *Evening Standard*.[9] Another boycott, established in Cardiff against Jack Arnold by George Fry, was effective, but expensive. Fry's address to a mass meeting of ordinary people was so persuasive that Arnold could book no more dates in all Wales. But the action he brought as a result cost the Association over £2,500.[10]

These, however, were the exceptions. The power of the Association was growing. Certainly contractual obligations were still broken; certainly, there were wage scandals like that of the Fred Neilson company at Maidstone, or Jack Leno who paid his chorus girls one week no more than two shillings and sixpence each; certainly, companies were still being stranded in dire circumstances. But it only took a visit from Lugg or one of the organisers, for the defaulting managers, in most cases, to capitulate and to do what they were asked. Usually it was Lugg who went: week after week he reported to the Council satisfactory rightings of wrongs. sometimes half a dozen at a time. Indeed, such reports became so frequent, that the Council framed a formula, officially finding that there was a trades dispute concerned and empowering the Secretary to take any steps required for its satisfactory conclusion. This it needed only to recite solemnly on each occasion, and the due power of action passed. On only one occasion was it necessary to pursue matters so far as to authorise a strike: that was at Salisbury on 26 January 1924; it was a very small affair, and instantly effective.[11]

So it is wrong to say that the Actors' Association did nothing: it did much; it hit out, hard and heroically. In the first five years of its existence as a trade union, it recovered no less than £57,731 for its members,[12] mostly in small sums. That is not done without much work; hard and constant work; and capable work too, which showed other results. Local trades and labour councils willingly collaborated with such valiant fighters. Permanent branches were formed at Liverpool, Manchester, and Glasgow; temporary ones at Newcastle and elsewhere. The Closed Shop caught the imagination. Other unions rallied round it. Arthur Bourchier, a manager whose company was already 100 per cent A.A., favoured it and volunteered to chair a special meeting at the Haymarket Theatre. At that meeting the Closed Shop was explained and propagated; and Lugg made one of his finest speeches. The Federal Council, subject to ratification by the three unions which composed it, resolved to support the policy whenever and wherever success seemed possible.[13]

Nor would it be true to say that, at any rate to begin with, the Actors' Association had any bitter feelings toward the Stage Guild. From the start of the breakaway, they expressed a continual desire to come together and discuss differences. When they were invited to the Criterion Restaurant in June 1924 with an opportunity for 'placing before the Stage Guild a statement of their intended policy', they accepted at once with less than a day's notice. What happened that time does not appear to be on record; but Lugg's able advocacy again won the Council's praise.[14]

The result of this meeting was an invitation from the A.A.'s side that both bodies should hold a public debate, under a neutral chairman such as Sir Edward Marshall-Hall or the Duke of Atholl, on the pros and cons of the position and the policy of each. This, however, was flatly refused by the Stage Guild.[15]

While the Council was deliberating what next could be done, a letter arrived by hand from Donald Calthrop, offering his services as mediator. This the A.A. accepted, and another meeting was arranged, to the great pleasure and approval of many actors and actresses who had attended an open meeting at the Kingsway Theatre called by Calthrop himself the previous day, and who did not understand why, when there was so much to be done for ordinary stage folk, two rival bodies, each claiming to think of ordinary folk, were inhibited by rivalry or passion from doing very much at all.[16]

The Stage Guild was more cautious. It first stipulated that neither the A.A. Secretary nor their own secretary should address this meeting, nor even attend it. This proviso was so unusual, indeed unreasonable, that it can be explained only by an un-willingness to expose their own members to the persuasive gifts of Alfred Lugg. Calthrop himself did not like this; he asked the Guild to withdraw it, on the grounds that it might 'endanger the harmony of a first meeting'. But the Council of the A.A. were so anxious for the meeting to take place, and so confident in their own cause, Lugg or no Lugg, that they did not insist on the withdrawal, though they suggested mildly that both officials might perhaps be present in a consultative capacity only.

At the Kingsway Meeting, Bronson Albery, a prominent member of the Guild, had publicly proposed that both bodies dissolve and form a new organisation altogether. In preparing its agenda, the A.A. asked whether the Guild would be willing to carry this out, if the A.A. did? The Guild replied with two further stipulations: there must be no independent chairman, and no verbatim minutes.[17]

Staggered by this insult to Calthrop, the Council asserted that he ought to act as chairman, and that it would be helpful to have a professional stenographer in attendance; but, they said, they would not allow the absence of these, if the Guild really insisted, to debar the A.A. delegates from coming. To be quite sure of their line of action, the A.A. Council carefully instructed them in suitable action when they got to the meeting-place, which was the Shaftesbury Hotel.

When the delegates arrived, they were more dumbfounded than ever. Evidently the Stage Guild had mistaken moderation for weakness or worse. Vincent Carlyle was not allowed to take pencil notes: no kind of publication or publicity would be permitted. The purpose of the Guild's coming, it was explained, was not for a debate, nor even for a conference, merely for a friendly chat, committing nobody to anything and meaning as little as possible. There is something rather pathetic about the curious secretiveness, the small-scale cunning, this fund of ingenious surprise attacks shown by the Guild. When Soviet Delegations have adopted similar tactics with American and British diplomats, it has been called an oriental idiom, below Western standards, and probably hiding a weak case. Certainly on this occasion the Guild seemed as if it were hiding something; for the A.A. delegates made a formal withdrawal from discussion in disgust, and then at the Guild's invitation returned unofficially, swore mutual secrecy and entered on 'friendly conversation'.

There may have been adequate reasons, of which the historian is unaware, for this extraordinary series of twistings; or there may have been some indefinable fear on the part of the Guild that subjects might be exposed in a manner prejudicial to them. In the absence of its Minute Books to clear it, the Guild remains under a cloud on this matter: much to the chagrin of the chronicler who would be objective.

The friendly conversation, however, turned out so innocuous that it was the Guild which broke the vow of secrecy some days later, when Gerald du Maurier, one of its Vice-Presidents, wrote to the A.A. asserting four points of policy on which both sides were agreed: registration of Managers; an agreed Touring Contract; a

Minimum Wage; and the 'betterment of the general conditions of the profession'. His proposal was that both bodies should try to attain these as separate associations, and 'by pacific means instead of by measures which will cause widespread distress through unemployment'.[18] An interesting letter; and perhaps not innocent of a sinister sting in its tail, lashing at the Closed Shop. For what unemployment would the Closed Shop bring, except by a deliberate counter-attack, by victimisation, from the managers' side? In a later letter he demanded the abandonment of theatre boycotts.[19] Any chance of an amiable get-together was now impossible. Nothing had been achieved by the A.A.'s overtures, except a subtle revelation of an unpleasant stiletto blade.

Two more attempts were made. Walter Payne, for the Society of West-End Managers, brought two groups of representatives together, but their talk ended vaguely where it vaguely began, in a discussion of a standard contract. Early next year Actor's Equity of America offered to mediate from across the Atlantic, provided that a trade union of some kind was maintained as a result of their mediation. But of all questions that was the one that the Guild would least consider; no progress could be made that way.[20]

I have written these chapters wrongly if the reader is seeing all the managers at the back of the Guild and none at the back of the Association; it was quite otherwise. The Association had many manager friends. Andre Charlot, always fair to his employees, issued a special rehearsal call for an A.A. representative to make the company 100 per cent trade union. Sir Arthur Carlton of Worcester, behaving very well over pantomimes, asked the Council to draft a dispute or strike clause for his contracts. Percival Broadhead, secretary of the Provincial Entertainment Proprietors and Managers (known as P.E.P.), not only assisted in getting minimum pay agreed, but lent his theatre at Newcastle free of charge for a meeting which Bourchier was to address, and paid all expenses for a similar one at Preston.[21]

But it would be equally wrong to overstress the importance of these in numbers. Since February 1924 the relations of the Council and the Touring Managers, by then known as the Incorporated Association of Touring Managers, had worsened. Taking a hint from du Maurier's first letter, the Council had suggested discussions to agree a Touring Contract. After six weeks' silence, Louis Casson replied 'that in view of the I.A.T.M. having a contract in general use, although not binding on its members, we feel that there is no necessity to re-open the subject with the Actors' Association'. However, there is a point at which illogicality can become insulting, and this reply passed that point; so it is not surprising that the Council now decided to have nothing further to do with the Touring Managers.[22] But the Touring Managers had still plenty to do with, and to, the Council. They published a remark in their trade journal which the Council, and Frank Gray of Glasgow, at whom it was aimed, thought actionable. So did the law courts; £100 damages were awarded in May 1925.[23]

The West End Managers, however, seemed to be more amenable. It appeared that they had come to see the need for the licensing of all theatrical managers, and were much interested in a bill that had been drafted at last for presentation to the House of Commons. But in the course of committee, discussion and bargaining, all the important provisions proposed had been dropped overboard or rendered ineffective. This was discovered by Gilbert Hall, then the A.A.'s assistant Secretary, only on 30 April 1925, when it was too late for any democratic controls to operate, since any further amendments had to be handed in by that night. The Council therefore sent its suggested amendments aimed at making the Bill worth the passing, up to the House of Lords: compulsory public advertisements by such managers as did register; touring managers to disclose certificates on demand; resident managers to be guilty of an offence if they allowed unregistered touring managers the use of their theatres; and so on. They even sent a personal appeal to the Prime Minister, Stanley Baldwin. It was not a Government Bill.[24] But they did not know parliamentary procedure; and though they believed their suggestions to be good, wise and necessary, they did not know what form of tact or bargaining was necessary to make them into democratic law. Would it be better to leave the mauled Bill as it was, rather than risk losing all by attempting to better it? They did not now think of turning to the trade union movement for help. They asked Arthur Bourchier to consult Lord Haldane who was Lord Chancellor at the time.

Knowing very little of party politics, and imprudently steering clear of them, they ran themselves aground, as non-party men must always do, and were left high and dry on shoals they did not know existed. There is something noble, saintlike and pitiable in Fisher White's firm refusal to allow agitation for the reformed Bill in Hyde Park. It might look like an attack on the Government, he said.[25]

Party politics were becoming aggressive, serious, dangerous; so was trade unionism: it is of vital importance to remember this through what follows. Costs were rising: employers were trying to reduce wages. The T.U.C. in July of this year backed with the Miners' Federation in its first act of defiant resistance: it seemed a thing confined to miners, at most to manual workers; but it was to spread and affect everyone in the nation. Real emotions were to rise on political themes, even in comfortable suburban back gardens. The General Strike of 1926 was threatening, when motor cars labelled 'T.U.C.' passing through shopping centres would be greeted by respectable folk with fear and hatred, contempt and disgust. And the Actor's Association was affiliated to the T.U.C.! Unto the Jews a stumbling-block, and unto the Greeks foolishness! 'Workers', said Sir Frank Benson, 'have no right to interfere with the theatrical profession.'[26]

The same social and political strains that bore upon experts, technicians, chemists, engineers, as paid employees of big concerns, weighed also upon the players, especially successful ones. They were on both sides and on neither; for they heartily deplored the idea of class warfare and would not believe it existed. They looked upon strike leaders as un-British, as potential traitors, for thus the popular press and some unscrupulous politicians taught them to look. For this reason, many actors viewed the A.A.'s paid organisers with a distaste approaching horror. The organisers in return sometimes behaved crudely, with impatience, without tact, as overworked organisers may often do before a prejudice they have no time or strength left to break down. This was a bad mark for the A.A.; it lost them many members as the economic conditions of the country grew worse and worse.

Now the transfers from A.A. to Stage Guild began, openly and in bulk. Godfrey Tearle was among the earliest and the most valuable: others followed, hard workers, like Frank Irish. Notabilities, like O. B. Clarence, more and more of them persuaded over, convinced. Others wavered and wobbled. Even the Association's solicitors resigned. One of the least explicable of turncoats was H. R. Barbor, who had been handling publicity for the A.A., and wrote a useful little account of its first struggles against the Stage Guild. He had even tried to bring about an amalgamation of the A.A. with the V.A.F. Yet within four months he was attacking the militant policy of the A.A., and Alfred Lugg personally, in an American trade paper called *Billboard*. He insinuated that his correspondence had been tampered with.

It was not a rot setting in, but a run. They took to their heels with one accord, like the late friends of the Soviet Union at the mention of Moscow gold. Indeed, the same story was circulated about the A.A.; only the gold was supposed to come from Germany and to be used for illicit political purposes. If this is not very edifying to watch, neither is it very funny. It delayed the progress of the plain actor for a dozen years, maybe a score. Every new member of the Stage Guild was one mark more to the managers. Even those who left the A.A. without joining the Guild were helping the managers' side: we can see that now; they could not. They were blinded by the scapegoats: Cook in the General Strike, Alfred Lugg in the actors' world outside the A.A. and to some extent inside also. But the Council stood loyally by him.[27]

With vanishing memberships came the problem of vanishing funds. Ways and means were tried, as they are tried in the humblest societies of all: sweepstakes, competitions, whist drives, and the like. But the police advised the abandonment of the first; and the others brought little in. A whole series of whist drives yielded only a few shillings each night. The financial position, always difficult, became dangerous. More and more drastic economies were thought of; the branches at Manchester and Liverpool were closed down. The Glasgow branch lasted longer, for it was paying its way longer; but at last an appeal from Mrs Frank Gray for £20 had to be answered with a telegram to close down there also. Room after room at St Martin's Lane was done without and sublet. The office staff was continually being given notice, retained, and given notice again, changing like a barometer in an English August.[28] A gift of £5,000 offered by Actors' Equity of America, which had come to see that the relations of the A.A. to the Stage Guild was exactly that of Equity to the 'Fidelity League' used by the American managements in the same way in 1919, was first proudly postponed, at last gratefully accepted as a temporary lease of precarious life.[29]

The cost of a paid organising staff was high. It was decided to share organisers with the N.A.T.E. That was a profound mistake; for this was the stage-hands' union, a militant union of workmen, which ultimately used strike action. In the sensitive condition of opinion at that time it would have been wiser, as Charles Farrell suggested, to share organisers with the musicians, many of whom were educated men; but his motion to that effect failed to find a seconder.[30] In February 1924 Bromley Davenport had risen and denounced the trade union policy of the Association; it could not be applied, he held, to a luxury profession like acting. Minimum salaries encouraged incompetence among undesirables, and federation with other trade unions kept really representative people out of the A.A. As nobody else on the Council agreed with him, he resigned in June. The Council intensified its campaign.

With ever dwindling funds, running out of ammunition, a brave assault was made on the resident managers' stronghold. In the interests of the old Standard Touring Contract dispute, boycott methods were contemplated.[31] But already there were signs of other weakening. Robert Young, a hitherto faithful servant of the Association, began to suggest that the Closed Shop was an obsolete aim. This earned him the charge that he was under the influence of Bronson Albery, if not actually in his pay; but his arguments won, for all that. Boycotts were abandoned. Bourchier, that last despairing help in time of trouble, was again approached. Perhaps he could get an 'award' contract, by peaceful means, by arbitration, maybe under Lord Askwith? Let him try anything, anyhow, at any time.[32]

But of course he could get nothing of the sort. Conquerors do not grant partial claims by peaceful means when they have their enemy on the run and wish to annihilate their claims and them together. This reversal of policy was fatal; it was the last *coup de grâce*, administered by the victim himself, because it was wrongly timed. In industrial affairs, a retreat well timed and widely publicised can achieve an objective very similar to a victory; but not a retreat in disorder, with fugitives deserting in open daylight and overwhelming casualties; and never a retreat *in aim*!

Now the Actors' Association stood for little for which the Stage Guild did not also stand, and with a clearer prospect of success. Result: a drastic drop in membership. From 3,440 in 1925 to 418 in the following Spring. Even the staunch-hearted Ben Webster dropped his arms and fled.[33] At Council meetings, less and less business was done; for there was less and less to do. General protests were given voice; hopeful requests were drafted; the organisation of theatrical landladies was discussed.[34] The meetings themselves which had before lasted a whole afternoon and then been adjourned, contracted to an hour and a half. The minutes became shorter and more laconic; you can tell today by the look of them, the story of disillusion and decay. They were badly typed by amateurish fingers, because the paid staff had gone. In the summer of 1925 the odour of dissolution was heavy in the air.

There was still a gallant flicker or two. In December the old trades dispute formula was brought out and recited solemnly, defiantly; and power of action duly passed to the secretary. But on investigation, there was found no case to proceed against – fortunately indeed! A senile Napoleon issuing dummy orders of the day to annihilate an imaginary foe would be a dismal spectacle. Yet Lugg could still carry off a thing or two with a swagger. In February 1926 he was in Cardiff talking bravely of Workers' Control; able still to kindle sparks in the wettest wood.[35]

It was getting about that the old firm was failing; that the Association at last was done for and bankrupt. The rumour was false; but by the autumn of 1925 it was very plain that the end was not far off. At length one Wednesday afternoon in March, sitting sorrowfully over the facts, the Council for the second time in the Association's history had to decide to call a General Meeting and wind up their affairs. No motion to that effect was required. The Councillors merely mutely and miserably accepted the report of the Chairman's committee. With equal lack of comment they heard from Ada Roscoe that a basket of crockery had been stolen from the ladies' room.[36]

On Sunday, 28 March the members were called to a Special General Meeting at the Shaftesbury Hotel. It was intended to place their resignations in the members' hands, and maybe maintain some sort of a shell, some sort of reminder of great ideals with an accommodation address. But they could not even do that; there was not a quorum of members present.

This pathetic inability even to give themselves their own quietus must be unique in trade union history. And yet by the strange laws of human relationship it was just because not enough people were enough interested to attend the funeral, that the corpse was enabled not only to revive but to grow strong and lusty. If a quorum had appeared, the Actors' Association would have vanished. If the Actors' Association had vanished, the Stage Guild could have applied for a Royal Charter, which in such circumstances it would very likely have obtained. A Royal Charter being incompatible with trade union status, in time some actor's union might conceivably have been founded in opposition to a body surveying the welfare of the profession as a whole. But its task would have been herculean, its growth snail-like, and its fulfilment long, long delayed.

As it was, however, this miserable fiasco at the Shaftesbury Hotel, so depressing to those present, so discouraging to all actors and actresses with any comprehension of industrial laws, was of vital importance in the founding of Equity itself. The Actors' Association did not go out into the night: the night was black around it. Blacker indeed it could hardly have been. But every night comes ultimately to its end: and it is one of the pleasures of history to record that once again, and just when light was needed, at the deepest point of blackness a new star was seen.

Notes and References

1. G. Carlton Wallace in a letter to the author.
2. H. R. Barbor, op. cit. Introductory notes by Sybil Thorndike and C. B. Cochran. p. viii.
3. Stage Guild, *Report of the Grand Council*, 1924–5. Letter of A.A. to American Actors' Equity, 26 March 1925, incorporated in Council's minutes of that date.
4. *Minutes of the Stage Guild Managers' Section*, 26 July 1926. Correspondence between G. Carlton Wallace and J. Norman Berlin, in the former's possession.
5. 26 July 1926.
6. *Minutes of a Meeting held at the Opera House, Manchester*, 25 November 1925. In the possession of the A.T.P.M.
7. Reported in *A.A. Council Minutes*, 23 February, 12 and 26 March 1923.
8. Ibid., 19 March, 3 April 1923; 25 September, 9 and 16 October, 13 November 1924.
9. Ibid., 11, 13, 23 September 1924; 9 October 1924; and Lugg at A.G.M., 1 February 1925.
10. Ibid., 10 September to 28 December 1924.
11. Ibid., 26 February, 26 March 1923; 10, 24, 31 January 1924.
12. George Fry at A.G.M., 1 February 1925.
13. *Minutes, etc.,* cit., 13, 27 March, 3 April, 1 May, 21 August 1924.
14. Ibid., 18 and 19 June 1924.
15. Ibid., 19 and 26 June 1924.
16. Ibid., 3 July 1924.
17. Ibid., 29 July 1924; and correspondence incorporated in the Minutes of 12 July 1924.
18. Ibid., incorporated in the Minutes of 2 August 1924.
19. Ibid., incorporated in the Minutes of 7 August 1924.
20. Ibid., 19 January 1925.
21. Ibid., 5 November, 14 and 17 December 1923; 21 August, 30 October, 6 November 1924.
22. Ibid., 14 February, 27 March 1924.
23. Ibid., 7 July, 14 August 1924; 21 May 1925.

24. Ibid., 7 February, 30 April, 21 May 1925. In its filleted form the Bill was passed in July and became operative on 1 January 1926. See *The Stage*, 15 July 1926.
25. Ibid., 18 June, 17 July 1925.
26. H. R. Barbor, op. cit., p. 5.
27. *Minutes, etc.,* cit., 13 September 1924; 22 January, 5 and 12 February 1925; 13 August 1923; 9 February, 5 March 1925.
28. Ibid., 1 October 1925.
29. Fisher White at A.G.M., 1 February 1925. Alfred Harding, op. cit., pp. 173 seq.
30. *Minutes, etc.,* cit., 21 February 1924; 12 November 1925.
31. Ibid., 25 February, 13 October 1924.
32. Ibid., 13 November, 27 November 1924.
33. Ibid., 20 January, 27 March 1926.
34. Ibid., 16 December 1925.
35. Ibid., 10, 17 February 1926.
36. Ibid., 17 March 1926.

CHAPTER THIRTEEN

The Making of Equity

I distrust British actors as Trade Unionists.
J. Fisher White

Week after week a caretaker committee met and carried on the business of a skeleton Association in a room at 50 Whitcomb Street, till the Annual General Meeting in June should decide what was to be done. Fisher White was in the chair, and the Council entirely depended on him. When he had to be absent acting or producing, question after question was shelved till he could come back and tell them what to decide. One of his letters to the Council when he was away in the cast of a play appropriately named *Conflict*, advised them on things to be done, and was respectfully, almost reverently, copied out in full in the minutes.[1] It has a faintly apostolic feel, as to a remote and ingenuous congregation of saints.

Alfred Lugg had gone. Ada Roscoe was the secretary, able to consult Lugg on points of routine and procedure, about which nobody knew as much as he. Now the minutes are handwritten; perhaps the new secretary could not type, or perhaps the typewriter had been sold.

In July 1926 came a change of Councillors. Fisher White firmly maintained that all the old members must be disqualified, however valuable their service had been; so that a new start could be said to have been made with new activities and new ideas. Among the new Councillors elected at the A.G.M. were Balvaid Hewett, Madge McIntosh, Rathmell Wilson, George Rollitt, Wilfrid Walter, D.

Lewin Mannering, Harry Zeitz and Neil Porter. Lewis Casson was much missed; he now ranked as a manager and could not serve.

But alas! the new activities were as few as the new ideas. The winding-up of the Entertainments Federal Council, which meant that the A.A. was no longer joined with theatre musicians and theatre staffs; advertisements in the *Daily Telegraph*; appointment of delegates to an N.A.T.E. discussion on films; forwarding to other entertainment associations of a charge brought by American Equity against the management of *The Vagabond King* at the Winter Garden Theatre; a few claims by members; these are practically all the transactions from autumn 1926 to spring 1927. Attendance grew sparser; minutes became mere headings and are seldom signed; between October 1927 and March 1928 there are no minutes at all. Once when Fisher White was away, nobody had the heart to take the chair. Now when he was present, only finance was discussed.[2] Finance was desperate: the membership was still declining; several large debts were owing. When the National Union of Corporation Workers asked for the repayment of its loan of £500, the only reply to be found was that at present no payment was possible. It looked as if despite the reprieve of 1926 the whole organisation would have to wind up, this time finally.[3] Then by surprise a new era opened.

It is always dangerous to impose a symmetrical pattern on history, which never repeats itself; and even parallels are seldom perfect. But there is at least a likeness between the triangle of Valentine the Guide, Raleigh the Philosopher, Lugg the (impetuous) Friend and a new triangle now appearing. Fisher White was wide and shrewd, but cautious too; the dramatic author Ian Richardson, like Cecil Raleigh, wrote stimulating articles in the press; and a flood of new ideas and enthusiasm swept into the Council in the person of Russell Sedgwick, an actor who was making his name in unusual plays like those produced by Peter Godfrey at the little subscription 'Gate' Theatre Salon.

Sedgwick was internationally minded; a member of the Executive Council of the Actors' International, he brought a knowledge of French, Danish, German-speaking and other foreign actors' associations into the A.A. Council's debates, besides being himself of American birth[4] and specially interested in American Equity. He was the motor, giving Fisher White fresh momentum and sometimes, indeed, requiring a brake. He started up in the very nick of time in March 1928, when he first came before the committee to report on a Conference in Paris of an 'International Union of Persons Connected with the Theatre'. He was formally inducted into the committee in August, and put forward an original and exciting scheme for legislation to reduce theatre rents, admission prices, and agents' fees, and to introduce pensions and contracts modelled on the long-term Continental type.[5]

New blood was timely for another reason. Ever since October 1926, Godfrey Tearle, now Chairman of the Artists' Section of the Stage Guild, had been pressing for complete amalgamation. This had been taken up on the Association's side in a letter to *The Era* by Ian Richardson, who, not being on the stage himself could view actors from the perspective of distance. Let them abandon internal wars, he argued, in the face of so many blows at their common interests from outside: Variety, Twice Nightly shows, Cinema, Broadcasting, and perhaps in the future Television! Himself a loyal member of the A.A. and an ex-Councillor, he pleaded for a fusion of the rivals, and an application for a Royal Charter; after which the new Incorporated Body could effect the licensing of both managers and actors, and the enforcement of minimal pay. This was an extension of the ideas of Jenkyn, Henley and Irving.

Now Royal Charters cannot be granted to sections of any profession, but only to a profession as a whole. The A.A., being a trade union, excluded managers. The Stage Guild, though including managers, could not claim to represent the whole profession so long as the A.A. survived in however reduced and dilapidated a form. Therefore the Guild must either destroy the Association or absorb it. To destroy it was difficult without rousing the whole trade union movement; and, in any case, a corporate body can be destroyed only by an act of corporate suicide. The faithful few were too faithful for that. Neither, so long as Fisher White remained, was it easy to absorb it.

The Guild put forth feelers. If it applied for a Royal Charter, would the A.A. consider a fusion? Godfrey Tearle's letters throughout this period have a most genuine, friendly, big minded feel to them. He looked for common aims, not differences. Indeed, he wrote the only point of difference was whether an actors' protective association should or should not be trade unionist. The biggest of all points, admittedly; but a single one. Could the A.A. not send a deputation to the Guild's offices at Great Newport Street, to discuss it? Fisher White was cautious. First he took legal opinion about the likelihood of the Guild ever getting a Royal Charter. Goddard, the solicitor, was dubious. In any case it would take years. Nor was White satisfied of the ethics of a trade union allowing a non-trade union body to get a Royal Charter, and then amalgamating with it. Neither could he see anything but folly in admitting commercial managers to such a Chartered Institute. They would jump at the Charter, and flood out the Institute.[6]

So on the 6 November 1926 he went round to Great Newport Street determined to insist on both groups forming sections of their own inside an altogether new body, with equal representation on a common Grand Council. It was George Rollitt's idea that any such new body, if it were achieved, might in conformity with the American counterpart which did admit managers, be called *Actors' Equity of Great Britain*.[7] Informal this meeting was, and friendly; with a very different atmosphere from that of the fiasco of two years before; but it was just as abortive. The two sides seemed to be agreeing; but the common ground vanished when they tried to measure it subsequently in writing. Tearle put on record that the A.A. was willing to wind itself up and join the Guild. Fisher White at once replied that his party had agreed to no such thing. It would join the Guild only as a separate section within it.[8] This from the Guild's angle was not to be thought of. Such members of the A.A. as still remained members were the militant ones, the trade unionists. As a recognised separate section they might well be expected to attack the managers from within, and disrupt the Guild altogether – fifth-column tactics. Tearle had to insist that trade unionism must be dropped, as contrary to the Guild's articles of association. But he conceded that Fisher White's was the more accurate wording of what had been agreed. 'I know', he concluded in his sane and serious rejoinder, 'that "Unity" is our adopted watch-word. If we can keep that aim in view, then I am sure eventual fusion must follow as the night the day.'[9]

All through 1927 and 1928 letters passed from Association to Guild and from Guild to Association. Both sides wished a way out of the impasse. Both sides wished fusion; for separately both were impotent, and the conditions of the ordinary player, which was the aim of the best members of both, were deteriorating. In January 1928 Martin Harvey went so far as to say that in winning its fight, the Guild had unwittingly destroyed the power of the artist to maintain a standard contract![10] Now it was the members of the Stage Guild who were beginning to lose confidence in their institution. No fewer than 450 managers, acting managers[11] and musicians had left, almost in a body. Although a total membership of 3,000 was still claimed, resignations and omissions to renew subscriptions were reducing this to an effectual figure of 1,555. There was an annual deficit of nearly £1,000. The Guild, in short, was rapidly dropping to the exhaustion level of the A.A. Like rival explorers fighting in a malaria swamp, both sides were dying and neither was capable of either slaying the other or even of struggling back alone to normal life.

What had happened was that the actor members of the Guild, to quote Godfrey Tearle, looking back across twenty-three years, were beginning to realise that a contract which *could not be enforced*, made obligatory upon *all* managers, was nothing but a joke. Many welcomed the new power that an influx of A.A. members might give them. They even overruled the Managers' Section on the Grand Council. The managers on their side put forward a counter suggestion for a further section of managers which they hoped would even up the balance of power in their favour again; but the Guild would not agree. The managers saw that the game was up; they could bluff the profession no more; so they resigned.[12] At the A.G.M. of the Stage Guild, questions were asked about the numbers of managers who had gone. The answers were evasive; and very few indeed were the managers that remained to stand for election to the Council. It was solemnly resolved that the Council should investigate the progress, and tell the members. By October 1928 a new managers' section was formed, including Alfred Denville, Nicholas Hannen, the Nettlefolds, Godfrey Tearle, Sybil Arundale and Gertrude Kingston. The policy of this new section was to develop a 100 per cent Stage Guild membership in all companies and to enforce the agreed Stage Guild Contracts.[13]

The progress of the Guild was weakened toward a Royal Charter, lacking the Association's name. On the other hand, the going of the managers removed one large obstacle from the path of the Association toward fusion. Individuals on both sides had the sense to see this; especially Godfrey Tearle in the Guild, and Russell Sedgwick in the A.A. Tearle's was the brain that saw the need for fusion; Sedgwick was the spark that kindled the forest fire which sent both combatants staggering to safety in each other's arms. Fisher White, too, saw the advantages of a joint Charter. No hide-bound doctrinaire, he wrote to Sedgwick: 'A Chartered Body is what you make it', and the power a Royal Charter might give to expel an unworthy member, as doctors or solicitors do, would be 'as strong a weapon as any trade union could acquire, let alone a trade union of actors'. To this he added the bitter words at the head of this chapter.[14]

Sedgwick wrote to the Artists' section of the Guild proposing the formation of a new body altogether. This offer was at once declined by Louis Casson, for it would mean the extinction of the Guild. But within a few days the Guild made a separate move; it planned an open meeting of the profession and invited the A.A.[15] If this meeting ever occurred, there is no record of it; very likely the Guild changed its mind. Possibly the General Secretary thought this no good time to consider tackling outsiders; the Guild's own constitution and finance were giving it quite enough worry. Fisher White therefore did some exploring. He went to the Ministry of Labour, to interest them in the fate of certain chorus girls who were being criminally underpaid; it was a fate which was so very much on his mind that when he came home to Inverness Place in the evenings he would talk about little else.[16] The best way out, he thought, was a revision of the Theatrical Managers Registration Act. The way Joynson-Hicks had filleted this, it had proved as valueless for its purpose, as many knowledgeable people had prophesied when it was passed. But revision, the Ministry officials told him, would get little hearing, unless it were backed by a body representing a large majority of the profession. They went further, and frankly recommended that the A.A. should amalgamate with the Guild and press for a Royal Charter. Fisher White also had an interview with F. J. Nettlefold, one of the Guild's Vice-Presidents. 'I found him doubtful about the Charter,' he reported to Sedgwick, 'and cock-a-hoop about the Guild.'[17] That was likely bluff.

But Nettlefold was going to East Africa after Christmas, and Fisher White hoped his colleagues on the Guild Council would be more amenable than he; for at last a Conference had been arranged between the rival organisations at the Guild's offices on 31 December. The Guild was represented by the hardy Conservative H. A. Saintsbury, the Liberal Felix Aylmer, and O. B. Clarence for the artists' section; by Godfrey Tearle for the attenuated managers'; and by the sane deliberate Bronson Albery for the Grand Council. The General Secretary, Norman Berlin, was its heavy artillery; a tough fighter.

The A.A. team included J. Fisher White, Bromley Davenport

(having returned to the fold), Harry Zeitz a popular and able figure, D. Lewin Mannering a good committee man, and George Rollitt. Their secretary was an eager and spirited amateur, Ada Roscoe, no match for the redoubtable Berlin. Fisher White was easier in mind for his previous explorations; and because both sides were ready to be firm, a number of initial agreements were reached: the Valentine Contract was fair for London, but the A.A.'s Touring Contract was fairer than that used by the Guild, insofar as it was ever used. Tearle insisted on the admission of managers, in order to acquire the comprehensiveness needed for a Charter, but Albery was for excluding commercial managers, as a *quid pro quo*. The main thing, he said, was fusion.

The permissibility of strike action was not so easy to decide. Both Albery and Tearle deplored strike action. So did Fisher White; he said all trade unions did, though they sometimes had to use it. No bar to agreement was raised if neither 'A.A.' nor 'Stage Guild' were the title of the new body. Both sides agreed that if a Charter were refused, amalgamation might still be profitable; it might lead to the setting up of an industrial council under the Labour Ministry.[18] This was suggested by Fisher White, knowing the Ministry's attitude. Another meeting was needed before the points agreed could be accurately defined and the delegates report to their respective bodies. This took place on Wednesday, 3 April 1929, with Godfrey Tearle in the chair. Here Sedgwick replaced Lewin Mannering; and O. B. Clarence was absent.

Trade unionism was still an obstacle; a constitutional one. It was forbidden to the Stage Guild; it was incumbent upon the A.A. The Guild demanded, therefore, that the A.A. dissolve. The A.A. required as compensation that its members should exist inside the Guild as a separate section; and if the Charter were too long delayed, it should have power to call a general meeting, and alter both policy and constitution of the Guild. This strong demand sounds in my ears with the voice of Russell Sedgwick. But whether strong or not and even though it threatened the whole Guild with possible disruption, it was acceded to, so anxious was the Guild for an agreement and fusion. Tearle even added that since trade unionism was a matter of conscience to the A.A., and the Guild's constitution was unalterable, both parties ought to dissolve, and form quite a new body.[19]

When the A.A. delegation left Great Newport Street to both sides it must have seemed as if fusion were practically accomplished and would henceforth be painless. Yet the progress they had made was to be wrecked as completely and by exactly the same manoeuvre as had wrecked the partial agreement of November 1926; only with less ingenuousness, and a much nastier air about it. Some power behind the scenes, which I do not identify, was determined to break up the A.A.

The written interpretations of what had been agreed differed profoundly; both sides claimed legal necessity for giving no ground at all. Letters passed, growing more and more exacerbated; emotional words were used. In the Association's phrase, 'the amazing conduct of your Grand Council in repudiating its whole agreement and the cool suggestion that the A.A. should disband for the benefit of the S.G.' a tone is to be heard which is less the balanced sageness of Fisher White than, I think, the hot voice of Russell Sedgwick.[20] But the exasperation is understandable; for the third time it looked as if the Guild were wasting the A.A.'s time and their own with self-contradiction and legalistical quibbles.

'They are living on F.J.N.'s money', Fisher White concluded in February, 'and bound therefore to abhor and destroy trade unionism.' This seems to have been true. A statement made by Equity in a letter of 5 October 1932 that the Guild's rent, payment of officials and general conduct of business depended on Nettlefold's subsidy went unchallenged: and when union was finally established he sent £75 to Equity as Guild money, though he was not treasurer. Not easily moved to wrath, Fisher White was, to use Sedgwick's phrase, 'volcanic in his indignation'. To the Guild the A.A. seemed a stubborn rump of doubtful ethics and questionable intelligence, whose main object seemed to be self publicity. But that did not stop Godfrey Tearle from continually pleading for fusion and the renunciation of pettiness. He was himself growing tired of the Guild, the more he knew of it; and the time was ripe for fusion. But the ears of too many were stopped, with matter of various kinds.[21]

There come moments in the history of men and of institutions, when obstacles due to principle or to prejudice, to legalism or to misunderstanding, can be removed only by dynamite and blasting. Such action, though it is in the interest of the multitude who can see no other way out, is seldom taken unaided by the multitude in a civilised community. It is generally engineered by a few, aware of the feeling of the many, and gifted with the power to turn chance to choice. Being opportunist, such action is swift and covert. It is the basis of revolutions, big or small: its opponents cannot see it as other than chicanery, self-interest, or the dictatorship of the few. But history looking backward does not award all credit to the one side, nor all her honours to the other. Sedgwick was not a political revolutionary in the accepted sense; nor perhaps a politician, in the pejorative one. He burned with zeal for the good of the ordinary actor, because he saw in a healthy theatre 'a great instrument for the imaginative integration of the human soul'.[22] He was not a fanatic, though. In the 1920s all the best brains, under the lead of Middleton Murry in his pre-Christian, pre-Communist, Keatsian phase, were much obsessed with integration. Sedgwick kept always before him as a motive to all his acts, the ultimate establishment of permanent theatres, with or without state or municipal subsidy. Sedgwick was well-versed in the behaviour of the soul when still disintegrated. Felix Aylmer was quite right when he called him 'an unblushing Machiavelli'. A Machiavelli in miniature he was; unscrupulous for the sake of his scruples. He saw that blasting was inevitable; chance gave him both charge and detonator.

In the first week of September 1929 a musical show called *Open Your Eyes* – yet another instance of the happy nomenclature of fortune! – collapsed at Glasgow in the third week of its tour. It had been mismanaged all along; and the company refused to open at Glasgow unless their salaries were guaranteed. A representative of Moss Empires did guarantee them; but at the end of the week the tour was terminated, and all the artists put out of work after autumn had begun and other engagements were unobtainable.

No new, and no unusual, story: but in this case the victims were of high rank; Joseph Coyne, Robert Hale, Geoffrey Gwyther, Marie Burke, Vera Pearce. The eyes of the profession opened very wide indeed when it turned out that the Theatrical Employers' Registration Act, designed to cover such actions, did not in fact cover them. The defaulting of this syndicate was not 'abandonment' within the meaning of the Act, for they had not in fact left Glasgow. Further, the syndicate had never been registered at all; it had got each of the five stars to join the company by the cheap trick of saying the others would; further still, its entire capital proved to be £100; and it had been registered under the Companies Act four weeks too late even to qualify as a theatrical employer.[23] As luck had it, the Executive Secretary of Actors' Equity of America, John

Emerson, happened to be in the United Kingdom on a visit with his wife Anita Loos. Sedgwick saw at once that by putting these two events together, a big drive for membership might set the A.A. on its feet again, all the more since the Stage Guild was doing nothing about the Glasgow default because none of its members had complained. That was a symptom itself, and galling to Godfrey Tearle, who pleaded again for fusion.

Sedgwick had been writing bulletins to *The Stage* about the doings and plans of the A.A., and in them had given publicity to Robert Young, an A.A. member, who had won a Labour seat in the House of Commons at the 1929 Election, and was known as the 'Actors' M.P.' of the time. Young had been co-opted on the Council; and Sedgwick and he, unchecked by Fisher White who was in New York, and abetted by Hannen Swaffer, the controversial theatrical journalist of the *Daily Express*, marshalled their joint forces. Swaffer in the Press stressed the connection between *Open Your Eyes*, American Equity, and the A.A.; and persuaded Emerson to carry out Sedgwick's plan.[24]

The A.A. called a big open meeting of the profession and invited the Guild to attend. The Guild could not well keep out; now that the Managers had left it, Felix Aylmer saw a way to implement his long-cherished plan of converting it to trade unionism from inside. Dame May Whitty herself confessed she no longer opposed trade unionism in principle; and it was Bronson Albery who lent the New Theatre for the purpose of fusion on Tuesday 8 October. The house was full; for the rank and file of the Guild members opposed trade unionism in a quite irrational way; pure lip-service to a social convention.[25]

That morning, the unblushing Machiavelli had breakfast with Emerson, arranged that he would stress the importance of trade unionism and describe how American Equity had begun and developed. Young would follow, with an appeal for a full-membered actors' trade union. Not to make the plan too obvious, from the floor Sedgwick would ask Emerson's advice about the steps to be taken at once; to which Emerson would reply: 'Scrap your two rival organisations and build a new one from the ground up'.

There was as a matter of fact little time for questions and discussion; and Sedgwick had to get his reply written across the question he sent on paper to Emerson later. But, as Emerson said, that did not matter. There was no doubt, if this meeting was at all

representative of the attitude of the profession; and neither the
A.A. nor the Guild could have packed the theatre. Marie Burke,
'The Jeanne d'Arc of the British Theatre', as Sedgwick first called
and then made her, startled them all with her revelations. Felix
Aylmer speaking in his usual grave, statesmanlike style for the
Stage Guild had no difficulty in getting acceptance for a positive
motion that deplored the inability of the law to restrain the bogus
manager. Hannen Swaffer amused, stimulated and re-assured
them with his witty egotism. A solid core of achievement and determination came from John Emerson, which lost nothing in force
from the fact that he had temporarily lost his voice and his
'message' was put over by Marie Burke at his side.

Great and compelling though all these were, it was Young who
made perhaps the most impact, when he rose to move:

> That this meeting urges the Actors and Actresses of this country to
> form and unite in one effective organisation and abandon every
> consideration which might prejudice this result.

It was carried enthusiastically, with only two dissentient
hands.[26] So far, so good: the blasting had opened a passage, and
the eager multitude pressed forward; but the passage was narrow;
their leaders jammed in it. That same afternoon the delegates of
the A.A. met the delegates of the Stage Guild by appointment at the
little Shaftesbury Hotel in Seven Dials. The former consisted of
Lewin Mannering, who was voted into the chair, Bromley Davenport, George Rollitt, Russell Sedgwick, and Robert Young, M.P.
The Guild's contingent was larger than usual: Felix Aylmer, Henry
Hallett, Robert Cunningham, Dame May Whitty, and Violet
Farebrother. The two unmatched secretaries attended as before.

The object of this little meeting was to obtain agreement on the
exact legal position of the A.A. if it entered the Guild. At least, that
was its apparent object. But some Guild members suspected a
trick; after the display of power at the New Theatre, could it be that
the A.A. just wished definitions?

Unfortunately Young's speech at the New Theatre had included
a violent appeal to disband the Guild. Still working cautiously on
difficult ground, Aylmer had agreed to that meeting on the understanding that nothing of the kind would be attempted; he felt
very naturally that he, and the Guild by him, had been betrayed.
Tempers were on edge; and it was not long before Sedgwick was
being openly sarcastic at Felix Aylmer's 'nobility in the matter of

definition'. Our unblushing Machiavelli was proudly dominant in this encounter. So roundly did he champion American Equity, that Robert Cunningham had to express his distaste for anything American as roundly. Emotional tones are infectious. Even more roundly Cunningham generalised about the Guild itself. Its Grand Council, he explained, was moribund, with activity limited to organising charitable events. It was the actors who were in actual control; the managers mattered no more; there were only twenty-six of them left. This laid him open to the retort that if such were the case, then twenty-six managers had as many representatives on the Guild Council as 1,500 actors. When Sedgwick asked whether, supposing the A.A. did join, this proportion of managers would be reduced, there was no reply. None was possible. Nor was the atmosphere lightened by Young's almost gibing request for the Guild Council to take a referendum of its members. This, said Aylmer, very understandably, would be taken by his Council as an insult.[27]

Neither side, of course, was in proper mood for sane or fruitful discussion. The elated Association overplayed its hand; the Guild, offended by the demagogy of the morning, took refuge in a patrician-like reserve. I would like at this point to print in full a letter written to Sedgwick by Felix Aylmer a short while later. Not only does it display the writer's fine diplomatic mind lunging thrusts no less deadly for being calmly contemplated first – which was to prove of such enormous value to the organised profession in later years; it also explains with succinct clarity the attitude of the best members of the Guild at this vital moment:

Dear Sedgwick,
I misled Dame May the other day, because I was not at the moment able to explain my position. I will gladly meet you any time to talk over things, but any further discussion of the fusion question should take place with someone likely to be of use in the matter.

For my own part, I am resigning all official position in the Guild. I should have followed Tearle immediately, if it had not seemed to me possible that the breakdown was due to misunderstandings that might be cleared away. It is now clear to me that, whatever the intentions when negotiations were opened, both sides have now come to treat the matter entirely frivolously.

The Guild's action, in accepting Mote's letter to you unedited, showed an incapacity for negotiation of the highest order. After this, your willingness to resume negotiations showed considerable dignity under provocation. It only became apparent when the meeting took place that your acceptance of our invitation was only a subterfuge, since you were quite unwilling to be drawn into any discussion or criticism. The impression I took away from the meeting was that you were merely on the look-out for copy to strengthen your position in the public eye. Moreover, Young's speech at the New Theatre meeting, attacking the Guild for impotence and proposing its abolition, after we had agreed that the speeches were to be non-partisan, and I had even gone so far as to ask for recruits to the A.A., proved to all doubters that the reputation for trickery that body had gained in earlier days was still richly deserved.

For your delegates to come to the fusion meeting, hot from the other, and to quote the applause elicited by Young's motion to a group, who were behind the scenes of the whole affair, as a mandate from the profession to abolish the Guild, was a piece of impertinence of which I cannot speak with patience.

Who but a fool doubts that any motion which advocated a burial of the hatchet and a fresh start, in all charity and brotherly love, would elicit just such applause? To such an audience it would not matter a twopenny damn whether you were proposing to absorb the A.A. in the Guild, or the Guild in the A.A., or, I would almost say, fuse the two in a new Night Club.

That sort of platform trick may fool some people but it does not impose on me any more than the calm attempt on behalf of your present executive, to appropriate the credit for the past achievements of the A.A. – effected by Valentine and Lugg, with the support of most of the present members of the Guild.

In spite of all this, on Tuesday last, I made a final appeal to the Artists' Council to reconsider the original agreement. It was turned down without one single argument that would hold water for a second being advanced against it.

I am now convinced that neither side has any serious desire for a fusion, nor can I see any prospect of the existing Executives proving capable of managing the united body if fusion were achieved.

I shall therefore retire into my shell again for the time being, and shall pray for the growth of grey matter in the profession and the appearance of a pair of Valentines, Luggs, Emersons and Gillmores.

So I will talk if you like but am afraid I can offer you little but gall or wormwood!

Yours,

FELIX AYLMER

This letter was dated 7 November 1929, and written from 8 The Mount in Heath Street, Hampstead.

The reader will perhaps have noticed the absence of Godfrey

Tearle from the recent pages. He was on tour, in Belfast, Manchester, and other places; nor was he altogether unwilling to be out of London at this juncture. For some time he had been viewing events with misgiving, and the leadership of the Guild with something more. Indeed, Fisher White had been going again and again to Tearle's flat: the Stage Guild was a snare, he said; only a trade union could do anything for the actors, whose conditions were even more intolerable than ever. At last he convinced Tearle himself of this, and Tearle made one last and mighty effort to persuade his colleagues to fuse. But it was no use: and what little chance there had been disappeared after the New Theatre meeting. When Tearle had verified an account of the Shaftesbury Hotel meeting which Sedgwick sent him, he made up his mind to resign. To scrap both associations would, he said, 'put the lid on theatrical organisation in England'.[28]

But it also looked as if this lid had already been put in that position by scrapping neither of them. Further proposals from the A.A. for discussion not unnaturally met no response from the Guild; yet there was a mandate, of some kind, from somebody, to do something toward founding Equity.[29] The newspapers of the time all take this name, and its implications, for granted; as it might be summer time, or the Loch Ness monster, or any other semi-magical thing already too familiar to need any explanation. There can be little doubt that the majority of folk in the profession did want a new trade union altogether. As Cunningham said at the Shaftesbury Hotel, quite a large section of the Guild were in open sympathy with the Association; and those in neither party were anxious for both to go ahead. The profession seemed to view the higgling and niggling conduct of both groups much as an elephant might view the squabbles of two groups of mice disputing their right to precede him.

Another mass meeting was called, this time by permission of Matheson Lang, at the Duke of York's Theatre, on 1 December. A neutral host was found, in the Entertainments and Kindred Industries Association, a federation of many theatrical and other trade unions created by A. M. Wall. He and Sedgwick persuaded the other A.A. Councillors that a new body was necessary, and arranged a big affair with all the honours: high officials of foreign stage organisations would be present and speak, the German Association, the French Union des Artistes, the Danish Actors' Guild. Wall would take the chair.

At this last arrangement, Robert Young refused to appear. Wall was Secretary of the London Trades Council and had been at one time a Communist although later a bitter opponent. Young was a Labour M.P. and even in those days Labour M.P.s were not allowed to share platforms with such people. However, at a party in his own house he was persuaded to withdraw his objections, and as the event turned out made a very good and important speech, pleading that the prime object was the formation of Equity, and any side issues must be disregarded.[30] Young's party scruples soothed, the A.A. went to the Duke of York's Theatre in as much trepidation as did the Stage Guild. What next would go wrong? Was there any chance at all of doing anything? To both sides failure seemed inevitable. An unwise word from the Guild would wreck the meeting; so would too eloquent a one from the Association. The question, for or against trade unionism?, had still been decided by nobody; yet failure now would be fatal for ever.

Publicity had been strong. Quantities of large well-printed leaflets were distributed, calling on people to join. Posters had been taken by Sedgwick personally to every stage door in London. The press was backing it (except the *Daily Telegraph*), especially the *Express* and *The Stage*. There was a more than capacity house. Tide and the expectation were high.[31]

Marie Burke rose as first speaker. She spoke well and reasonably being a person of quick intelligence and fully grasping what was afoot. She pleaded for the art of the theatre to be treated as a business, not as a mere pastime. But she was followed by the foreign speakers, piloted and interpreted by Charles Landstone, who had some trouble with a self-important Prussian; they naturally referred to such things as closed shops and trade union status, and told what good things they had found them to be – and nearly wrecked the meeting that way. It was true that such a direction had been widely publicised, and most of the audience must have expected it; but not unnaturally the Stage Guild's anti trade union view had also to have a hearing; and Nicholas Hannen, coming from the wings, gave it one, a very rousing and stirring one; because he held up Irving's pencil like a holy relic and accused the actors of turning their managers and friends out of their Guild although Irving, their first president, was a manager. His moral was that since all disputes always ended in conferences, it would be best if everyone joined the Stage Guild right away.[32]

Again the probability of success stretched and thinned to near snapping. Stage folk are impressionable, and appeals to loyalty at their public meetings seldom receive anything but sympathetic and obedient respect. They gazed at the relic as if it were ecclesiastical. Many of them repented past errors; and if forms of application to join the Guild had at that moment been handed round, doubtless scores would have filled them in.

But this was not only a question of sentiment; for all of them it was also one of bread-and-butter and security; and fully as many were uneasy about the Guild's aims and achievements. Next, Robert Young spoke sensibly; demanded an organisation that would have the complete confidence of the profession, a form of trade union that would exclude politics by not affiliating to the T.U.C. He said the Home Secretary, J. R. Clynes, had himself advocated this in a letter which Young now read aloud; it was an effective counter-focus for many eyes to the pencil of Sir Henry Irving. He had got Clynes to write the letter himself; it was tantamount to an attack back at Wall and Sedgwick, but it sobered the meeting. However, during Hannen's speech there had been several interruptions of dissent, and Young unfortunately made use of these to claim that the Guild no longer had the confidence of the profession, because it was organised too weakly. Many loyal Guild members present objected to this; and again tension stretched and thinned. Again it might have snapped, if Young had not skilfully side-stepped. What was wanted, he explained, was trade unionism 'without any entanglements'. Hannen Swaffer then followed his new lead. He attacked the A.A. as carefully as Young had attacked the Guild, because 'a few of its members displayed too much zeal, and the great majority too little'. Coulson Gillmore, President of the Film Artists' Guild, sensing the feel of the meeting welcomed more boldly the idea of an Equity that would be strong enough. From the Chair, A. M. Wall, big, ponderous, with greying hair and an imposing moustache, summed up with a plea for formation.

The question was thereupon laid open for discussion, and pandemonium rushed in. Speakers from both sides protested their loyalties, defended their pasts, attacked the opposition: historical mud began to fly; tempers rose, the waves dashed about the rocks. Then, a climax and cynosure for everyone, up from the back came a figure to speak. When this was recognised as the exiled scapegoat Alfred Lugg, a storm of cheers, jeers and hisses burst out. Lugg faced it with unflinching bitterness; he said he preferred their hisses to their cheers, knowing what both were worth. 'Are you to be trusted to form any kind of union?' his challenge rang out.[33] He was blunt; he was arrogant; he was insulting: but in a few minutes the hissing stopped and the cheers went on. It was the managers who killed the Actors' Association, he said, by forming the Stage Guild. When they had done that, they killed the Stage Guild too and threw the Valentine contract on the dust heap. Why shouldn't this new Equity be a trade union? It was the only form of organisation for actors now possible. There was never a doubt of his effect. He had lost nothing of his powers of persuasion. But the Guild had plenty of life yet. Now it was the greatly respected aged Ben Webster who gave the meeting consolidation and momentum. Everyone quietened down as he made his way slowly on stage from one of the boxes.

Although Ben Webster had wavered on occasion, he had never lost his sense of values. As recently as October, in condemning fusion if it meant losing trade union status, he had written in a letter: 'The A.A., or some new body if you like. But not the traitors who wrecked us – not intentionally, I quite believe, but from sheer ignorance.'[34] He knew he must now plead for moderation and calm reflection. Fighting speeches were over; now action must ensue. Let them then, he advised, form the Equity association first, and consider trade union affiliation afterwards: for in the meantime all the things that Valentine had won for the actor were being lost again.

There must have been many present that day whose thoughts went back to August 1918 and the surprising trade union vote at the little theatre in Maiden Lane. Many of Valentine's friends must have felt as though he were present today, gently reproaching them. Eleven years gone; and nothing added to his work: the building he had broken his heart and health to put up, lying indeed in ruins; ground lost; the actors not yet organised, disorganised; wasting their powers and years in needless schisms.

But if the dead can return to earth in wisdom, he would have approved as well as reproached. He would have approved of Fisher White, steadfast in his honourable devotion to a strong actors' society, sagely walking into martyrdom for the sake of the ordinary actor, losing good engagements, being told he would never again be employed, sinking into poverty so severe that he had to walk to meetings to save the fare. He would have approved of Godfrey Tearle, honest, sensitive, finding the truth in his own powerlessness. He would have approved of Lugg, waiting in obscurity for time that would never now turn ripe for his matchless gifts. Many he would have approved, on both sides. Many he would not have approved; among the self-important leaders especially; among the self-seekers lusting to become leaders; among the managers, profiting by the demoralisation they had largely themselves caused.

Most of all, I think, he would have approved and trusted the rank and file. Valentine had a sense of historical timing. He would have known, this day at the Duke of York's Theatre, that now or never a united organisation must be formed. The worst industrial crisis in world history had begun: all over the globe, in every form of employment, owners and managements were concentrating their forces, economising, rationalising, breaking whatever form of employee power they could, to save their firms. For years to come no theatrical employer could afford to be generous; for years the actor would be doomed if he did not take this last chance. Many had been the attempts to unite the ordinary player, all had failed. There comes a time when derision and despair make any further attempt finally impossible: if this one had failed, it must be the last of all. Valentine would have known that. I am sure he would also have known that the ordinary actor would take the chance; because ordinary people are not fools, and they act, in accord with a historical necessity.

After the sage words of Ben Webster, bitterness subsided into common sense. The motion was put from the chair, that a British Actors' Equity Association be formed. It was carried at once. It was not only carried, but to most people's surprise it was carried without dissent. With the rival leaders bowing politely to each other, if somewhat disconcerted, at the head of the Pass, the way lay open to the Promised Land, and the struggling mass poured through.[35] If there is any truth in Samuel Butler's lines

But meet we shall, and part, and meet again,
Where dead men meet, on lips of living men,

then most undoubtedly that day at the Duke of York's Theatre, Sidney Valentine made a round of greetings – grateful, proud, and happy.

Notes and References

1. *Minutes of the Council of the A.A.,* 5 June 1926.
2. Ibid., 17 September 1926.
3. Ibid., 4 March, 12 July 1927.
4. Letter from Russell Sedgwick to John Emerson, London.
5. The scheme is given in full in the Minutes of 10 August 1928.
6. Letter from Godfrey Tearle to A.A., 2 October 1926, copy in *Council Minutes,* 11 October 1926. See also *Council Minutes* 16 and 22 October 1926.
7. *A.A. Council Minutes,* 16 October 1926.
8. Report of meeting in Minutes of 8 November 1926.
9. Letter from Godfrey Tearle to A.A. Council, 22 November 1926.
10. *The Stage,* 18 October 1928.
11. The term *acting managers* requires some little explanation. I am indebted to Mr Jack Isaacs for its elucidation. It was an old term, going back to the time of Colley Cibber at least, when it referred to managers who also acted, rather than to actors who also managed. Later, however, in the nineteenth and early twentieth centuries, the term was applied to the front-of-house manager or business manager. It is now obsolescent, if not obsolete.
12. Letter from Godfrey Tearle to the author, 3 April 1951. It should not be thought, however, that the S.G. had been inactive toward the actor all these years. On the contrary, a glance at the *Stage Guild Bulletin,* its weekly organ, will show a many-sided activity over artists' difficulties, medical attention, and so on. But its usefulness was strictly limited in range.
13. *The Stage,* 2 August 1928. *Stage Guild Bulletin,* 23 October 1928.
14. Letter from J. Fisher White to Russell Sedgwick, dated Brighton, 9 July 1928.
15. Letter from E. L. Marples, sec. of the Artists' Section, 3 July 1928. And letter from J. Norman Berlin, Gen. Sec. of the Guild, to Ada Roscoe, Hon. Sec. of the A.A., 30 June 1928.
16. Anna Fisher White, his widow, in conversation with the author.
17. Letter from J. Fisher White to Russell Sedgwick, 18 December 1928.
18. Minutes of the Meeting, 31 December 1928.
19. Minutes of the Meeting, 3 April 1929.
20. Letter from the A.A. to the S.G., 9 August 1929.
21. Letter from Fisher White to Russell Sedgwick, 3 February 1929. Letter to the *Sunday Express,* 22 September 1929. *The Stage,* Editorial, 26 September 1929. In the matter of Nettlefold's financial subsidy see correspondence Equity and Stage Guild, 12 July to 7 October 1932.
22. Russell Sedgwick, autobiographical notes, unpublished.
23. *The Stage,* 19 September 1929.
24. Hannen Swaffer, *Daily Express,* 2 October, 6 October 1929. Russell Sedgwick, op. cit., pp. 11–13.
25. Felix Aylmer in a letter to the author, 7 April 1951.
26. Letter from Godfrey Tearle to the author, 3 April 1951. Letter from Russell Sedgwick to John Emerson, undated, but 8 October 1929, with reply by Emerson. *Evening News,* London, 8 October 1929. *Daily Express, Daily Chronicle, Daily Mail,* 9 October 1929. *The Stage,* 10 October 1929.

27. Letter from Felix Aylmer to the author, 30 March 1951. Report of this meeting (itself somewhat heatedly composed) in *Minute Book of the A.A. Council*, 8 October 1929.

28. Letters from Godfrey Tearle to Russell Sedgwick, from Belfast, 20 September 1929, and from Manchester, 11 October 1929. Also to the author as cited above.

29. Letters from the A.A. to the S.G.: one undated, but demonstrably 14 October 1929; the other 28 October 1929.

30. Minutes of preliminary meeting of the A.A. Council; and MS. notes on two postcards jotted down by Russell Sedgwick.

31. *The Stage*, 28 November 1929. The *Daily Herald*, 2 December 1929.

32. Hannen Swaffer, 'The Tragedy of a Great Actor', *Sunday Express*, 8 December 1929.

33. *Morning Post*, London, 2 December 1929.

34. Autograph letter, from Ben Webster to Russell Sedgwick, Glasgow, 4 October 1929.

35. *The Era*, 4 December 1929. *The Stage*, 5 December 1929. Russell Sedgwick's autobiographical notes. Letter from Charles Landstone to the author.

POSTSCRIPT

'In all labour there is profit', said Solomon; 'but the talk of the lips tendeth only to penury.' There were to be many lips talking and many threats of penury before the new Association got down to its labour. There were to be back-slidings and hangings-back; plots and counterplots; challenges and resistances; before Equity acquired the power that was necessary for its success. Unity, the Equity Shop, and other means to power took a lot of winning; and much trouble lay yet in store for the actors' leaders. But no Promised Land was ever yet reached along by-passes of others' making.

From this point forward the chronicler's path leads through the Growth of Equity rather than its Rise.* My story properly ends at the Duke of York's Theatre. For it was there that the forty-seven year struggle for an actors' protective association came to its end and fulfilment. What the ordinary actor and actress made of that association, and how they made it, is 'another story'.

* The original title of this book was *The Rise of British Actors' Equity*.

APPENDIX I

The Arts Council of Great Britain
4 St. James's Square,
LONDON S.W.1

CL/PJM   1st January 1951

Joseph McLeod, Esq.,
46, Queen Street,
Edinburgh.

Dear Mr. McLeod,

I ran into Russell Sedgwick the other evening and he reminded me that I had promised him that I would write to you and tell you of my own connection with the founding of Equity in 1929.

This connection, although vivid in my memory, is of no great importance to the history of the movement. You may, however, find that it has a certain interest, and it may help to fill in one or two blanks, in your records.

It came about in a curious way. In the early nineteen-twenties I used to earn a side income as courier, guide and interpreter for Thomas Cooks. In November 1929 I was manager at the Everyman Theatre, Hampstead, and it appeared that Sedgwick had approached Cook's for the services of a professional interpreter with knowledge of French and German for an international theatre conference. In those days it was the system at Cooks to dismiss all but a skeleton staff at the end of the tourist season, and to rely on free lancers for carrying out any commissions that came along during the off period. (I don't know whether they still follow these methods, or whether, now they are nationalised, employment with them is more stable). Knowing my interest in the theatre they rang me up at the Everyman and asked me whether I would like to undertake the commission. My salary at the Everyman was not very munificent – neither was the work so onerous that I could not leave the theatre at times when there were no performances. Moreover, I was curious as to the nature of this unspecified conference, so I accepted. It thus came about that I, who have always been connected with the managerial side of the theatre, was one of the small number of people connected with the birth of the Actors Trade Union.

I was ordered to report to Russell Sedgwick at Transport House, and when I met him I found that he was a young actor who was Secretary of the Actors Association. The conference was the annual International Conference of Trade Unions representing Theatre Workers, and it was being held in England in order to help English actors found a Trade Union on the model of American Equity. Altogether about eight people were present, representing Germany, France, Scandinavia, Belgium and Austria, but as far as my memory takes me, although good wishes were received from America, no delegate was present from that country. I have forgotten the names of the delegates, but I know that Sedgwick has the list. The German delegate – a typical Prussian, who was President of the Theatre Workers Union in his own country, was the Chairman of the Conference. He was an actor, and the Secretary was a charming little Austrian dramatist, who subsequently (in 1938) was brought to this country and supported by a special committee of Equity set up to help refugees from Hitler. Llewellyn Rees (now, as you know, Administrator of the Old Vic) who was in the 1930's Secretary of Equity, was, I believe, Chairman of this Committee and can give you further information on this issue.

The conference lasted three days. It was largely taken up with problems of the theatre, which have since then long been solved – the closed shop was one, the copyright of the actor in his mechanically recorded work was another one on which a long discussion, stretching out over a whole day, took place. In the meantime, Sedgwick was busy with the arrangements for a mass meeting to be held at the Duke of York's Theatre on the Sunday following the Conference. The Prussian Chairman was not an easy customer, and I had a great deal of trouble watering down his remarks in interpretation.

The delegates were entertained to lunch at the House of Commons. Mr. Trevelyan, then President of the Board of Education in McDonald's Labour Government, presided. Other M.P.'s present included George Strauss (today Minister of Supply) Ellen Wilkinson, Beckett (who subsequently ran away with the Mace and was interned under 18b) and Oliver Baldwin (now Lord Baldwin) who, much to my annoyance, insisted in interfering with my job and displayed his knowledge of languages with a most atrocious German. On the English theatrical side I can only recall Maurice Browne, then at the height of his career as a Theatrical Manager. Trevelyan made a speech in which he expressed the hope that English actors would follow the Trade Union lead of other countries. There was a most terrific row after the luncheon, because Sedgwick had arranged for the best English linguist amongst the delegates – a Danish actor – to propose the health of the Minister, instead of asking the Prussian Chairman to speak in his own language. When the fireworks had subsided the Prussian was still concerned with the fact that the Minister had been insulted, insomuch that the most important person present had not proposed his health, and I had to mollify him by promising him that due apologies would be conveyed to the Minister.

Other hospitalities during the three days were visits to the theatre, including boxes at the London Pavilion to see Cochran's production of

"The Silver Tassie" with Charles Laughton. This very Irish play by Sean O'Casey took some explaining to the foreigners. I was in need of an interpreter myself, most of the time. Incidentally, although it has nothing to do with it, I still remember Una O'Connor's lovely performance in this play. It was one of her last stage appearances in England prior to her departure to Hollywood.

On Sunday there came the mass meeting at the Duke of York's Theatre. I do not remember – and I do not think that I knew at the time – whether Sedgwick had organised this entirely by himself, or whether he worked with a Committee. Certainly, as I have said, he was Secretary of the Actors Association, but this Association was by then almost defunct and the Executive consisted apparently only of himself, and all his speeches throughout the Conference were concerned with the need of an Equity on the American model.

The international delegates met prior to the meeting at a hotel in Bloomsbury. The Prussian drew me importantly into a corner. He asked me if I had ever been an actor, and I had to admit that I had never been on that side of the footlights. Nevertheless, he said that he required some acting from me, which I must try and carry out. It was very necessary, he said, that his speech should make a profound impression, and he had therefore, taken the trouble to prepare it. At the same time, directly I read it I would realise the need for it to appear spontaneous, and he was therefore going to deliver it as if he were speaking extempore. He desired, naturally, to have a very accurate translation, and he wanted me to prepare it beforehand – but not to read it, so that nobody should know that the original speech was a prepared one. In fact he wanted me to appear to be taking notes whilst he was speaking and then hesitate and fumble for my words here and there, so as to give a definite impression that I had just heard the speech for the first time. All this I promised to do to the best of my ability.

The meeting at the Duke of York's was a crowded one. On the platform in addition to the foreign delegates and Sedgwick were many actors and actresses, of whom I can only recall Marie Burke. The subsequent first Secretary of Equity, Wall, made his first public appearance on the stage in connection with the movement. Lewis Casson and Sybil Thorndike were in the Royal Box, Circle level, audience right. The Prussian's speech went off very well, and although my experience as an actor has been limited to very occasional emergency appearances when some small part actor and his understudy have been missing, I certainly on that occasion gave the best acting performance of my life. The Prussian was immensely gratified, and took all the applause for himself, and Marie Burke, sitting next to me whispered me a special word of congratulation.

Wall, Sedgwick and Lewis Casson all made speeches. Although my connection with the movement ended at the close of the meeting and my further knowledge of its early days was gleaned from conversations with actors and newspaper reports, I think it is correct to say that Equity was really born that night.

I am afraid that this long letter is barren of any important historical facts. I hope, however, it may help you to glean some titbits of useful information. I presume you are in touch with Mr. Llewellyn Rees for information on weightier matters.

Sincerely yours,
Charles Landstone,
Associate Drama Director.

APPENDIX II

Lawn House
St. George's Avenue
Weybridge

30th March, 1951

Dear Joe,

Yes, by all means use the letter if you want it. It would, however, be better to avoid the use of Lugg's name in the passage about trickery. I suggest the substitution: "the reputation for trickery that body had gained *in earlier days* was still richly deserved". I don't think I ever shared the rather general opinion that he was not to be trusted and, in any case, he should not find the charge implied against him in a published record. The later complimentary reference does not effectively cancel the suggested slur. (And there is a law of libel!)

There is also a spelling slip. In the last sentence but one it should be "Gillmores", not "Gillmours". No doubt the mistake was mine in the original.

I am very glad you have found material for an interesting book. The arrangements were made while I was abroad, or I should have contributed to your material. I have preserved very little but it might be as well for you to look through the enclosed few letters for checking purposes.

I am personally puzzled by the lapse of time between Fisher White's letter to me of January, 1928, referring to "the formation of the new Association", and Godfrey Tearle's letter of Oct. 11th, 1929, foreshadowing his resignation from the Guild. I can only suppose that the A.A. made an attempt to re-organise itself before the final bust-up. I feel sure the Equity project had not been broached so early. Most probably you will know the answer.

My own position was equivocal. I never believed in the Guild and only joined on the ground that it was necessary to keep all the active people together and bring about the necessary conversion to Trade Unionism from inside. I tried to take the remnant of the A.A. with me but they were all last ditchers. Looking back, I am sure I was right, as there was continuous opportunity for pointing out to the Guild Council that their consistent failure to deal with problem after problem was always due to their lack of the Trade Union weapon. Early opposition dwindled, and when May Whitty finally admitted that she was no longer opposed to Trade Unionism in principle, the case was won.

My plan then was to choose the next spectacular case of a stranded company as the occasion to bring the two bodies together on the same platform, and negotiate a fusion, the condition of which, on the A.A.'s part was to be the registration of the combined body as a Trade Union.

Whether this would have worked, I don't know for, when everything had gone nicely according to plan, the New Theatre meeting was wrecked by the irruption of Young (on the platform), with his appeal for the disbanding of the Guild. As the Guild had only consented to appear on the same platform with the A.A. on the express assurance, given by me on the basis of Sedgwick's guarantee, that nothing of the kind would be attempted, I looked "a proper crook" and, in an attempt to recover my shattered reputation, kept quite clear of Equity during the formation period. I never heard the explanation of Young's behaviour. As he was not a regular attendant of the A.A. Council – I am not, indeed, sure that he was a member – Sedgwick may have overlooked him when explaining the conditions of the meeting. If it was a plot, it was a pretty dirty one. This explains my tone in the letter you are using.

I include Gillmore's letter in case it is new to you that the A.A. were depending on money borrowed from American Equity.

There is also the draft of a letter I seem to have done for the Guild. In the absence of a date, I cannot say when it was sent, but it indicates that the proposal to form a body on the lines of American Equity had been advanced before the New Theatre meeting.

I have a number of "Stage Guild Bulletins", but am not sending them as I expect they will already have come your way. If there is any other way in which I can help, please call upon me.

All good wishes and many thanks for undertaking the job.

Yours,
Felix Aylmer.

APPENDIX III

British Actors' Equity Association
Imperial Buildings, 56 Kingsway
London, W.C.2

GS/KS. 25th May 1951

Joseph Macleod Esq.,
46, Queen Street,
Edinburgh, 2.

Dear Joseph,

Thank you very much for your letter dated the 20th May.

Please thank your wife for her thoughtfulness. Needless to say I would not have minded seeing the book after Felix and Tearle. No, that is not strictly true! The typescript arrived yesterday morning and I read it through the lunch hour and am fascinated by it. I read the last two chapters first, and think you have done a quite brilliant job in catching the atmosphere of the incredible meetings which preceded the formation of Equity. I am not, of course, in a position to comment on specific points, by my first impression is that you have done exactly the kind of job I had in mind. Having whetted my appetite to this extent, I am very anxious for you to get going on the pamphlet on our later history. I look forward to meeting you on this question at the end of the summer.

As regards the postscript on the post card, I have asked Miss Bowles to do her best. Sidney Valentine's widow is still alive and is the recipient of a pension. We have been unable to trace her first name, but are in hopes of doing so through the Bank which pays out the pension. We will let you know if we have any success.

The whereabouts of Sidney Valentine's portrait are unknown. Would it be worthwhile making an appeal from the stage at the A.G.M. on Sunday?

Sincere congratulations and kind regards,

Yours ever,
GORDON SANDISON
General Secretary.

P. S. I am forwarding the notes and references to Tearle.

APPENDIX IV

19, Queen Anne Street,
W.1.

June 4th 1951

Dear MacLeod.

Sorry to have been so long in writing you. I've been rushed with casting for a production and rehearsals start immediately, so I'm still rushed! I have received the notes from Equity and they – and your typescript – will be sent off to you as soon as I can get to a Post Office.

The whole work is, to me, very exciting. Whether it can have a reading public, now that the whole thing has more or less settled down, seems to me problematical. However that's yours – and the publishers – affair.

One query on fact. Was it John Emerson the *President* and Frank Gillmore the *Secretary* of American Equity? I would have made a bet on this point.

The other thing I want to say and I feel rather strongly on this:—

It seems to me that for 20 years or more we were all working for *one thing*. I would crystallise it by calling it an *enforceable contract*.

To have described the early awful conditions which screamed out for this thing you have described – the rise of the A.A. and its fall. – The Valentine contract, which not being enforceable was in effect only a 'scrap of paper' – The rise and mess up of the Guild and eventually the merging, as it were, of actors and the decision to form a British Equity. But there you stop, I cannot help feeling that, in this book of yours, you should sum up and mention the *success* of Equity. Even if it were only in the form of an appendix. I mean you should show how we – *at last* – got a Standard Contract, an enforceable contract. And, in short, we won out!

This is only a rambling suggestion but I think the brochure you speak of should be included in this volume, otherwise we end up rather in the air just having formed a new association and we're rather failing "This is where we came in!" or am I worrying needlessly?

Anyway sincere congratulations on a work which must have been a real headache to compile.

Yours,

Godfrey Tearle

Index

Abud, Charles, 78, 85
'Acting managers', 173, 187
Actors' Association, 70 ff
Actors' Benevolent Fund, 48, 49, 53, 62
Actors' budgets, 34–5, 54, 102
'Actors' Equity of G.B.', 172, 182
Actors' Exchange & Mart, 64, 71
Actors' International, 170
'Actors' M.P.' *see* Palmer, Young
Actors' Newspaper Co., 75
Actors' Order of Friendship (USA), 67
Actors' Orphanage, 49, 53, 70
Actors' 'Pay for Play' League, 110
Actors' Protection
  Agency/Association, 58, 60, 64
Actors' Union, 89, 93–4, 101
Actresses' Franchise League, 93, 116
Addison, Dr (Minister of Health), 139
Adelaide Neilson Fund, 53
Ainley, Henry, 95
Albery, Bronson, 148, 159, 164, 174–5, 178
Alexander, George, 21–3, 30, 41, 43, 48, 82, 106, 116
Allen, Clifford, 113
Amalgamated Musicians' Union, 110, 129
Amateurs, 36–7, 59
American Equity, 129, 132, 146, 161, 164, 170, 177, 178, 180, 184, 191, 195
Anderson, Mary, 23
Applin, Arthur, 98
'Arnold Case', The 145
Arnold, Jack, 150, 158
Arthur, Robert, 28
Arundale, Sybil, 173
Ashwell, Lena, 23, 148
Askwith, Lord, 165
Austin, F. J., 134
Aylmer, Felix, 13, 174, 177–82

Bacon, Judge, 83
Baldwin, Stanley, 162

Bancroft, Lady (Marie Wilton), 17, 18
Bancroft, Squire, 16, 20, 21, 29, 30, 32, 48–9, 72, 86, 99
Barbor, H. R., 152, 163, 168
Barker, H. Granville, 23, 30, 86–9, 94, 100
Barnard, Lionel, 142
Barnes, Sir Kenneth, 14
Barrett, Wilson, 22, 32, 33, 48
Barrie, James, 23, 50, 118
Bateman, Virginia, 49
Bawtree, Arthur, 92–3
Bayliss, Lilian, 149
Bayly, Monte, 122, 147–8
Bedford, Henry, 94
Benevolent funds, 46
Bennett, Arnold, 137
Bennett, William, 28
Benson, Frank, 32, 70–3, 78, 87, 106, 153, 162
Bentley, Fred, 92
Berlin, Norman, 174
Billboard, 163
Black, Jessica, 140
Blashill, Thomas, 39
Blow, Sydney, 36–7
'Bogus managers', 59, 61–2, 65, 72, 80, 105, 141
Bolton, T. H., 86
Bottomley, Horatio, 31
Boucicault, Dion, 23
Bourchier, Arthur, 146, 148, 161–2, 164
Bowerman, C. W., 144
Bramall, Ellis, 28
Braythwaite, Lilian, 93, 115
Brighouse, Harold, 153
British Medical Journal, 38
Broadhead, Percival, 150, 161
Brooking, Cecil, 103
Brough, Fanny, 50, 72, 93
Brough, Lionel, 72, 82
Broughton, Phyllis, 93
Browne, Lennox, 38, 39

Browne, Maurice, 191
Buckstone, J. B., 22, 51
Burke, Marie, 177, 179, 183
Butts, Sir Alfred, 121

Calthrop, Donald, 88, 146, 159–60
Calvert, Mrs Charles, 52
Campbell, Mrs Pat, 32
Carl Rosa Opera Company, 139
Carlton, Sir Arthur, 161
Carlyle, Vincent, 141, 160
Carson, Charles L., 49, 58, 64, 68–9,
    71, 75, 82, 86
Carson, Kitty, 49, 50
Carson, Lionel, 58
Casson, Lewis, 88, 94, 95–7, 100, 104,
    114, 150, 170, 192
Casson, Louis, 139, 140, 145, 148, 150,
    152, 153, 161, 174
Challenor, Bromley, 142
Chapman, W. E. ('Ithuriel'), 77
Charing Cross Hospital, 40
Charlot, André, 161
Chartered Institute see Royal Charter
Chute, J. H., 17, 68
Cibber, Colley, 56
Clarence, O. B., 56, 163, 174–5
Clayton-Greene v. De Courville, 144
Closed shop, 91, 140, 145 ff, 158, 161
Clynes, J. R., 184
Coborn, Charles, 92
Cochran, C. B., 127–33
Coffin, Haydn, 104
Cole, G. D. H., 57
Collins, Arthur, 29, 53, 55
Collins, Horace, 14, 55
Collins, Wilkie, 51
Compton, Edward, 24
Compton Comedy Company, 118
Congress of Hygiene, 38
Conti, Italia, 91
Cooke, T. P., 52, 55
Courtenay, Foster, 71
Courtneidge, Cicely, 70, 132
Courtneidge, Robert, 70–2
Covent Garden Fund, 46, 48–9
Coward, Noël, 50
Cowley, Earl, 45
Coyne, Joseph, 177

Crystal Palace, 52
Cunningham, Robert, 179–80, 182
Curzon, Frank, 83
Cutler, Kate, 115

Daily Express, 178, 183
Daily Telegraph, 170, 183
Dance, George, 83, 131
'Danks' Case, The, 107
Darby, Edward, 28
Davenport, Bromley, 164, 174, 179
Davey, Peter, 116
Davies, Ben, 47
Dean, Basil, 104
Deeley, Frank, 83
de Freece, Sir Walter, 144
Denville, Alfred, 52, 155, 173
Denville Hall, 53
Derwent, Clarence, 103, 106, 108, 110,
    114
Dickens, Charles, 51
Diggory, 46
Dodd, Henry, 51–2
D'Oyly Carte, Richard, 80
Dramatic and Musical League, 93
Dramatic College, 51–2
Dramatic Copyright Act, 22
Dramatic, Musical and Equestrian Sick
    Fund Association, 47, 52
Dressler, Marie, 105
Drury Lane Fund, 46
du Maurier, Gerald, 49, 50, 153, 160–1
Dyall, Franklyn, 153

Edwardes, George, 29, 83
Edwards, J. Passmore, 50
Emerson, John, 146, 177–9, 181, 197
Entertainments Federal Council, 170
Entertainments and Kindred
    Industries Association, 182
Entertainments Tax, 115–16
Equity Club, 53
Era, The, 40, 117, 171
Evening News, 77, 127
Evening Standard, 158

Farebrother, Violet, 179
Farrell, Charles, 14, 164
Fay, W. G., 116, 119, 124

Federal Council, 146, 147, 151, 158, 170
ffolliott, Gladys, 91, 148
'Fidelity League', 164
Film Artists' Guild, 184
Fladgate, William, 28
Fleetwood, Charles, 57
'Flying matinées', 111
Forbes-Robertson, Johnston, 87, 153
Forde, Athol, 95
Forde, Frederick, 95
Frohman, Charles, 83
Fry, George, 147, 148, 158

Garden, E. W., 88
Garrick, David, 53, 57
Gas-workers' strike, 67–8
Gattis, The, 30, 83, 137
General Theatrical Sick Fund, 51, 52
Gerald, Frank, 93
German refugees, Committee for, 191
Gibbons, Arthur, 139, 153
Gilbert, W. S., 23, 78
Gillmore, Coulson, 181, 184, 197
'Glorious Eight' (Covent Garden), 57
Glover, J. M., 148
Goddard, Theodore, 134, 142, 172
Godfrey, Peter, 170
Grand Council (Stage Guild), 153, 173–4, 176, 180
Grant, Lawrence, 88, 93
Gray, Frank and Mrs, 162, 164
Gray, Walter G., 14, 54
Grein, J. T., 87
Grove, Fred, 103
Gurney, Edmond, 103
Gwyther, Geoffrey, 177

Haldane, Viscount, 162
Hale, Robert, 177
Hall, Gilbert, 162
Hallett, Henry, 179
Hannen, Nicholas, 173, 183–4
Harding, Lyn, 153
Hare, John, 21, 22, 30, 48, 72, 78
Harris, Augustus, 30
Hatchman, 71
Hawtrey, Charles, 106
Henley, W. E., 81, 106, 171

Hewitt, Balvaid, 169
Heys, Edwin T., 156
Hibbert, H. G., 27
Hicks, Seymour, 22, 23, 30–3, 36, 83, 89, 115
Hilton, Robert, 105
Hishin, Bernard, 137
Hollingshead, John, 25, 29
Horne, Sir Robert, 128, 129
Horniman, Miss A. E. F., 100, 146
Howard, J. B., 27
Hutchison, Percy, 121, 148, 155
Hyndman, H. M., 101

International Conference of Trade Unions representing Theatre Workers, 171, 190–1
International Copyright Agreement, 22
International Labour Organisation, 126
Irish, Frank, 163
Irving, Ethel, 84
Irving, Henry, 21, 22, 27, 48, 64, 71–2, 81, 82–3, 85–6, 89, 99, 118, 171, 183–4
Irving, H. B., 89, 106, 116, 121
'Ithuriel' see Chapman

Jackson, Sir Barry, 153
Jenkyn, Professor, 81, 171
Johnson, William, 105, 109
Joint Industrial Council, 139, 141, 143
Joint Protection Committee, 151
Jones, Henry Arthur, 23, 153
Jones and Douglas, 116

Karno, Fred, 145, 156
Kean, Edmund, 16
Kendal Company, The, 59, 72
Kendal, Madge, 17, 72, 93, 129
Kenneth, Keith, 147
King George V, 51, 108
King George's Pension Fund, 51
King, T. C., 20
Kingston, Gertrude, 37, 44, 93, 173

Landstone, Charles, 183, 190–3
Lang, Matheson, 49, 182

Langley Place, 50
Lawrence, Gerald, 14
Lawrence, Wingold, 19
Leon, Jack, 158
Lestocq, William, 72, 76, 83, 88, 98
Lewis, W. T., 57
Littlewood, S. R., 58
Lloyd George, David, 108
Loftus, Kitty, 144
London Actor Managers' Committee,
    67
London, Bishop of, 138, 141, 143
London County Council, 39, 138
London Standard Contract
    ('Valentine'), 131, 133, 137, 145,
    175, 185, 197
Londonderry House, 53
Loos, Anita, 178
Loraine, Robert, 128
Lord Chamberlain, 103, 138, 143
Lugg, Alfred, 14, 120–2, 124, 129,
    133–4, 138, 151, 157–9, 163–4, 166,
    169–70, 181, 184–5, 194
Lusitania (S.S.), 83

McCardie, Mr Justice, 144
McCready, William, senior, 14, 16
McCrindle, Alex, 9, 14
Macready, W. C., 5, 16
McDonald, Dr C. Knight, 14
McGowan, Major, 153
McIntosh, Madge, 169
McKinnell, Norman, 135, 138–40
Malleson, Miles, 113
Mander and Mitchenson, 13
Mannering, D. Lewin, 170, 175, 179
Martin Harvey, John, 106, 118, 153,
    156–7, 172
Mason, A. E. W., 21, 22
Match-girls' strike, The, 67
Mathison, Edith Wynne, 95
Matthews, Rose, 91, 93, 103–4
Maude, Cyril, 83, 106, 110, 118
Melville, Andrew, 26–7
Melville, Walter, 105
Miller, Gilbert, 121
Ministry of Health, 139
Moore, Eva, 153, 157
Moore, Mary see Wyndham

Morand, M. R., 71
Moreton, F. Leslie, 153
Morland, Frederick, 103, 111
Morning Post, 128
Moro, 80
Moss Empires, 108, 177
Murray, Harriot, 16
Murry, J. Middleton, 177
Music Hall Artistes' Railway
    Association, 91
Music Hall Union, 92
'Music Hall War', 92
Musicians' Union, 144, 146

National Association of Theatre
    Employees (later N.A.T.K.E.), 79,
    85, 105, 109–10, 117, 139, 144, 146,
    157, 164, 170
National Federation of General
    Workers, 170
National Union of Corporation
    Workers, 170
'Neilson, Adelaide', 45, 53, 55
Neilson, Fred, 158
Neilson, Julia, 21, 30, 43
Nettlefold, F. J., 153, 173–4, 176
Newcastle, Duke of, 30
Nossiter see Valentine, Sidney
'No play, no pay', 69, 74

O'Brien, Tom, 14, 85
Ocean Accident and Guarantee
    Corportion, 77
O'Grady, James, 120
Owen, Jackson, 145

Palmer, Charles, 139
Paxton, Sydney, 143
Payne, 71
Payne, Walter, 161
Pearce, Vera, 177
Pearman, Sarton, 155
Pelican, The, 30, 43, 48, 78
Penley, W. S., 68, 72
Phelps, Samuel, 52
Pinero, Arthur Wing, 23, 77, 153
Play Actors Company, 103
Players, The, 76, 79
'Playhouse Pay', 69, 74

Pope, W. MacQueen, 83
Porter, Neil, 170
Provincial Actors' Union, 92–3
Provincial Entertainment Proprietors'
    and Managers' Association
    ('P.E.P.'), 138–9, 161
Provincial Managers' Association, 66

Raleigh, Cecil, 91, 93–4, 101, 106, 114,
    170
Rean, Clifford, 131–2, 134, 138, 140
Rees, Llewellyn, 191
Referee, The, 89
'Reform Group', 94–9, 101, 104
Registration of Managers, 160–2, 168,
    174, 177
Rehearsal Club, 53
Réjane, Gabrielle Charlotte, 108
Rich, Christopher, 56
Richardson, Ian, 170, 171
Richardson, Professor J. H., 66
Roberts, Hugh, 147
Robertson (Lincolnshire Circuit), 16
Robertson, T. W., 21, 23
Rodway, Philip, 46
Rollitt, George, 169, 172, 175, 179
Roscoe, Ada, 166, 169, 175
Rothermere, Lord, 55
Rothschild, Baron, 55, 80
Rowlands, Abraham *see* Raleigh
Royal Charter, 81, 166, 171, 173–5
Royal Command Performance, 51
Royal General Theatrical Fund, 49
Russell, Bertrand, 113
Russell, Harry, 113, 155

Saintsbury, H. A., 174
Salvini, Tommaso, 17
'Samaritan Fund', 47
Sandison, Gordon, 13, 196
Sanitation, 35, 37–40, 49, 69, 72, 83,
    118, 126, 139, 145, 146–8
Saturday Review, The, 46
Savile, J. H., 25, 116
Saville, Eve, 14
Scott, Clement, 49, 50
Scott, Mrs Clement, 49
Scott, Harold, 14, 113
Seddon, J. A., 123

Sedger, Horace, 30
Sedgwick, Russell, 13, 170, 173–84,
    190–2, 195
Select Committee on Theatres, 37
Seyler, Athene, 50
Sharpe, F. B. J., 131
Shaw, G. B., 23, 116
Shortt, Edward (Home Secretary), 139
Sibley, Lucy, 93, 97, 98, 103, 108
Sim, General, 28
Simpson, Mercer, 18, 19, 25
Smith, C. Aubrey, 153
Society of West End Managers, 107,
    108
Sothern, E. A., 32
Sprang, Adnam, 115
Stage, The, 33, 36, 46, 58–9, 61, 63,
    67–8, 75, 78, 82, 86, 98, 104–5, 114,
    125, 132–3, 139, 146, 178, 183
Stage Directory, 163–4
Stage Guild, 152, 159–61, 163–4,
    172–92
Stage Operatives' Union, 64, 79
Stage Players' Complaint, 56
Stage Year Book, 94, 101
State Insurance Act, 102
Staveley, W. R., 119
Steerman, A. H., 119
Stewart, Athole, 153
Stilwell, James, 119
Stirling, Mrs Fanny, 47, 52
Stoll, Sir Oswald, 121
Sunday Times, 36
Swaffer, Hannen, 124, 178–9, 184
'Syndicate backers', 31

'Taff Vale Case' trade dispute, 90
Taylor, A. Dixon, 153
Tearle, Godfrey, 13, 115, 153, 155,
    163, 171–6, 178, 181–2, 185, 194,
    196
Teck, Duchess of, 53
Terriss, Ellaline, 23, 30
Terriss, William, 37, 72
Terry, Edward O'Connor, 29, 43,
    46–7, 62, 72, 88, 97
Terry, Ellen, 17, 25, 72, 93, 116
Terry, Fred, 153
Theatre, The, 82

THEATRES (London):
  Adelphi, 25, 30
  Aldwych, 22
  Alhambra, 121
  Avenue, 83
  Brixton, 83, 85
  Camden, 83
  Comedy, 28, 83
  Coronet, 83
  Court, 29, 87
  Covent Garden, 39, 46
  Criterion, 22, 30, 79, 83, 114
  Drury Lane, 29, 46, 56, 83
  Duke of York's, 22, 87, 182–6, 192
  'Dust Hole', 21
  Gaiety, 29, 78
  Garrick, 83, 156
  Gate, 170
  Globe, 22, 123
  Haymarket, 30, 114, 146
  Hicks', 22
  His Majesty's, 51, 105, 114, 129
  King's, Hammersmith, 139
  Kingsway, 159
  Lyceum, 25, 30, 46, 72–3, 83
  Lyric, 31, 71
  New, 178
  Olympic, 25
  Playhouse, 94
  Prince of Wales, 83
  Queen's, 22, 121, 131, 133
  Royalty, 80
  Sadler's Wells, 25
  Savoy, 30, 87, 121
  St James's, 21, 22, 30
  St Martin's, 144
  Shaftesbury, 71, 179
  Shoreditch, 27
  Strand, 46–7, 83, 118
  Terry's, 38, 88, 104
  Trafalgar Square, 22
  Vaudeville, 44, 83
  Waldorf, 105
  Winter Garden, 170
  Wyndham's, 83
THEATRES outside London:
  Birmingham, 23, 27
  Birmingham, Grand, 27
  Birmingham, Theatre Royal, 46

  Bristol, Theatre Royal, 27
  Derby, Grand, 27
  Dublin, Abbey, 116
  Edinburgh, Lyceum, 27
  Edinburgh, Theatre Royal, 27
  Glasgow, Theatre Royal, 27
  Liverpool, 28, 43, 116
  Maidstone, 145
  Manchester, Queen's, 40
  Margate, 118
  New Brighton, 116
  Newcastle, Royalty, 27
  Newcastle, Theatre Royal, 27
  Paisley, 116
  Perth, 116
  Portsmouth, 116
  Stratford, 145
  Swansea, Morriston, 53
  Swansea, New, 27
  Swansea, Star, 27
  Walsall, 27
Theatre Alliance (Managers), 104, 128
Threatrical Choristers' Association, 79
Theatrical Christmas Dinner Fund, 50
Theatrical Employers' Registration
  Bill, 144, 177
Theatrical Fire Fund, 47
Theatrical Garden Party, 50
Theatrical Ladies' Guild, 50, 54
Theatrical Managers' Association, 82,
  100, 104, 107, 115, 146
Theatrical 'Mart or Exchange', 64
Theatrical Syndicate, 67, 74
Theatrical Trust, Ltd., 77
Thorndike, Sybil, 88, 100, 152, 192
Thorne, Sarah, 37, 118
Thorne, Tom, 44
Toole, J. L., 40, 48, 72
Touring Contract, 131, 153, 161, 164,
  175
Touring Managers' Association (also
  called Association of . . . and
  Incorporated . . .), 105, 109, 114,
  121, 130–2, 137–9, 140–2, 145, 148,
  150–3, 156, 161
Trade disputes, 67–8, 79, 82, 85, 93,
  109–10, 127–9, 140, 142–4, 156–7,
  158, 163, 175, 177
Trades Disputes Act, 90

Tree, Sir Herbert, 104–6, 109–10, 116, 121
Troubridge, Sir St Vincent, 57
T.U.C., 92, 147, 163, 184
Tyack, H. S., 72, 76

'Unity is strength', 58, 61, 63, 122

Valentine Contract *see* London Standard Contract
Valentine, Sidney, 88, 116, 118–23, 126–36, 138, 153, 170, 181, 185, 186, 196
Valentine, Mrs Edith, 134–5
Vanbrugh, Violet, 50
Vansittart, Robert, 113
Variety Artists Federation, 92, 122, 128, 144, 146–8, 163
Vedrenne, J. E., 87
Vezin, Hermann, 36, 52

Wages, 18, 30–5, 46, 70, 75, 77, 88, 92–4, 102, 106–7, 109–10, 114–16, 123, 126, 130, 132, 145, 154
Wall, A. M., 182, 184
Wallace, G. Carlton, 13, 139, 152–5
Walter, Wilfred, 169
'Water Rats', 92
Weatherby, Frank, 139

Webb, Sydney and Beatrice, 67
Webster, Ben, 165, 185–6
Wentworth, Stephen, 121
West End Managers' Association, 104, 107, 109, 130, 137, 161, 162, 165, 185–6
Westby & Co., 83
White, J. Fisher, 88, 148–9, 162, 169–78, 182, 185, 194
White slave traffic, 107
Whitty, May, 88, 178–9, 194
Wilde, Oscar, 23
Wilks, 56
Willard, 33
Williams, J. B., 146
Wilson, Rathmell, 169
Wilton, Marie *see* Bancroft, Lady
Wyndham, Charles, 21, 22–3, 33, 48, 72, 79, 118
Wyndham, Fred, 43
Wyndham, Lady (Mary Moore), 49, 148
Wyatt, Frank, 22

Young, Robert, 149, 157, 164, 178–84, 195

Zeitz, Harry, 170, 175

Index of Plays

Anna Christie, 146–8
Arcadians, The, 71
Brighton, 79
Caste, 23
Catch of the Season, The, 23
Charley's Aunt, 68
Claudian, 24
Conflict, 169
Cyrano de Bergerac, 127–8
David Garrick, 33
Dorothy, 105
For the Crown, 32
Hamlet, 37
Julius Caesar, 51

Lady of Lyons, The, 18
Little Minister, The, 140
Little Old Mother of Mine, 140
Open Your Eyes, 177
Passion, Poison and Putrefaction, 50
Peterkin, 80
Romance of India, 108
Silver Tassie, The, 192
Vagabond King, The, 170
Very Idea, The, 144
Via Crucis, 157
When Knights Were Bold, 142
White Heather, 83